THE VOW OF STABILITY

THE VOW OF STABILITY

An ethnography of monastic life

Richard D. G. Irvine

First published in 2025 by
Scottish Universities Press
SUP Publishing CIC
International House
38 Thistle Street
Edinburgh
EH2 1EN

https://www.sup.ac.uk
Text © Author 2025

This work is licensed under Creative Commons Attribution-NonCommercial 4.0 International licence. This licence enables re-users to distribute, remix, adapt, and build upon the material in any medium or format for non-commercial purposes only, and only so long as attribution is given to the creator. Attribution should include the following information:

Irvine, R. D. G., 2025. *The vow of stability: An ethnography of monastic life*. Edinburgh: Scottish Universities Press. https://doi.org/10.62637/sup.bilp1551

Third-party materials are not covered by this licence. Please see the individual credit lines in the captions for information on copyright holders.
To view a copy of this licence, visit https://creativecommons.org/licenses/by-nc/4.0/

ISBN (Hardback): 978-1-917341-09-7
ISBN (Paperback): 978-1-917341-08-0
ISBN (PDF): 978-1-917341-11-0
ISBN (EPUB): 978-1-917341-10-3
DOI: https://doi.org/10.62637/sup.bilp1551

All external links included were live at the time of publication.

An electronic edition can be downloaded free of charge at
https://doi.org/10.62637/sup.bilp1551
or scan the following QR code:

This book has been through a rigorous peer review process to ensure that it meets the highest academic standards. A copy of the full SUP Peer Review Policy & Procedure can be found here: https://www.sup.ac.uk/peer-review

Typeset and designed by Palimpsest Book Production Limited, Falkirk, Stirlingshire
Cover design: Palimpsest Book Production Limited, Falkirk, Stirlingshire
Front cover image: © Richard Irvine.

'So it always is: when you escape to a desert the silence shouts in your ear.'

Graham Greene, *The Quiet American*

TABLE OF CONTENTS

Acknowledgements — ix

Part I: The nature of stability — 1

Chapter 1: The promise of stability — 3

Chapter 2: The architecture of stability — 31

Chapter 3: The rhythm of stability — 59

Part II: Prayer, private and public — 83

Chapter 4: Liturgical prayer and the limits of participation — 85

Chapter 5: Contemplative prayer and the problem of other people — 117

Chapter 6: Reading as prayer and learning to listen — 153

Part III: Flight from the world? — 171

Chapter 7: Work and pray — 173

Chapter 8: Abuse and the failure of responsibility — 201

Chapter 9: Leaving home — 221

References — 233

Index — 249

ACKNOWLEDGEMENTS

Twenty years have passed since I first took a bus to Stratton-on-the-Fosse and walked along the driveway to the guest wing of Downside Abbey. That moment of first encounter remains vivid, a fixed point in time, as so much else has shifted in my life. My children, James and Barry, had not yet been born, and I had not yet had the opportunity to learn from them. In taking so long to write, I have seen my own thinking and purpose reshaped by them and by my partner Clea Paine, and I am thankful for that. My parents Jim and Kath, whose care and love propelled me through my studies, have died. I owe them so much, and would like to have shared this book with them.

I began this project as a PhD student in the Department of Social Anthropology at Cambridge, and my first attempts to understand things took shape under the supervision of Leo Howe. I am grateful to him and also to Marilyn Strathern, Barbara Bodenhorn, and Joel Robbins for teaching me what anthropology can look like. I have since moved to Scotland to teach at St Andrews and there I am grateful for conversations with Tom Ovens and Adam Reed that have helped me approach the ethnography from a new angle.

The book would probably never have taken its eventual form had I not had invitations to workshops convened by Maya Mayblin on the Catholicity of Desire, and by Nicholas Lackenby on Time and the Anthropology of Christianity. Having to produce the ethnographic outlines I presented at those workshops gave me the kick up the backside I needed to get on with the job.

Finally, I am grateful to the community at Downside for their hospitality, for their perseverance with me and for giving me the opportunity to learn. Dom David Foster and Dom Anselm Brumwell, monks of Downside Abbey, were kind enough to offer comments on an earlier draft of this manuscript. I am very grateful for their insight and critical feedback; it goes without saying that I take full responsibility for the ethnography offered here and for any errors that remain in the text.

Several of the monks who were the most generous to me and who pushed me in my understanding are now dead. It is to them that I dedicate this book. May the souls of the faithful departed, through the mercy of God, rest in peace.

PART I

The nature of stability

CHAPTER 1

The promise of stability

Scene of death

The body of a monk lies prostrate on a funeral pall. Requiem candles stand lit at the corners of the pall. Around the body, the monastic family kneel in prayer. They chant the litany of the saints, praying for their brother, praying for Christ's mercy, asking Mary and the saints to join their prayers with them, calling on God to hear their prayer.

This mortuary ritual is a beginning. It is part of a rite of passage, the monk's solemn profession as a full member of the community. Enacting a death, the monk lies at the threshold, leaving a life in order to pass into a future. But he is not alone; he is surrounded by others who accompany him in prayer.

What kind of transformation is this death, and what is it a passage into? This book is a study of a contemporary community of Catholic men living, working and praying together in the shape of life set out in the sixth-century *Rule* of St Benedict. It takes as its focus the life of the monks who were resident at Downside Abbey in the south-west of England, a monastery of the English Benedictine Congregation. England is a land dotted with the ruins of great abbeys; monastic fragments fenced around and managed by the National Trust or converted for use as parish churches, cathedrals, or private houses. Through these heritage sites Catholic monasticism comes to be interpreted as something associated with the past – a chapter of English history that came to an end during the reign of Henry VIII, the dissolution of the monasteries, and the Reformation. In this context, an ethnographic study of monasticism today strikes an apparent note of discontinuity with contemporary English life. Yet the monk lying on the funeral pall does not *leave* the present. Rather, at this moment of death, what is laid bare is the nature of a present at the threshold of eternity. And it is to that present which the monk returns, challenged to live, day by day.

One starting point, then, is to say that the study of Benedictine monasticism offers an anthropology of everyday life from a point of view where the routine is experienced in relation to the absolute. In many respects, this connects with other work within the anthropology of Christianity, where Fenella Cannell (2005: 346) has drawn attention to 'the juxtaposition of the numinous and the banal', challenging the idea that Christianity is characterised by the discontinuity between the immanent and the transcendent, a turning away from this world for otherworldly goals (see also Cannell 2006). Indeed, as Webster (2013) argues, transcendence and immanence are rarely understandable as two opposed poles; rather, transcendence comes to be experienced as immanent, a presence in the fabric of everyday life. Of course, it may still seem somewhat counterintuitive to turn to the monastery for examples of continuity between the search for the transcendent and life in the world; indeed, in allowing that, even as we pay attention to immanence, there remains an 'undoubtedly powerful ascetic current in Christianity', Cannell (2005: 342) suggests that 'the most obvious examples come from monasticism'. Yet, rather than stressing a radical discontinuity with concerns of this world, as we shall see, English Benedictines frequently sought to draw connections between the central concerns of the monastic life and general human challenges of living; and a central theme of Benedictine life was the encounter with God within the everyday and ordinary.

In a garden beside the abbey church, one of the monks had carved into a rock the words *Deus totus in omnibus et singulis* – God is whole in all things and each thing. The monk who carved these words gave some indication of why they were significant to him during a conversation over tea with some guests who, like myself, had been taking a walk in the garden and saw the rock set back among the flowers. He told us that the words come from St Thomas Aquinas[1] and, discovering them in the course of his reading, he was amazed, hearing something at the very core of the life he had committed himself to at his own solemn profession. Within the routine of the monastery, he explained, God is encountered through everyday acts of working, eating, interacting. By comparison with the dramatic tales of superhero saints who performed miracles or achieved great feats of asceticism, the daily life of the monastery set out in the *Rule* appears rather prosaic. Yet through the Benedictine routine, the monk learns that God is not simply to be sought out in the extraordinary but is encountered in the ordinary. God is whole in places like gardens, in acts like carving.

'How does the monk pray? In the way he lives! When does he pray? Always! Where does he pray? Everywhere!' (Vermeiren 1999: 54). I was directed to these words during the first weeks of my fieldwork at Downside back in 2005. The abbot, who had translated into English the book from which the words were drawn, loaned me a copy, explaining that it had played an important role in his coming to understand the Benedictine vocation. A study of the *Rule* of St Benedict and the early monastic texts in whose context the *Rule* emerges, the book suggests that the Benedictine life was and is one of continuous prayer; within the monastic *horarium* (or time-table), prayer and daily activity are closely interwoven, such that prayer comes to permeate all aspects of the monk's life. Such an approach challenges any rigid distinction between the sacred and the routine. Each night, as I listened to the abbot reading out a chapter of the *Rule* of St Benedict to the community before Compline, the final point of collective prayer in the day, I became more and more aware of how God was understood to be present even within the minutiae of monastic management – here, after all, was a way of life in which the cellarer was instructed to regard the monastery's kitchen utensils as if they were sacred vessels of the altar.[2]

1 *Summa Theologica*, First Part, Question 8.
2 *Rule* of St Benedict, Chapter 31. In the *Rule*, the cellarer is the monastic official in charge of food, drink and kitchen supplies.

It is significant that the *Rule* is heard at the end of the day, to be taken into the night. The *Rule* plays a key role shaping a routine that in turn shapes the monk's form of life. As Giorgio Agamben (2013: 69) has observed, a distinctive feature of monastic life is the way in which rule and life are bound together: monastic rules 'performatively realize the life they must regulate'. One way in which the *Rule* of St Benedict does this, as a contemporary monk of Downside has argued (Foster 2021), is in generating a *community of listeners*. From the very first words of the *Rule*, it is a call to listen: 'Listen, my son, to the precepts of a master, and incline the ear of your heart.'[3] And crucially, the task of listening is located in a collective setting, a 'school of the Lord's service', as St Benedict puts it. This offers one route to understanding, as Agamben sets out to do, how a *Rule* becomes a form of life, rather than simply a subjection to a norm. The *Rule* is both a call to listen and a framework of collective listening through the shape of the everyday. Again, this is urged in the *Rule*'s prologue – 'What is there sweeter than this voice of the Lord inviting us, dearest brethren?' – and this daily listening is enacted through the life of community.

So what is set out in the *Rule*? It describes a community which is both economically and constitutionally self-contained, ruled over by an abbot elected by the monks. It lays out a pattern for common life, focused around set times of liturgical prayer, as well as shared meals, eaten in silence as one of the monks reads a book aloud. Time is also allocated for spiritual reading and manual labour. The English Benedictine historian David Knowles (1940: 4) suggests that in the monastery described in the *Rule*, 'If an average is struck over the whole year, the monk is found to be engaged for some four hours (or a little less) in the liturgical prayer of the oratory, for some four hours in meditative reading or prayer and for some six (or more) in work which is either domestic, or strictly manual, or the pursuit of some simple craft.' All of this gives a sense of the pattern of the *Rule*, but not of its core impulse, which was repeatedly described to me as the 'charism of community living': 'tending to others, being open to the moments of grace that come from living alongside others'.

---

3 *Rule* of St Benedict, Prologue.

The monk who gave this description echoed it a decade later, when he offered a 'Thought for the day' over YouTube as part of the community's public outreach during the COVID pandemic,[4] when a UK-wide lockdown meant that the doors of the monastery were closed to visitors. Recorded sitting in front of a bookshelf in the *novitiate*, where he now taught the *Rule* that he had once been taught, he emphasised that St Benedict's words are directed towards *cenobites*: those who live in a community. To live together requires the openness to *listen*, which we hear in the very first word of the *Rule*. Listening seems a simple thing to do, but actually allowing someone else's words into our heart means 'we have to let go, and this requires effort'. It is this deep listening which the monks bring to prayer when they gather as a community in the church, but also to their moments of personal prayer and the prayerful reading of scripture. 'And we shouldn't forget it's the listening that we should try and exercise in our relationships with the brethren.' This growth through listening, 'sticking at it' through a lifetime, was at the core of the daily social life of the monastery, but it also had relevance beyond the monastery walls. We are 'called to live in community, and listen to one another, and exercise patience, love, and understanding. So as we live through these difficult days... we need to exercise the patience and the wisdom that St Benedict outlines for us. We're all being asked to listen with our hearts and show compassion towards our brothers and sisters at home, our neighbour in our country and in the world. In St Benedict's own words, no-one is to pursue what he judges best for himself, but instead what he judges better for someone else.'[5]

Perseverance

There was a particular significance to these words being shared in the *novitiate*. This is the space where each monk of the community,

4 See Irvine (2021a) for an ethnography of the monks' digital outreach during this period.
5 *Rule* of St Benedict, Chapter 72.

and the generations before them who now lie in the cemetery, began their formation – the process of becoming part of a household, shaping a life in response to the desire for God.

When a man seeks to enter the community, he arrives first as a guest, giving the abbot and the novice master an opportunity to meet him, get to know him and consider his application. If his application is accepted, he is invited to live with the community as a postulant, usually for six months. Postulants often live in the *novitiate*, normally under the guidance of the novice master, and participate in community life; this is understood as a period of discernment, giving both the community and the postulant an opportunity to consider his calling.

Following this phase, he may ask to become a novice. If admitted, he is 'clothed' in a ceremony where he puts on the monastic habit[6] and is given the name of a saint as a new name to accompany his new identity as a monk.[7] This is a continuation of the process of discernment, but also a time of study – at this stage primarily of prayer, of the liturgy and of the *Rule* and the constitutions of the English Benedictine Congregation. Every three months, in a short ceremony, the novice comes before the abbot in the presence of the whole community. The abbot addresses the novice: 'What is it you ask for?', to which the novice replies, 'Perseverance.'

If the monk perseveres over his year as a novice, he is asked whether he wishes to proceed to a simple profession; this is a formal and public commitment to live in the monastic state for a fixed period of three years (which can be extended). A formal application

---

6   While 'habit' here obviously refers to monastic clothing, the historic proximity between 'habit' as a form of dress and 'habit' as a way of life is explored by Agamben (2013: 13–14). In a sense this is reflected in the process of taking on more elements of monastic dress through the process of formation. Although, as a postulant, a simple form of habit is worn, the 'clothing' at the start of a *novitiate* is the first point at which the monk wears full monastic dress, with the exception of one item: the cowl, worn over the habit on solemn occasions, which is given to the monk for the first time at his solemn profession.

7   Significantly, the name is an addition, not a replacement; baptismal names are still used by the monks when they refer to their full names.

is written, to be considered by the abbot and voted on by the whole community before the novice can proceed to this profession. The novice also makes arrangements for somebody (of his own choosing) to take over responsibility for any property or income he may have during that time. He then leaves the monastery, to spend time on retreat in preparation, before returning for the rite of profession.[8] There, the monk vows – before the community and before God – to live according to the *Rule* and the constitutions of the Congregation.

The monk promises *stability*, understood in the sense of personal perseverance, but also as a commitment to stability of place: to remain in a particular community, to bind oneself to it and not to wander from it (Rees et al. 1978: 139–41). As we shall see, this has a particular historic significance for English Benedictine identity, with stability as a value that has been actively defended in the face of forces drawing monks out and away from the monastery. (In Chapter 2, I discuss the monastic architecture as a deliberate assertion of stability at a time of debate around English Benedictine identity.) Crucially, it is by means of this rootedness that monks grow through a lifelong commitment to their specific community. As the Australian monk Michael Casey (2005: 244) has explained, this makes social interaction with those closest at hand 'the ordinary means by which the image of Christ is reformed in us'. In this way the 'whole cosmic drama of salvation is transferred to the microcosm of the monastery' (2005: 240).

The monk promises *obedience*. In its most specific sense, this is a promise to live in obedience to the instructions of the abbot as *paterfamilias*[9], whose role in turn is explicitly framed by the *Rule* as part of a listening relationship with the whole community.[10] In a more general sense, it is understood as the imitation of Christ's obedience in listening to the will of his Father (Rees et al. 1978: 190–1).

8 See Yeo (1982) for a detailed account and juridical analysis of monastic profession in the English Benedictine Congregation.
9 See Nuzzo (1996: 874): 'this concept of father of the monks is directly parallel to the Roman concept of *paterfamilias*, where the senior male of the family was its "singular authority figure"'.
10 *Rule* of St Benedict, Chapter 3.

The monk promises *conversatio morum*. This resists straightforward translation, and different attempts have been made within the Congregation to explain its meaning (see Yeo 1982: 312–16). Fundamentally, this commitment reflects the communal basis of Benedictine monastic life, and Christopher Jamison (2006: 116), formerly Abbot of Worth, another monastery within the Congregation, provides a useful working definition: 'If you look up the word conversation in some dictionaries, you find a clue to the meaning of conversatio. There you discover that the first now obsolete meaning of conversation is living with somebody ... So this Benedictine vow is a resolution to live with others, specifically with other monks, and hence to live the monastic way of life.' In her ethnography of an American Benedictine community, Guarino (2018: 12) explains that *conversatio* is 'about process and change in pursuit of and supported by the stability of the monastic family', a dynamic which she links to the blending of sound in the liturgy as monks find their common voice (2018: 77).

Following this simple profession, the monk continues their life with the community and the study of theology and philosophy. After three years in this temporary state, they decide whether they wish to apply for the lifelong commitment of solemn profession, at which they make these vows in perpetuity.[11] If the abbot and community agree to accept the monk's application, following this rite of profession the monk is bound to the community until their death.

The ritual process of solemn profession – at the heart of which is the scene of death described at the start of this chapter – follows the tripartite model of rites of passage identified by Arnold van Gennep (1909), with phases of separation, margin, and aggregation. This model has, of course, been a rich source of inspiration for anthropological thinking. Turner (1969: 95) famously places an emphasis on the dramatic potential of that marginal (or liminal) phase when the initiate lies 'betwixt and between', at a distance from the structures of everyday life in ways that oxygenate the

---

11 This period may be extended by the abbot beyond the period of three years, but, according to the constitutions of the Congregation, should not last for longer than nine years.

fundamental human bonds of participants – indeed, Turner considers the stripping and levelling impact of Benedictine monasticism as an example of the 'institutionalization of liminality' (1969: 107). From this point of view, the expression of vows sustains the monk's location on the threshold throughout their life. Taking rather a different stance, La Fontaine (1977) argues that such rites of passage are occasions that demonstrate the legitimacy of authority and validate the traditional knowledge that underlies power. Indeed, we can recognise that in a monastic profession, we are in the presence of the authority of the *Rule* and the abbot, embodied in the vows of the monk. Turner and La Fontaine therefore draw our attention to two significant aspects of the social dynamics of the rites, each of which threatens to obscure our view of the other. Yet there is another aspect expressed by van Gennep, which is the potential to link the movement through life with wider movements beyond the human. Time and again he returns to the resonance between human and cosmic rhythms – indeed, this is the specific note on which van Gennep (1909: 279) chooses to end, connecting the passage of humans with the great rhythms of the universe. From this perspective, the rite of passage is not only an individual movement through a social process, but also a point of dynamic relation with the cosmology that gives this process substance. At any rate, this is certainly what we see in the rite of solemn profession.

The day before their solemn profession, the monk enters the chapter house to find two chairs in front of him: over one is laid the clothes he wore as a layman before entering the monastery; over the second is the monastic habit. This is one last sign of the separation the monk is about to make complete, an indication of the life the monk can return to. If he chooses to persevere, he writes out his vows, to be placed on the altar during the rite of profession.

This rite takes place during the community Mass, and often an appropriate feast day is chosen for the occasion. The monk chants his vows and places them on the altar, to be signed by the abbot and the secretary of the council of the monastery. In the current form of the rite the monk offers a sign of peace to the whole community who have become his brothers; in previous forms he would kiss the abbot's hand as an indication of his filiation. Before the altar the monk then chants the *Suscipe*:

Suscipe me Domine secundum eloquium tuum et vivam, et non confundas me in expectatione mea

– 'Receive me, Lord, according to your word, and let me live, and do not confound me in my hope.' These words are chanted three times by the monk; on each occasion the whole community repeat the chant, adding their prayers to his. Two particular aspects of this chanting were pointed out to me by members of the community. The first was a resonance with the liturgy of the Easter Triduum, the celebration of Christ's death and resurrection; it was pointed out to me how the threefold repetition of the *Suscipe* before the altar, intoning the chant on a higher note each time, reflects the threefold repetition of the chant when the cross is carried to the altar on Good Friday, 'This is the Wood of the Cross'; and again at the Easter Vigil in the night before the dawn of Sunday when 'Christ our Light' is chanted three times as the paschal candle is carried forward. It is also a future echo of the death of the monk: his brothers will sing the *Suscipe* for him once again, on the day of his funeral.

The liminal status of the monk at this point of transition is clear, as he prostrates himself on the funeral pall, with his face, hands, and feet covered. A life is being left behind – but the monk has not yet fully taken on their new identity. Following the rite of profession, after the monk has stood from the funeral pall, and has been blessed with holy water and clothed anew, his hood is pinned up in place and he is led away for three days of silent retreat in isolation.

Recalling this silent retreat, the monks emphasised three different aspects to it. The first was the symbolism of death and resurrection with and in Christ. It was generally described as 'going to the tomb', the significance of the three days of retreat being a reflection of Christ lying dead in the tomb after his crucifixion and rising again on the third day. In this light, the rite of profession expresses the infinite significance of the Easter mystery within the specific bounds of an individual life cycle and the microcosm of the monastic community. Secondly, it was pointed out to me how this time in the tomb reflects the dynamics of monastic life: the rite of profession taking place in the context of a conventual Mass reflects the communal character of monasticism, but the time in the tomb shows the fundamental place of solitude and silence before God – an expression of the pulse of private prayer and contemplation within the rhythm of Benedictine life (see Chapter 5). Thirdly, some monks described the psychological aspects of the isolation. 'I remember this very strange dissonance. I remember thinking "I want to go home", and every time … this realisation like a bell, "you are home", and this continued … And I remember thinking again and again "I am alone", then having this incredible sense that I was not alone.' Another stressed the 'starkness' of time 'in the presence of death, contemplating your own death with little to distract you'.

After the three days of silent retreat, the monk's hood is ceremonially unpinned and a celebration meal is held to welcome him into the community as a Solemnly Professed monk. Through the process of profession, then, the monk has enacted a social death, leaving the world he inhabited as a layperson. He sheds aspects of his identity and commits his future to decisions that are no longer his alone, but made in response to instructions under the vow of obedience. He renounces the possibility of married life for the celibacy required by the vow of *conversatio morum*, and he sinks his own individual property and income into that of the community, and having access only to that which he is granted for use by the abbot. Yet, having left the world, he returns to it in an intensely social way, embracing for the rest of his life new family ties[12] and responsibilities. In this sense, the significance of individual death within the rite of passage marks change of status, and also makes plain the power of the institution. Yet the ritual lays bare something that has always been present: the relationship of a human life to the infinitude of time and space. Through the vow of stability this confrontation precipitates in the everyday routine of a finite domestic sphere.

---

12 See also Qirko (2004) on the relationship between fictive kinship and celibacy in the context of religious communities, and the significance of ritualised familial cues.

The guest in the monastery

So far I have described the process of becoming part of a household. Where does the anthropologist fit into all of this?[13]

This problem was raised in the earliest days of my research, before I had even entered the field. While I was still in the planning phase, I met with an English Benedictine monk visiting the university to preach a sermon. As the conversation turned to my research, and I attempted to explain what it was that I was looking for, it seemed that he was broadly sympathetic to my research project: he agreed it was worth investigating how the elements of life in a monastery fitted together. He was interested in how and why the monastic institution sustained the ideal of community, and the place of the monastery in relation to wider society. Nevertheless, he expressed some confusion about an ethnographic methodology, feeling that it carried a risk of self-indulgence, and so he asked: how could I be sure that I was not just playing at being a monk?

The problem for him was that ethnography seemed to involve imitation without commitment. I could attempt to follow in the footsteps of the monks through the day, join in where I could, share where they would allow me. But always, of course, with the intention of upping and leaving when the fieldwork was done. Some anthropologists, it should be said, have set a precedent for far greater levels of commitment in this kind of fieldwork. Joanna Cook, who carried out 15 months of fieldwork in a Thai Buddhist monastery, spent a year of this time as a professed Buddhist nun. She describes her ordination as a formal but also intimate marker of involvement, telling us how a senior nun whispered a reminder to her of the kinship ties that now bound them within the monastery (Cook 2010: 242). However, this example flags crucial contrasts with the fieldsite I was entering. Cook's mode of participant observation was made possible in part by the understanding that monastic profession can be an interim process in a longer life cycle. However, this would have been alien to the Catholic idea of solemn profession being a lifelong,

---

13 I have also reflected elsewhere (Irvine 2010a) on the dynamics of fieldwork within the monastery.

transformative commitment; and even vows at simple profession are made in the hope of persevering.[14] Temporary immersion could cut against the character of stability, and the intimacy of kinship was located in that commitment to shared time. My own transient presence represented a mobility and ephemerality of relations[15] that ran contrary to the bond that stability creates until (and beyond) death.

Yet guests – and hospitality – occupy a particular place in Benedictine monasticism. The *Rule* notes that monasteries are 'never without' guests and instructs how they are to be received. Accordingly, guests were built into the structure of the monastery, with rooms for guests occupying the upper floor of the east wing, facing the monk's living quarters across a courtyard. Monks and guests converge in the abbey church and the refectory, where they pray and eat together (though seated separately). On the desk in each guestroom was a printed information sheet, which begins with a quotation from Chapter 53 of the *Rule* of St Benedict: 'Let all guests be received in the Person of Christ, so that He will say to us: "I was a stranger and you received me."' The information sheet continued: 'We welcome you to this place of prayer, whoever you are. You represent Christ coming to our community as our guest and as a pilgrim.' It went on to offer some practical information, including an outline of the monastic *horarium*, a reminder that 'silence is to be savoured', and some indication of the running costs of the guest accommodation, for which donations are welcomed. Here, the monastery opens itself to the outsider. This hospitality becomes a further social domain in which gospel values form the monks' lives. As the American Benedictine Kevin Seasoltz (1974: 441) remarked,

---

14 Indeed, when the Catholic Church's Code of Canon Law of 1917 instructed that perpetual Benedictine profession be preceded by a period of three years in temporary vows, the very concept of temporarily vowing stability was deemed a contradiction by some Benedictines. Yeo (1982: 325), an English Benedictine monk and canon lawyer, remarks that this development represented a 'radical departure from the Benedictine tradition'.

15 What Wittel (2001) describes as a network sociality, a disembedded individual-centred relation of shifting connections, in contrast to relations grounded in an enduring collective.

'At the last judgement, Jesus will reveal to everyone the mystery of this hospitality. Through and in the visitor, Christ himself is welcomed or sent away, recognized or unrecognized, just as when he came unto his own people.'

Yet the outsider in the monastery remains an 'ambivalent' presence (Seasoltz 1974: 446). The presence of a guest is an opportunity for encounter, and for contact and witness (Fortin 2003), communicating the monastery's values to the society beyond the cloister – yet this presence also carries a risk of disruption which could undermine those very values. As Pryce (2018: 90) describes in her ethnography of the interaction between monastic communities and contemplative seekers in America, this leads to a 'dialectic of enclosure and openness'. It is within this dynamic that the anthropologist seeks a zone of involvement.

Given the expectation that guests are only present for a short period of time (few stay beyond a week), my own position carrying out research over a year was particularly anomalous; a problem resolved to some degree by the monks giving me the opportunity to live in a small house on the monastery grounds, only a couple of minutes from the abbey and so with ease of access to the daily routine, but sufficiently separated to prevent my continued presence becoming disruptive (and wearisome) beyond the point of tolerance. From here I would make my way along the driveway each morning to the massed limestone of the abbey church, carrying the ring binders I had been loaned so I could participate in the liturgy. Along with the early hour of rising, the scale of the building was something I never became habituated to, the pillars leading my gaze up to the vaulting high above. As was generally the case with guests, I was spatially separated from the monks in the nave of the church, but joined with them in chanting the psalms, following their movements, standing, sitting, kneeling, bowing. Of course, there were no consequences attached to sleeping in, arriving late, or missing any of the liturgical hours. It was my own choice to follow their pattern of prayer, and so I was only accountable to myself. Sometimes, especially at the start and end of the day, I would be the only person in the church apart from the monks, alone in the body of the church and engulfed by the space.

So the monastic *horarium* (see Chapter 3) gave structure to my day, a sense of shared time. Yet at the same time there was a structural sense of separation, a boundary between ways of life, notwithstanding my own Catholicism. What was interesting was the way in which learning and dialogue were made possible through this boundary.

A solid oak door marked the entrance to the monastic enclosure. Above the door, a plaque bears a single word, booming out in block capitals: SILENCE. This was a locked boundary, but it was passable for guests (including myself). Indeed, following the monks as they moved from abbey church to refectory at mealtimes, the door would be held open in welcome, allowing me to make my way into the cloister. Still, the sign calling for silence indicated a transition. What kind of restriction is this demand – or should it be read as an invitation? Wichroski (1997: 227), in an account of fieldwork in the monastery of a contemplative order of nuns, describes how the nuns' insistence upon silence at first reinforced for her the 'realness' of the barrier between the community and the outside world; yet, in that environment, she came to understand that this was itself a form of communication, recognising the flourishing of community within that shared silence. To pass through that door was to acknowledge, and to be included in, a particular kind of environment[16] – one most obvious in the silence at mealtimes, where the focus on listening rather than speech was apparent. Within this space, the body adapts, taking special care not to disturb the state of prayerful recollection. Yet, as some of the monks made their way hurriedly towards breakfast, casting down their cowls on the first available surface in an effort to get to the refectory as rapidly as possible, it also became quickly apparent that this was real human life, cutting across stereotypes of solemnity. In the first days of my fieldwork, this point was put across by one of the older monks, gesturing to the sign that called for silence as we were about to pass under it. 'Yes, the sign seems austere. But the abbot who put

---

16 Jonveaux (2018: 86) notes that the condition of monastic silence combines two elements: the limit on authorised speech and habituation to the absence of sound.

that there kept the temperature at 27 degrees by way of copious amounts of coal, so his heart was in the right place.'

So entering this space meant learning a shift in how to pay attention, but also learning about the value placed on moderation. This was most apparent in the daily teatimes when guests and monks joined together in the refectory in the afternoon, a relaxed time when this convivial aspect of community living came to the fore – joking, sharing stories and recollections, discussing the events of the day.

If prayer structured my day and teatime lightened it, there were still many hours to fill – the hours of work, the other key aspect of monastic discipline twinned with prayer in the Benedictine motto *ora et labora*. Here, not being subject to any vow of obedience, I had to make my own arrangements. And so I immediately responded to the invitation of the monk running the carpentry workshop when he asked if I'd like to help there, wandering each afternoon into the works yard. The memorial cards requesting prayers for the soul of former members of the community, the image of the annunciation, and the fading postcard of an icon of the Blessed Virgin Mary, all marked this place of work as a place of prayer, in which the repetitive movements of plane, spokeshave, and sanding block became meditative acts within a life in the service of God. Of course, this all sounded suitably monastic for the purposes of participant observation. But this kind of manual labour (as discussed in Chapter 7) was somewhat peripheral in the life of the community, where (as we shall see) time was primarily directed towards pastoral work: the care of parishes and the running of a school. Perhaps my 'playing at being a monk' had led me towards an idealised form of monastic labour, rather than towards the primary forms of work with which the community was concerned. Yet these hours in the workshop, and the patience shown to me there as I tried to reach basic competency, were precious. The comings and goings as people brought work or came to help out or just to eat chocolate from the tin kept in the rafters (a stash of chocolate gifted by parishioners) were, of course, a wonderful opportunity to speak freely, ask questions and get to know people. But it was also an immersion in the materiality of life in the monastery – repairing the chairs of the refectory, making shelves to accommodate more books for the library – and even the materiality of monastic values. It was in the care and attention to the process of work, even the deliberate care given to cleaning the workspace afterwards, that I came closest to understanding how material processes are granted spiritual significance in the daily life of the monastery; the deliberate prayerfulness of the everyday.

If time in the workshop allowed me to learn through a somewhat outlying activity, hours spent in the library helped me to grasp matters that were considered core to the monks' identity. From my first arrival at Downside, having expressed an interest in gaining some background knowledge through working in the archives, it became clear that the voices of the monks of the community through time were not mere background, but participants in live ongoing discussions, and that historic debates continued to shape contemporary frames of reference. My request to use the archive was general and open; the response was specific and directed. Without much in the way of discussion or explanation, the archivist led me down the concrete steps to the lowest floor of the library, where he unlocked two cupboards, pulled out a couple of boxes of documents, placed them on the desk above the cupboards and left me to work. The documents related to a constitutional debate in the English Benedictine Congregation between 1880 and 1900. Of all the books and folders that surrounded us, why this starting point?

Platt (2012) describes how the boundaries between field and archive are breached by encounters where the voices of the dead become part of dialogue with the living. From this first introduction, I rapidly learned how integral the library and archive were to the ethnographic method. The importance of the controversy the archivist had opened to me was soon clear – it was a debate about where the focus of English Benedictine activity should lie: whether monks should be directed towards missionary work for the conversion and pastoral care of England or whether this external focus undermined the stability and community of the household itself (I return to this below, and in Chapters 2 and 7). These remained live questions. This initial immersion through the archivist in matters that concerned the monks themselves became integral to the direction of my research, a foundation that helped me to identify core ethnographic concepts and gain a historically informed basis for conversations in the field. This was crucial for navigating the monks' own relationship with institutional time: their historical consciousness was a source of connections and comparisons that shaped social relations for the present and future. A living relationship with the past gives some explanation for why a great deal of this book takes as its ethnographic material the writings of past members of the community and other historical and archival materials. Here was a fieldsite in which communications were frequently footnoted. These sources are ethnographic precisely because the monks directed me to them, taking these historic voices as points of reference in an ongoing conversation. And this is indicative of the temporal scale on which a study of monasticism needs to operate. Recognising, with the historian Fernand Braudel (1972: 21) in his call to attend to the *longue durée*, that events at a specific point of time are 'surface disturbances, crests of foam that the tides of history carry on their strong backs', in the monastery we find that in the temporal scope of the ethnographic present expands into centuries of institutional history and theological debate. The chapters that follow, weaving together fieldwork and historical sources, work within this ethnographic *longue durée*. Ongoing discussions are understood as part of enduring debates; monastic stability incorporates the individual monk's life cycle into a history that spans generations.

The mission and the cloister

A core concern in the study of monasticism – explored at length by Max Weber (1968) in the posthumously published *Economy and Society* – is the relationship of monks with wider society. The scene with which we started this chapter is an act of withdrawal, and this solemn profession is highlighted by Weber as a formal expression of the monks' world rejection (1968: 529). Ascetic practice and monastic silence marks separation from the world beyond the cloister (Jonveaux 2018). This appears not only to be a division of labour but also a division of orientation, between those who have withdrawn from the world in pursuit of the Kingdom of God and the remaining mass of the population who must maintain the world by getting on with the duty of production and reproduction (Troeltsch 1931: 242). Yet this formal withdrawal from the world (Weber 1968: 542) is rarely complete: the monk often relies on the world they have 'rejected' (for example, for sustenance and recruitment) and directs their attention to it, while a wider laity often look to the 'virtuosic' presence of the monks. The virtuoso, according to Weber (1963: 151–65), is someone recognised for their particular talent and skill (in this case, for prayer and living the religious life), who combines this with the intensive practice required to cultivate this talent (see also Goldman and Pfaff 2014). This virtuosity attracts a wider public who look to the monk as an expression of religious values and practice in their midst. They may even be drawn to short-term engagement with monastic discipline as a means of orienting and trying to make sense of their lives in the world, as with lay participation in Sherpa Buddhist monastic rituals (Ortner 1978) or American contemplative Christians on monastic retreat (Pryce 2018). As Tambiah (1970: 109) describes in his account of Thai Buddhist monasticism, here a 'symbiotic relationship' emerges between monk and lay congregation: what Silber (1995) describes as a 'virtuoso-society complex'.

But there is a tension: this can lead to a redirection of the monastic impulse. Instrumentalised by society and 'absorbed' by the Church (Troeltsch 1931: 241), monks become a resource to be directed to external ends: 'asceticism is completely reinterpreted into a means, not primarily of attaining individual salvation in one's own way, but of preparing the monk for work on behalf of the hierocratic authority – the foreign and home mission and the struggle against competing authorities' (Weber 1968: 1167). In this redirection is a danger of dilution and compromise with the world (1968: 1175–6).

How has this tension played out in English Benedictine life? The opening scene of this chapter saw the monk on the threshold, but the early days of my fieldwork were inflected by quite a different scene – monks at the very heart of English Catholic society. In October 2005, the Downside community travelled from Somerset to London to celebrate Mass in Westminster Cathedral. They processed through England's mother church, the sound of monastic chant rising into the domes. Filling the cathedral were parishioners of churches served by the monks, former pupils at the monastery's school, and many others drawn into the orbit of the monastery. This was a Mass of thanksgiving marking their 400th year as a community, but also an opportunity for the monks to reflect on and express their place within the nation. Here in the capital were the ripples of the monastery's presence in English Catholic life.

In his homily, the abbot recalled the community's history of service to the Catholic Church in England, most poignantly in the memory of 'six of our brothers who died a hideous death, condemned by the state as traitors, and honoured by the Church as martyrs'. Missionary work in England played an extremely large role in the life of the English Benedictine Congregation when it was reconstituted following the reformation.[17] Monastic communities of Catholic exiles were founded in continental Europe as centres for the reconversion of England. The Papal Bull[18] *Plantata*, issued in 1633 by Pope Urban VIII, ratified the Congregation's missionary mandate, confirming that the monks should, when making their profession, take a 'Missionary Oath', by which monks solemnly accepted the President of the Congregation as having the authority to transfer them the mission. These were the roots of the 400-year history being celebrated: the monastic community of St Gregory the Great was founded in Douai in 1606, then a notable centre for Catholic exiles (Bossy 1975: 12–17), as a house from which to send monks for the mission in England. It is this sacrificial witness that is embodied in the community's martyrs.

While honouring this history, the abbot nevertheless pivoted to a different kind of 'mission', not expressed through external labour but through the life of the community itself. This was a 'family founded by men fired with the desire to keep the faith alive in England', but he believed it was the life of the monks *as* a family

---

17 For the early history of the Congregation during this period of exile, see Lunn (1980) for the period from 1540 to 1688, and Scott (1992) for the period from 1685–1794.

18 An official decree issued by the Pope.

which shone a light in the world: the 'charism of community living' discussed earlier. Here the monastery is presented as an exemplary centre, showing a communal life that transgresses social norms while elevating new, potentially even utopian, norms (see Jonveaux 2018). In the words of the abbot, 'A monastery shows the beauty of a way of life which does not involve careerism and getting promoted; the beauty of a way of life which does involve being liberated from rivalry and power struggles. They show the beauty of a community life which is structured by mutual deference and obedience, of a community where no one is in the centre, where there is an empty void, which is able to be filled by the glory of God.'

Here the abbot reflects a longstanding position within the community, as expressed by one of his predecessors, Cuthbert Butler (1919: 382–3), second Abbot of Downside, who wrote that 'the real use of a monastic house lies not in activities and usefulness' but in its place as a 'reservoir of religion' in the midst of society. This was a position that took shape in the debates around English Benedictine identity at the end of the nineteenth century (see Irvine 2010b). By this stage the community was no longer in exile on the continent, and in fact had been at home in England for a century – the events of the French Revolution, policies suppressing monastic orders, and finally the declaration of war against Britain by the revolutionary government made life in France unsustainable, while freedom to worship as a Catholic was granted in England by the 1791 Catholic Relief Act. Forced to leave Douai in 1793, the community based themselves temporarily in Acton Burnell, Shropshire, before settling at Downside in 1814. Yet, in spite of the return of the monastic houses to England, the fundamental understanding that the purpose of the monastery was to provide priests for the mission, and the structures that supported that arrangement remained unchanged. This led to an identity crisis.[19] On the one hand, the missionary vocation of the English Benedictines was vigorously defended by those who saw the reconversion of England as the Congregation's fundamental task, enshrined in its identity

---

19 I have written elsewhere (Irvine 2010b) about the debates within the Congregation at this time, and discuss them further in Chapter 7.

and constitution at the point of its revival. On the other hand, there were those – including Cuthbert Butler – who felt that this external focus undermined their vocation to live a monastic life. In particular, the existence of a missionary oath was seen to contradict the vow of stability, detaching the monk from the monastery of his formation and fragmenting the household as a place of spiritual growth. Following the Papal Bulls *Religiosus Ordo* (in 1890) and *Diu Quidem* (in 1899), the missionary oath was abolished and the monasteries gained constitutional status as autonomous households. In fact, there was little change to the nature of the work undertaken by English Benedictines, generating an ongoing tension (see Chapter 7); but the emphasis on the family life of the monastery as the essential feature of Benedictine identity, with any external works viewed as secondary to this, came to be expressed with a particular tenacity in the wake of this history.

So the affirmation of the monastery's relation to society as a 'reservoir of religion' invokes not only the abbey's life as a liturgical centre (see Chapter 4), but also the role of the monastery as an exemplar, in the sense described by Humphrey (1997) and developed by Robbins (2018: 191) in relation to institutions: 'moral sensibilities are developed ... by means of people's encounters with the values they find actually existing and experientially available in the exemplary figures and institutions of their social surround'. As Evans (2023: 454) has put it, exemplars are 'arguments for what ought to be rendered in hopeful statements about what is'. In this way, the monastery is a living expression of Christian social life. However, in contrast to Weber's model of the virtuoso, which places emphasis on that which is exceptional, what is striking when we consider the idealised picture of monastic life presented by the abbot in his homily at the anniversary Mass is that his words are attractive precisely because they lie within reach. The way of life being spoken about is not meant to exclude the rest of humanity: it is to show a possibility of what could be.

Here it is important to note a characteristic emphasis on moderation, as can be seen in Cuthbert Butler's account of Benedictine life, which contrasts the severity and austerity of early monasticism with the *Rule*'s provision for 'sufficient food, ample sleep, proper clothing' (Butler 1919: 40); the focus is not on acts of severe asceticism through which the individual pursues a 'personal advance in virtue ... prolonging his fasts, his prayers, his silence' (1919: 13), but rather 'the sanctification of the monk was to be found in living the life of the community' (1919: 45).

Over tea one spring afternoon, a monk told me about a letter he had received from a man asking to stay in the monastery through Lent so that he could experience the rigours of severe fasting. 'I hate that kind of thing. I wrote back and told him that if he was interested in fasting, he probably wouldn't find much of it here.' He defiantly munched on a biscuit, and his frustration with the assumption that the monastic life must be characterised by extreme austerity was palpable. Benedictine life was, for him, not about pushing those kinds of limits. Certainly, the monastery observed certain elements of abstinence in continuity with the wider church, such as abstaining from meat on Fridays, but not in a way that made a show of their asceticism. Another monk responded with a recollection of his own from the 1950s: a 'very severe' visitor to the monastery asked the guest master whether he might borrow a hairshirt. The guest master, somewhat bamboozled by this request for a form of penitential garb that was quite alien to his experience of monastic life, nevertheless decided to play along and went away saying he'd have a look in the store, coming back with the answer that he was very sorry but all twelve were in use.

Around the time of this conversation, an ornately carved misericord had arrived in the workshop in need of repair and reattachment, having broken off from the choir stalls. A misericord is a wooden ledge on the underside of the folding seats of the choir stalls, aiding those monks who need support by taking some of their weight of the long periods of standing in the liturgy; the name comes from the Latin *misericordia*, meaning mercy. As a demonstration of kindness to those who through age or illness were weaker on their feet, the misericord embodied the humane characteristics of the *Rule* to which my attention was repeatedly drawn: its moderation and recognition of human frailty. As Maya Mayblin (2017) has argued, there can be a tendency for anthropologists to overemphasise the role of discipline within religion, and within Catholicism in particular, in a way that overlooks the constitutive role of lenience and mercy. Whereas Talal Asad (1993) characterises Catholic monasticism as a regimen of ascetic discipline for the construction of obedient wills, a central aspect of the monks' self-representation was the compassionate realism of Benedict's 'little Rule for beginners',[20] setting down 'nothing harsh, nothing burdensome'.[21] This crucial point was driven home on the 'ask a monk' section of the monastery's website, in response to a question on the eating habits of monks: 'A monk, therefore, is not some sort of super-Christian, but rather an everyday sort of Christian trying his utmost to live out his baptismal vocation in a monastic community.'

Departure

On 28 August 2020 the community announced that they had decided to leave Downside and seek a new place to live. In March 2022, on the feast day of their patron St Gregory the Great, they celebrated their final Mass in the abbey church, before moving to Southgate House in the grounds of Buckfast Abbey, Devon, another English Benedictine monastery, as a 'stepping stone' while they reflect on their longer-term future as a household.

Given the importance of stability – and, in particular, stability of place – to English Benedictine identity, such a move sounds a dissonance with the nature of the monastic commitment. When a life cycle becomes so intimately bound around a particular location, what does it mean to leave home? And yet the decision to move was made as a family; and when the monk promises stability, it is a lifelong commitment to the household of their profession. For a community to move together is to maintain those family bonds, albeit there is a poignancy to leaving behind a place where so much of that collective belonging has sedimented.

Such a move also recalibrates the relationship between the monastery and society, leaving behind such a prominent and visible

---

20 *Rule* of St Benedict, Chapter 73.
21 *Rule* of St Benedict, Prologue.

symbol of the place of monasticism as the abbey church. In some ways this is the culmination of decades of divestment: in 2015 the community reorganised its local parish commitments around the single parish church within the village of the monastery, leading to the closure of five churches in Somerset and a sale of church buildings, and in the subsequent years it has handed over responsibility for its parishes elsewhere in England. Within the school established by the monastery, for many years monastic involvement in teaching had been limited, but in 2014 the school appointed its first lay headmaster and in 2019 the school formally became independent of the abbey. In other words, the monastic community had effectively withdrawn from the forms of apostolic labour that had been a principal focus across centuries of its history. From one perspective, such retrenchment could be seen as the culmination of the shift away from an external focus to an emphasis on the life of the household itself – the very thing that had been sought by the reformers at the end of the nineteenth century. Yet, of course, this was also a matter of logistics. The monastery had been built to house a community of 50, but that number had dwindled and the community had aged. When I began my fieldwork in 2005, Downside was a household of 28 monks; by 2024, there were only 14.

Further factors had a bearing on the decision to move. In 2018 the Independent Inquiry into Child Sexual Abuse reported on numerous allegations of abuse carried out by members of the community in addition to a case of sexual assault that had led to the arrest and imprisonment of one of the monks. Moreover, the Inquiry reported on how the community had sheltered offenders and sought to protect its own reputation, while failing to act to protect children at the school. The formal separation of school and abbey came in the wake of the recommendations of the Inquiry, and this separation was followed by a period of discernment in which the community considered its future.

In the face of the pain and destruction caused by abuse, what is the point of anthropology – especially an anthropology which deals primarily with aspects of an institutional life that focus our attention elsewhere?[22] I have no easy answer to this. I have often wondered what worth the picture of religious life gained through this study can have in such a context. To speak, as I have above, of the role of such a community as an 'exemplar', is to plunge the reader into an atmosphere of distrust, rightfully wary of 'objects of suspicion whose exemplarity will necessarily be revealed as illusory given sufficient time and information' (Evans 2023: 448). The gap between the ideal and everyday practice is of course a key space for anthropological analysis, and tensions within and between elements of monastic life are an important part of this ethnography. That the monks have long recognised and reflected on a tension between the external focus of work such as the school and the stability of household living, and the potential problems this generated for the community, provides some relevant background to these events and to the question of the community's future; this is the focus of Chapter 8. But it would be inaccurate and inappropriate to present my research as though I had set out to address moral failures. What I present here instead reflects an ongoing relationship; an attempt to get to know people better, to understand them on their own terms, a responsibility both to listen and to speak honestly. The ethnography embodies not only an initial year of fieldwork, but a continuing critical conversation over many years subsequently, a process of reflection in dialogue with the monks about the moral, ritual, and institutional framework of a human community and its lived relationships. I have taken that framework seriously while attending to its tensions. I will leave it for the reader to decide whether that task is valid.

The central theme of this ethnography is stability – the possibility of belonging and growing through relationships rooted in place and enduring through time. Yet stability understood in this way is a way of responding to a human need, not an accomplishment in itself. It is an expression of perseverance.

In the chapters that follow, I examine how that promise of stability

22 See also Engelke (2007), who in his conclusion reflects on one of his key informants being convicted of multiple counts of rape; he too has no straightforward answers to this question.

is grounded in time and space. Chapter 2 examines the architecture of the monastery as the expression of a desire for community living, but also as an expression of continuity in the landscape and the endurance of the Catholic Church: a witness to a particular way of living. Chapter 3 then focuses on the time discipline of the monastic *horarium* and the rhythm of prayer. It describes how in the movement through the day time comes to be experienced as a relationship rather than an abstract quantity. In these chapters we therefore see how the ideal of stability takes material form, while beginning to reflect on some of the pressures placed upon this ideal.

The next group of chapters examine in detail the dynamics of prayer in the monastery, and how the different elements of prayer connect and disconnect. Chapter 4 focuses on monks' shared public prayer. I discuss the leading role monks in the community took in advocating liturgical reform and resisting the idea that monasteries should become 'museums' for out-of-date forms of liturgy; but, showing how these reforms have been contested, I also reflect on some of the monks' concerns that the transcendent potential of the liturgy has been undermined. The central theme of this chapter is participation: to what extent does a focus on the individual intentionality of a participant build conscious community, and what are the possibilities for a sense of collectivity that transcends the individual? Chapter 5 explores the crucial presence of contemplative prayer in the monastery. This is a space of solitude and silence that draws attention to the central tension of engagement and disengagement at the heart of monasticism. Crucially, it is expression of the perseverance that characterises stability, a wilful act of love even as thought and feeling seem to dry up. Yet it is also, paradoxically, an unsettling, an expression of perseverance into the unknown. Chapter 6 examines *lectio divina* – the 'slow, contemplative praying of scripture' – and the challenge of developing a community of listeners.

In the concluding chapters, I return to the theme of the monastery's relationship with society. Chapter 7 examines the role of work in the monastery, and recognising the emphasis placed by the English Benedictine Congregation on external work, I discuss how the problem of accommodating such work within the framework of a life of stability is shown to be a recurrent problem in the history of the Congregation, the monastery, and the lives of the monks themselves. Chapter 8 focuses on the failures of the monks' responsibility and revisits the core elements of the monastic commitment in the wake of the harms identified by the Independent Inquiry into Child Sexual Abuse. Finally, in Chapter 9 we focus on the community's departure from Downside. What does leaving home show us about the nature of monastic stability?

A focus on stability allows us to recognise a desire for rootedness and belonging, the sense of direction through the growth of relationships in place – a growth that is sometimes a joy, sometimes a pain, full of moments of brightness but also of difficulty. It locates the life of a community not in any particular moment or in specific historic events, but as a thread of continuity through time. Yet this continuity is not simply the comfort of familiarity; it is an unsettling of the ordinary and the everyday through its relationship to eternity. Stability is a work of perseverance open to the unknown.

CHAPTER 2

The architecture of stability

A statement of sacred space

'Are our religious houses places of sanctity, sanctuary, and hospitality? Do they witness to the centrality of prayer in our lives? Do they suggest that our lives are consecrated to God?' In the week before the feast of All Saints, habits of different styles and colours converged upon Downside as the monastery hosted a day of recollection for brothers and sisters of the various monastic and religious orders present in the diocese. As those attending reflected, prayed, and ate together over the course of the day, the abbey, and its grounds, performed its role as a place of retreat and hospitality. So when the abbot addressed the gathering, it seemed fitting to reflect on the character of monastic architecture as both a metaphor for and a visible expression of the religious vocation.

Beginning by pointing out that the word 'paradise' comes from the Persian for enclosed garden, he continued: 'The cloister is the nearest example of the garden of contemplation. Tending towards the centre the walks of the cloister inform the space not only of the garden but of the whole building which surrounds it. It is a statement of sacred space.' This model informed not only the religious house but also those who lived there, working to cultivate in themselves 'an enclosed space which reflects … the whole of creation. In this sense the religious is an intense focus of the abiding love of God.' Key to this image of the enclosed garden was a contrast between the space for contemplation and an uncertain world beyond its threshold. 'The religious life seen as a personal life of holiness lived out in a sanctuary set aside for the silent search and worship of God is still a compelling image and one which makes increasing sense to a world which seeks to find meaning and blessing ... If you ever visit a beautiful monastic cloister the enclosed garden seems a paradisal respite from a hostile world, an oasis in a desert. Finding space and solitude is an unsurprising fixation in a world dominated by noise and too much busyness.'

What is the significance of architecture for our understanding of monastic life? I begin with the abbot's words because they focus our attention on the cloister as an expression of a particular form of life and a witness to that life. They do so in a way that hinges on an opposition between the sacred space and a world beyond in search of 'meaning and blessing'. Taking its cue from these words, this chapter considers how core monastic values might be materialised in the buildings of the monastery. In particular, by examining the history of the buildings at Downside and the kind of life contained within them, the focus is on how stability – as a monastic vow, but also as a value to be witnessed – comes to take physical form.

Here the abbey church with all its imposing presence is a good place to begin. Scale has an impact. This physical encounter with such an imposing building in a rural location was itself a key factor in the monks' social presence. The tower of the abbey church is visible from miles around and physically dominates the small village in which it is located. Following the signs to the visitor entrance, you are taken along the full length of the building's exterior, making apparent the sheer quantity of limestone involved in its construction. This construction embodied a certain set of aspirations among the community: to make a home – and in making a home, to stake a claim to an identity that was truly *at home* in England and within English society and history.

On a certain level, what I am proposing here is to read the buildings in terms of their symbolic meaning. Of course, this kind of emphasis on the representational value of buildings has been subject to critique, and with good reason. As the anthropologist and architectural theorist Albena Yaneva (2012: 21) has written, 'If you find yourself asking "what does this building mean?" and "what does the architect want to say?", you will have picked the wrong questions! The only questions you need to ask are: "how does this building work?" and "how was this building made to work?"' The point she wishes to drive home is that representational thinking reaches an impasse when the architectural is reduced to something that can be explained as a manifestation of other factors. Instead, the focus should be on the worlds buildings generate and the worlds that set them to work. I agree with this perspective: I am interested in how the architecture of the monastery plays an active role in the shaping and reshaping of the monastic life, and at the same time how monks' lives become enmeshed in the set of buildings. Yet it is not possible to completely abandon a symbolic discussion of what the buildings might communicate. This is, first of all, because of the intentional incorporation of symbolic expressions – scriptural narratives, doctrinal concepts, and stories of saints – within the fabric and decoration of church buildings; a point which Hall (2000) relevantly elaborates in relation to Victorian churches. But it is also because the buildings are intentional interventions in society. They are ways by which parts of the community sought to make specific identity claims – within internal debates about the monastic life, but also to the world at large. It is therefore ethnographically important to follow these claims. In a different minority context – Muslims in the Netherlands – Oskar Verkaaik (2012, 2020) has described the way in which mosque design is a process of *negotiation* of identity, asking what it means to be Muslim in Europe (and specifically in the Netherlands) today, and the forms of materiality and visibility this might require. Here, debates around design cannot completely evade questions of representation: what kind of identity claims emerge through the building in the context of the world around?

Accordingly, this chapter considers the role of monastic architecture in the context of social change (see also Irvine 2011a): the status of Catholicism as a minority form of Christianity within English society; aspirations for a future to which the monastery might witness; and shifting (and competing) understandings of the monastic vocation within all this. The focus will be on the monastery as an *architecture of stability*, both through its imposing assertion of endurance within the landscape and in how it was put to work in the process of giving stability material form.

Endurance in the landscape

Beyond the initial impression of the abbey church's imposing and engulfing scale, it is also one of a building that asserts antiquity. In the words of one of the monks who published an architectural history of the abbey: 'It is not a medieval church ... And yet to the perceptive stranger visiting it to-day, there is no doubt that it possesses the atmosphere of a medieval church' (James 1961: 6).

This should be understood as the desired effect of a number of design decisions made in the late nineteenth and early twentieth centuries – there was a deliberate intention to evoke the past in the present. It was, from the first, intended to be imitative of medieval architecture. Aidan Gasquet, the prior who initiated the building work in the 1870s, was himself a medieval historian. The architects he engaged, Archibald Dunn and Edward Hansom, drew heavily on the Gothic architecture of French cathedrals, especially Amiens, which Dunn had studied (James 1961: 10). The drawings prepared by Dunn and Hansom, complete with processions of tonsured monks, demonstrate the medievalist imagination at work. The very use of the pointed arch, characteristic of the Gothic style of architecture, is a nineteenth-century revival of a form of building that had fallen into abeyance with the shift to classical styles of architecture between the sixteenth and eighteenth centuries. Dunn and Hansom's Gothic Revival design shaped the construction of the west wing of the monastery, providing living quarters for the monks but, of the grand church envisaged, only the transept was completed – setting a footprint for the scale of what was to follow – in addition to the ambulatory (the walkway around the envisaged east end of the church) and some of the radiating chapels.

A second phase of building emerged following the election of Edmund Ford as the first Abbot of Downside. As we shall see, throughout his time as monastic superior (first succeeding Gasquet as prior, and then becoming abbot when Downside was raised to the status of an abbey), Ford championed stability as central to an authentic monastic vocation, and the further development of the Church should be understood as part of the assertion of these ideals. He enlisted the services of the architect Thomas Garner, who had left an impression on Ford through his work to restore the 'Slipper Chapel' at Walsingham in Norfolk as a place of Catholic pilgrimage. Given the importance of Walsingham as a major pilgrimage destination and site of devotion until the Reformation, when the main shrine was dismantled as an act of iconoclasm in 1537, what is worth noting is that this was a task which showed the architect's sensitivity to the task of restoring the suppressed glories of England's Catholic heritage,[1] something which resonated with the task of restoring the place of monasticism in England. Although many of the community remained attached to aspects of the Dunn and Hansom plan, Ford championed Garner and, in particular, his adherence to more specifically English forms of Gothic architecture. Garner designed and oversaw the construction of a square east end for the abbey church, which he felt was far more in keeping with the architecture of English medieval churches; his design was largely based on the Perpendicular Gothic style of English churches in the fifteenth century (1961: 42–7). In this way, the linkage between the abbey church and the specifically English history that it was intended to be part of became increasingly explicit.

Garner died in 1906, before his full scheme could be completed. The work was instead continued by Giles Gilbert Scott from 1922 to 1925. After unsuccessfully presenting two plans for the nave, which the community rejected as too disconnected from what had gone before (Stamp 2011), Scott implemented a third scheme, blending his own work with Garner's designs and their proportions.

1 See Coleman (2000) on the revival of pilgrimage to Walsingham and its perceived importance to the revival of English Catholic identity and the 'reconstruction' of forms of heritage suppressed at the time of Reformation. While the 'Slipper Chapel' was not the location of the pre-Reformation shrine, but rather a chapel on the way to the shrine itself, today it remains the 'Catholic National Shrine' and thus the focus of Catholic pilgrimage to Walsingham.

However, the west end of the church was not completed, as the community could not decide whether they wished to extend the nave of the church further and so opted to build a 'temporary' plain west wall so as to delay the decision (James 1961: 75–6). This wall still stands.

There is an obvious social and political context to these aesthetic decisions, a theme not lost on the architectural historian Nikolaus Pevsner in his description of Downside Abbey as part of his county-by-county architectural survey, *The Buildings of England*: 'If ever there was excuse for building in period forms in the C20, it is here … The whole of the abbey church has become the most splendid demonstration of the renaissance of Roman Catholicism in England' (Pevsner 1958: 71). This is architecture that asserts a status after centuries of absence.

'Rebuilding Glastonbury'

We get a sense of this desire in visions of the future voiced during construction. In 1882 Laurence Shepherd – an English Benedictine monk at the time serving as chaplain to the nuns at Stanbrook Abbey – was invited to give a series of retreat talks to the community at Downside. We know from contemporary records that the ideas he expressed generated a great deal of excitement (as well as controversy) among the community.[2] Shepherd urges the monks to embrace and embody the rich history of English monasticism, 'the ten hundred years history of glory in England' prior to the

---

2 In the archives at Downside Abbey, the papers of the Second Abbot of Downside, Cuthbert Butler, include a typescript manuscript from 1905 titled 'The Downside Movement' (item 1435), in which he remarks that Laurence Shepherd's retreat 'had a great effect on many of us, certainly it had on me' (18). A more hostile reflection on the retreat from within the community can be found in the papers of Alphonsus Morrall (item 453); as we shall see, in contrast to the enthusiasm which Butler shared with some of the younger monks, Morrall's position was more resistant to calls for reform in the English Benedictine Congregation at this time.

Reformation.[3] He evokes the tremendous learning, the hospitality and, above all, the solemn celebration of the liturgy of the medieval monks. He looks around him and, finding the community at Downside 'engaged in the grand work of Building a House to God',[4] he envisions the building work as a restoration of the spirit and place of monasticism in England. 'If I have talked too much as tho' I were dreaming, dreaming that St. Gregory's of Downside was getting turned gradually into Glastonbury, it is pardonable.'[5]

The idea of 'rebuilding Glastonbury' is a potent one. As a site of lost monastic grandeur and deep legend,[6] the great monastic ruins at Glastonbury, some 15 miles away on the other side of the Mendip Hills, exerted a magnetic pull on the monks' imaginations. Aidan Gasquet, under whose leadership the construction of the new church at Downside began, had also written about Glastonbury Abbey as a symbol of England's monastic heritage (Gasquet 1895). Glastonbury connected the history of monasticism to the thread of British history. It was the resting place not only of King Edmund I and King Edmund II, but also, according to legend, the burial site of King Arthur. In folklore, Glastonbury was said to have been visited by Joseph of Arimathea, the man who had taken Jesus down from the cross and entombed him. For Gasquet, these legends did not need to be verifiable in order to be significant – they simply stood as a clear indication of the link in the popular imagination between monastic life and England's history as a Christian country: 'Here, and here alone on English soil, we are linked not only to the beginnings of

---

3 Laurence Shepherd, 'Notes of the Retreat given at Downside 1882', 115, Stanbrook Abbey Archives.
4 Shepherd, 'Notes of the Retreat given at Downside 1882', 121.
5 Shepherd, 'Notes of the Retreat given at Downside 1882', 147.
6 See Bowman (2004) on the mythology around Glastonbury's place as the 'cradle of English Christianity', the early-twentieth-century revivals of pilgrimage to Glastonbury seeking to reconnect with this heritage and the subsequent growth of New Age spirituality in the town around the monastery ruins. Prince and Riches (2000) have provided an ethnographic account of late-twentieth-century Glastonbury; while their focus is primarily on these New Age religious movements, it testifies to the continued allure of Glastonbury's sacred geography.

The architecture of stability

English Christianity, but to the beginnings of Christianity itself' (Gasquet 1895: 4). With the dissolution of the abbey in 1539 and the subsequent execution of Richard Whiting, its last abbot, for treason, this link was all but severed.

Against the backdrop of this historical rupture, it is little surprise that monks came to be seen as something alien. The community made their home at Downside at a time when Catholicism itself was treated with a great deal of suspicion and even hostility (Ralls 1974; Paz 1992). Catholics, it was claimed, owed their allegiance to a foreign power. In the mid nineteenth century, the sermons of Cardinal Wiseman – appointed first Catholic Archbishop of Westminster in 1850, following the restoration of the Catholic hierarchy in England and Wales – in which he expressed admiration for those condemned as treasonous in this world and crowned as martyrs in the next, were used as evidence by the Conservative Member of Parliament Charles Newdegate, who argued that the Catholic hierarchy was a threat to the security of the state (Arnstein 1982: 168–70). Newdegate was hardly unique in holding this view. An established church (as existed, and still exists, in the form of the Church of England) intertwines religious authority with the authority of the state. Loyalty to Rome could all too easily be construed as disloyalty to Queen and Country. How can one claim to be both 'Catholic' and 'British' at the same time?

As for monasteries, we can see the particularly acute suspicion in which religious and monastic orders were held at this time. The view of celibacy and enclosure as unnatural forms of asceticism fuelled a growing literature depicting apparent acts of depravity within the cloister. Ingram (1991: 783) details the 'professional leisure industry', which satisfied the public appetite 'for stories about the misbehaviour of the Catholic priest and his lascivious practices in confessional and convent … a great torrent of public performers in the character of "escaped nuns" and "reformed priests" toured the British Isles lecturing to delightedly shocked audiences with accounts of their own "personal experiences"'. The portrayal of monasteries as sinister presences in the English landscape is exemplified by false allegations against the Cistercian Abbey of Mount St Bernard, Leicestershire, after a man named William Thomas

Jeffreys claimed to have been held at the monastery against his will; his claims of captivity, detailing the cruelty of the monks, were published in 1849 in a pamphlet titled *A Narrative of Six Years' Captivity and Suffering among the Monks of Saint Bernard, in the Monastery at Charnwood Forest, Leicestershire*. The angry reaction of locals, who threatened to blow up the monastery, shows the clear potential of such tales to inflame tensions and prejudices (Paz 1992: 122). At the heart of such suspicions are claims that monasteries were 'Popish prisons', essentially foreign and forever incompatible with English values.

'Rebuilding Glastonbury' in this context is to claim continuity in place of rupture. Positioning the abbey as a restoration of past glories rather than some kind of foreign body, the architecture becomes a way of asserting the *Englishness* of monastic life. There were indeed occasions during my time in the monastery where members of the contemporary community sought to make this point and used the building to help drive the point home. Taking me to one of the side chapels, dedicated to St Vedast, one of the monks showed me the stained-glass window depicting Pope Gregory the Great blessing St Augustine of Canterbury before he set out for England in 596 AD. The monastery founded by Augustine in Kent 'began 1400 years of Benedictine history in England. The history of England is bound up with the history of monks living according to the *Rule*. Part of being English is not shouting out about being English and making a song and dance about it. But there are very few parts of English life that can claim a 1,400-year history and I think that is something we should be proud of'. Reflecting this, the intention throughout these phases of construction was to build 'a Downside which should vie with great pre-Reformation abbeys in dignity and magnificence' (James 1961: 72). The Church is packed full of connections with that pre-Reformation history.

One point of connection is in the stone used: oolitic limestone laid down in the Lower to Middle Jurassic has long been exploited as a building material in the region, and so the buildings exist in clear relation to the geology underfoot and to the economy of the region. There were several disused quarries in the vicinity of the monastery that served as landmarks when planning walks for times of recreation. It was such quarries that had provided the stone for many of the great churches in the region, including Glastonbury Abbey, but also Bath Abbey and Wells Cathedral. So the very material roots the abbey in place and lays claim to a continuity with the building of the great churches of the county. This sense of material connection with the past through oolitic limestone sits at the very heart of the church: the altar around which the community gathered to celebrate Mass each day was built from stone taken from the grounds of Glastonbury Abbey.

Other points of deliberate connection with pre-Reformation monasticism can be found in the decoration and furnishing of the abbey. The vaulting of one of the largest side chapels, dedicated to St Benedict, is bossed with the Arms of the principal Benedictine monasteries prior to their dissolution. The choir stalls to which the monks return throughout the day for the cycle of liturgical prayer are reproductions[7] of the choir stalls at Chester Cathedral, itself a former Benedictine abbey. We are left in no doubt of the lineage within which the community placed itself.

What we see is a tremendous effort to build in such a way that it might appear that monasticism in England *had never gone away* – to make buildings of the late nineteenth and early twentieth centuries appear consistent with the English history they lay claim to and, in so doing, to make them appear at home, rather than something rendered alien by the historical chasms of reformation and dissolution. As we have seen, the architecture not only connects the monastery with pre-Reformation forms but seeks to demonstrate their continuing vitality. One of the most commanding displays of the abbey's claim to continuity is its tower, completed in 1938 and based on a design by Giles Gilbert Scott. The design of the tower is deliberately imitative of the pre-Reformation church towers of the county. The 'Somerset Tower' is a recognisable style that consists in its simplest form of a buttressed square tower, topped with a parapet and pinnacles at each corner (Wright 1981).

---

7 In 1930, scale drawings and photographs of the Chester stalls were sent to Ortisei in South Tyrol, where they were reproduced in the workshop of Ferdinand Stuflesser. The stalls were completed in 1933.

Church architecture throughout the county between the fourteenth and sixteenth centuries shows the development and elaboration of this theme. Scott, in completing the tower of the abbey, crowned it with pinnacles and located it firmly within this tradition.

While the scale of the abbey dominated the countryside below, the community were nevertheless proud of the fact that the pinnacles of the great tower were in no way dissonant with Somerset's history: coming into view, they would be in keeping with the other great churches of the county, and not alien to the landscape around. Indeed, one member of the community gave me a pamphlet he had written (Lambert 1997) taking the reader on 'a journey around the ornate parish church towers of the Somerset Mendip hills'. After providing photographs and historical notes for seven towers of the period 1350–1550, he ends with the tower at Downside nearly 400 years later, not only as a continuation of the county's indigenous forms, but something of a dramatic culmination. After reflecting on the height of the tower (166 feet), second only to the stately tower at Wells Cathedral (187 feet), his pamphlet concludes, 'These men of masonry and prayer are seen to have high and noble aspirations. Both professions are native to the Mendips.'

Counterfactual architecture

Such appeals to continuity with the past place the monastic architecture squarely within the domain of the 'invention of tradition'. The historian Eric Hobsbawm (1983: 2) developed this concept as a way to explore 'responses to novel situations which take the form of reference to old situations'. This is fundamentally a process of legitimation: especially in the face of social change and apparent rupture, institutions root their values and norms in the sense of authority that comes from endurance through time and the appeal to an 'unchanging and invariant' past. In a different context, Maurice Bloch (1968, 1986) has illustrated how ritual structures can give the impression of transcending the present. The brightly painted and decorated tombs of the Merina in Madagascar with their walls of stone and cement 'demonstrate in material form the victory over time and also over movement. Tombs are emphatically placed in a particular highly significant place and they are there for ever' (1986: 169). In doing so, they give material form to an ideology of descent which 'remains still amidst the vicissitudes of time', legitimating the authority of the ancestors over the present life and its activities by creating the impression of 'a group which is unaffected by day to day events and which continues to exist as generations come and go' (1968: 100).

The use of medieval forms at Downside should be seen as an assertion of the endurance of the past into the present. Indeed, it is striking that one of the first examples Hobsbawm (1983: 1) offers to illustrate the invention of tradition is the use of Gothic Revival architecture: the choice of Gothic for the nineteenth-century construction of the British Houses of Parliament, and the choice to rebuild on the same plan following the Second World War damage. At times of rapid social change, disruption and shifts in political representation, the authority of the 'mother of parliaments' was asserted through the adoption and repetition of a style which conveys its long history.

But does legitimation through continuity with the past fully account for the work the buildings at Downside were doing? Here, I suggest reading the abbey as *counterfactual architecture*; that is, architecture that critiques the present by asserting what could have been under different circumstances.

While highly influential, the concept of the invention of tradition has been critiqued – including by Terence Ranger (1993), co-editor of the volume which introduced the concept – as potentially closing off a recognition of processes of creativity and contestation in the use of 'tradition' (see also Post 2001). Moving beyond a static conception of tradition, Neveling and Klein (2010) have drawn our attention to the future orientation of such inventions: how by highlighting negative developments in the present, appeals to tradition are not simply attempts to make it seem that the past never went away, but can generate ideas of what the future should be like.

Returning not only to the pointed arches at Downside, but also to Hobsbawm's example of the architecture of the Houses of

Parliament, the Gothic Revival provides an interesting case in point. Augustus Welby Pugin – the architect responsible for the design of the Houses of Parliament, and whose advocacy of the Gothic style was particularly influential in ensuring its revival[8] (Hill 2007) – presented architecture as a visible manifestation of truth and error.

In the context of his own conversion to Catholicism in 1835, this becomes a way for Pugin to demonstrate the wrong turning that English society had taken following the Reformation. His famous work *Contrasts; or, A Parallel Between the Noble Edifices of the Fourteenth and Fifteenth Centuries, and Similar Buildings of the Present Day; Showing the Present Decay of Taste* is an illustrated polemic that attempts to demonstrate the moral superiority of Gothic forms. The message of his work is clear: 'on the eve of the great change of religion, we find Architecture in a high state of perfection,[9] both as regards design and execution' (Pugin 1841a: 5), but, from then on, the story is one of catastrophic decline. We read of suppression, spoliation and desecration, avarice and greed, and the loss of religious unity and pious feelings; for Pugin, these were the primary social effects of the Reformation. This moral decline, suggests Pugin, is clearly evident in the degeneration of architecture, and he sets out to prove this through a series of illustrations

---

8 A. W. Pugin had, in fact, been commissioned to draw plans for monastic buildings at Downside, and he made several drawings for this work between 1839 and 1842 (O'Donnell 1981). However, a lack of funds meant that it was only later in the century that building work could begin on a new church and monastery complex, by which time new plans had been drawn up by Dunn and Hansom.

9 This claim that architecture had reached a point of perfection arises from his insistence upon two great rules for design (Pugin 1841b: 1): 'First, that there should be no features about a building which are not necessary for convenience, construction or propriety, Second, that all ornament should consist of enrichment of the essential construction of the building ... In pure architecture the smallest detail should have a meaning or serve a purpose; and even the construction itself should vary with the material employed, and the designs should be adapted to the material in which they are executed.' He goes on to state that 'strange as it may appear at first sight, it is in pointed architecture alone that these great principles have been carried out'.

contrasting pre-Reformation and nineteenth-century architecture. Parochial churches, chapels, altar screens and memorials are all catalogued in ways that seek to elevate the beauty of the old forms and the ugliness, banality and incongruity of the new forms.

Pugin does not restrict his contrasts to aesthetic comparisons; that he is presenting social commentary is made clear by his contrasts of pre- and post-Reformation cities (the latter filled with factories, workhouses, a lunatic asylum and a 'socialist hall of science'). Monasteries are presented as crucial to the pre-Reformation order: 'It would be an endless theme to dilate on all the advantages accruing from these splendid establishments; suffice it to observe, that it was through their boundless charity and hospitality that the poor were entirely maintained. They formed alike the places for the instruction of youth, and the quiet retreat of a mature age; and the vast results that the monastic bodies have produced, in all classes of art and science, show the excellent use they made of that time which was not consecrated to devotion and the immediate duties of their orders' (1841a: 7). The failings of the current age are illustrated by drawings contrasting the care for the poor provided in a monastery with the nineteenth-century workhouse, complete with chained inmates, a watchtower in the style of Bentham's panopticon and the ominous notice: 'a variety of subjects always ready for medical students'.

To bring the discussion back to Downside, so far what I have been arguing is that the abbey church emphatically declares the endurance of monasticism, while making an ambitious claim in its scale and grandeur for the contemporary status of Catholicism and its capacity to revive pre-Reformation glories. From this perspective, 'invention of tradition' does more than just assert continuity. We might even consider the architecture of the monastery as an exercise in counterfactual history. It poses a set of provocative 'What if?' questions: What if Henry VIII had not dissolved the English monasteries? What if the Reformation had never happened?

To assert stability here is certainly to suggest that Benedictine monasticism endures and persists in place while generations come and go but, by suggesting that buildings might be treated as 'counter-factual', what I am saying is that the architecture invites contrast between a vision of the traditional order and the present world. Pugin (1841a) ends his *Contrasts* with an illustration of the architecture of the nineteenth century placed in a balance and weighed against the architecture that preceded the Reformation. Surrounding the illustration is an inscription of words from scripture (Daniel 5: 27): 'They are weighed in the balance and found wanting.' In a similar way, the monastery serves an agitation of memory (see also Irvine 2018): challenging to the contemporary shape of things by proposing a different vision of *what might have been* – and, crucially, *what could still be* – which stands in contrast to *what currently is*.

Longing for a home

So far, the focus has been on the relationship between the monastic architecture and the world around it. What is its place in the life of the community itself?

To begin to answer this, let us return to Laurence Shepherd 'dreaming that St. Gregory's of Downside was getting turned gradually into Glastonbury' in his retreat talks of 1882. We have considered the wider social context of such dreaming, but what were the specific dynamics within the community at this time?

As we saw in the introduction, this was a time of transition for the community and for the English Benedictine Congregation as a whole. As was the case with other communities in the Congregation, the monastic community of St Gregory the Great had been founded in exile, establishing a house in Douai in 1606, from which it sent missionaries back to England to work for the reconversion of the land. Although the community had returned to England in 1794 and moved to Downside in 1814, as of 1882 this missionary focus had not fully shifted. The result was that residence in the monastery was, for most, a temporary feature of the life of the English Benedictine monk: a number of years in formation in the monastic house would be followed by a career serving parishes elsewhere, rather than living in community. A pamphlet published in 1880 by

Monsignor Weld, who had entered the novitiate at Downside, but left because of a dissatisfaction with the monastic life on offer, describes the problem which those who had made their profession as English Benedictine monks face: sent on the mission a few years after being clothed, the monk 'is ordered to quit his monastery, never more to return. They never do return.'[10] As he points out, 'A case is hardly to be found of one ever returning to his monastery'[11] after being translated to the mission.

This is the context in which Laurence Shepherd celebrates and urges a return to the glories of pre-Reformation monasticism: 'now, which of you having a mind to build a tower, does not first sit down, and reckon the changes that are necessary?'[12] There is little point in building a grand 'House of God' if the monastery does not adhere to monastic principles. The fact that he was urging a change of direction for English Benedictine life – away from a focus on training monks to leave the monastery and run parishes, towards a restoration of community living – explains the hostility of some within the community for whom this was an abdication of the responsibility the English Benedictine Congregation had taken on. A direct response can be found in the notes and diaries of Alphonsus Morrall, who had served as novice master before being sent to serve a series of parishes, and who was committed to this missionary identity for the Congregation: 'To talk about making Downside now what Glastonbury was in the 14th or 15th century is nothing but sentimentality. Let us strive to make Downside now, what we may hope that Glastonbury would have been now ... a monastery devoting itself in the true Benedictine spirit, to the reconversion of our country.'[13]

Among others, however, these aspirations found a receptive

---

10 Weld, *The English Benedictines* (1880), privately published pamphlet, 11, Downside Abbey Archives.

11 Weld, *The English Benedictines*, 5.

12 Laurence Shepherd, 'Notes of the Retreat given at Downside 1882', 121, Stanbrook Abbey Archives.

13 Alphonsus Morrall, remarks on Ford's 'Nine Demands', Item 453, Downside Archives.

audience, including the monks under whose leadership construction took shape. For the reform-minded, the development of the monastery buildings, including a suitably dignified church, was bound up with a desire for monastic stability. Aidan Gasquet, under whose leadership the foundation stones were laid, stated that stability 'is the key to the spirit of monasticism as interpreted in [St Benedict's] Rule, for by it the monastery is erected into a family, to which the monk binds himself forever' (Gasquet 1896: xiv). To enter a Benedictine monastery is to become part of a corporate body and to share in all aspects of life with that body, 'acting only through it, sharing in all the joys and sorrows of its members, giving and receiving that help, comfort and strength which come from mutual counsel' (1896: xii). Similarly, Edmund Ford, who engaged Thomas Garner as architect for the second phase of construction, wrote in a sketch of the Benedictine vocation which he circulated among the community that 'the normal life of Benedictines is the life of many living together, not for the sake of doing any particular work, but that they may carry out as far as possible the full teaching of Christ on the perfection of social life'. The ideal was that 'the monks … are bound together by ties which are particularly close. They are truly said to form a family.'

The building work can be seen as an embodiment of this desire for stability. Alongside the architectural grandeur which would assert Catholicism's presence in the landscape, these words show a more intimate side to the construction projects: the desire to make a home. When in 1899 the Papal Bull[14] *Diu Quidem* elevated Downside to the status of an abbey and set out instructions that the monastic houses of the English Benedictine Congregation should be self-governing, this gave renewed vigour to the historic task of 'rebuilding Glastonbury'. But it is a measure of the domesticity of the monks' aspirations that the phrase 'Diu Quidem' was quickly appended to the timely and welcome development of bathroom facilities at this moment in the community's history, and so came to be used as a euphemism for the toilet – a usage which continued a century on.

14 A Papal Bull is an official decree issued by the Pope, in this case Leo XIII.

The principle of connection

The arguments advanced by Gasquet and Ford continue to shape the self-representation of the monastic community to this day. To give just one example of this: in 2020, deep into the COVID-19 lockdown, the monks held a number of online Q&A sessions across YouTube and Instagram as a way of expanding their presence while the monastery was closed to guests. Fielding a question on vocations, and how to recognise if you have a calling to the Benedictine life, the monks gathered around the webcam reflected on the distinctive fact the Benedictine vocation was not to carry out any particular form of work. Instead, they were called to the 'charism of living in community', to grow to know God through living all your life with the same family of monks. This was the importance of the vow of stability, which one of the monks explained in this way: 'When I walk past the cemetery, I know that one day, God willing, I will be in there. Hopefully not too soon! I haven't booked my slot.'

Benedictine monks are men whose life cycles become wrapped around a particular place. The history of the abbey church could also be an intimate history for the community: one monk, a convert to Catholicism, first encountered Downside Abbey through its acoustic, hearing Midnight Mass on the radio one Christmas while in the RAF. In showing me the church, he was sharing some of his life story: first, taking me to the chapel of St Benedict, where he first received Holy Communion – pointing up to show me the coats of arms of pre-dissolution monasteries featured on the vaulting, his own personal history of arrival in the Church entwined with a national history of Catholic faith lost and found. A little further, we arrived at the Lady Chapel – 'a glimpse of heaven' – where, years later, he celebrated Mass for the first time as a newly ordained priest.

The importance of the monastic buildings as an architecture of stability is that they offer scope for an entire monastic life cycle to be passed in the same household; those at the early stages of their monastic development – postulants, novices, and juniors – had individual rooms in the novitiate section of the monastic accommodation, before moving along the west wing to live in rooms in the main living quarters with the rest of the solemnly professed monks. The west wing of the monastery also contained an infirmary, where sick and elderly monks could live under the care of the infirmarian, an official appointed from within the community specifically to care for those who are ill. The infirmary had its own direct link to the abbey church, opening out into a gallery, enabling continued participation in the community's ritual life.

Below the infirmary and the rooms of the monks (sometimes referred to as cells) was the chapter house, where the monks met together for chapters (meetings of all solemnly professed monks of the community) and conferences from the abbot. Alongside was the *calefactory*,[15] a kind of common room with armchairs and newspapers, where the monks spent periods of recreation and gathered together after supper. These private spaces for sleep and social and institutional spaces to meet were connected to the abbey church and the rest of the monastery buildings by means of the cloister.

The cloister is a core feature of Benedictine architecture, reaching back to the design of medieval monasteries (although in the case of Downside, in spite of the clear inspiration taken from medieval design, their cloister falls short of the medieval prototype by only enclosing the central garden on three sides; this is not the ideal four-sided yard entirely enclosed by monastic buildings). As the medieval historian Walter Horn (1973: 13) explains, the cloister is a form that expresses a particular idealised pattern of social life: aside from 'those rare occasions' when he might be called away from the monastery, 'the monk spent his entire life in this enclosed yard and its surrounding structures, which served as his living, eating, working, and sleeping quarters'. Horn points to the Plan of St Gall – a ninth-century manuscript prepared in the context of monastic reform synods held in Aachen in 816 and 817, sketching out an ideal arrangement of monastic buildings – as providing a prototypical answer to the crucial question of how a monastery should be designed. What

---

15 From the Latin *calefacere*, to warm; the name is retained from that traditionally given in Benedictine monasteries to the room with the fire where the monks would have gone to warm themselves.

The architecture of stability

we see in that plan is the much-replicated model of a cloister that connects the sleeping quarters and the refectory, surrounded by the various buildings and gardens which provide the resources the monastery needs to function. While, as we have seen in the introduction, English Benedictine monks do not aspire to such total containment, the cloister not only gives architectural form to the vow of stability, but also mediates it as a key element of *connection* in monastic life.[16]

For Horn, the historic emergence of the cloister is a clear indication of a move away from a monastic architecture in which individual monks' cells were disconnected with no linking passage, and in which the primary concern is the maintenance of individual space, and towards an increasing connection that generates social space and mediates interaction. It follows from a rejection of hermit-like forms of living and the acceptance of the *Rule*'s communal model based on shared and co-ordinated activity.

The cloister leads from the living quarters, alongside the abbey church, and to the east wing – the newest set of buildings within the monastery compound, concrete constructions in brutalist style designed by the architect Francis Pollen (see Powers 1999: 90–6) and built between 1965 and 1970. There was a family connection here: Pollen's sister was the wife of one of the monk's natal brothers. But his involvement in ongoing developments in the community as they adapted to this time of change in the Church and in society is clear from the range of commissions he had, including the reorganisation of the sanctuary of the abbey church to reflect the liturgical reforms following the Second Vatican Council (see Chapter 4), and the construction of a new monastic church for Downside's daughter house at Worth, which was to become an independent abbey. The design implemented for the east wing of the monastery consists of a bank of large windows, with the rooms overhead jutting out in V-shaped

---

16 See also Yaneva (2012: 110) on the architectural as a type of connector, rather than a container; here I am making the point that the cloister is not purely a *representation* of stability, but a *mediator* of its social possibilities.

concrete bays.[17] At the same time, a radiating octagonal structure in glass and concrete, linked to the west wing by a passageway, was built to house the monastery library. There is no question that the assertively modernist style of these developments appears to jar with the rest of the monastery's architecture and its assertion of continuity with the past through the Gothic form. Yet the numerous revisions of the design – ensuring that it followed the levels of the existing buildings and so could connect with and continue the cloister – show the continuing commitment to the architecture of stability, finally fulfilling the need to have proper space for eating, study and hospitality within the monastic buildings, integrating all aspects of the monks' daily life as envisaged by the *Rule*.

The library contains 150,000 volumes, intended to provide for the needs of not only the current community, but also future generations of monks. In this way the library is also associated with stability, in that it exists independently of the lifespan of individual monks; monks come and go, but the books stay. As the then librarian explained to me during my fieldwork, managing a monastic library involves thinking on a timescale of centuries. He envisaged that some day in the future, even when the bodies of all of the community living today lay buried in the monastic cemetery, there would still be monks – as well as researchers and other visitors – sitting in the library that overlooked their graves, consulting the books there. 'When you are dealing with a living collection, you have to think beyond the present day', beyond the lifespan of the current monks and into the future. (Or, to put it in the slightly less reverent terms of another of the monks: 'buying more books in languages that none of us can read'). The librarian continued to order books for the library from his bed in the infirmary in the days leading up to his death from cancer in January 2007 – a fitting demonstration of his commitment to the community beyond the present.

---

17 The community kept open the possibility of adding a further floor on top of the east wing buildings, with the result that they contained a set of 'stairs to nowhere'.

Eating in silence as a family

The key element of the east wing itself is the refectory, where the monks gather together to take their meals. Though contained within a modernist shell, this is also a key space of stability and is furnished in a way that speaks of continuity with the past. On the walls of the refectory are portraits of past abbots and other historically significant members of the household; ancestors whose contributions to the ongoing history of the community still loom large, whose writings are still studied and referred to, whose personalities are still subjects of conversation. The presence of these ancestors endures and, here in the refectory, we see them as ongoing participants long after their death.

As the place where the monks gather to eat together as a family, the refectory is central to the desire for stability (see Irvine 2011b). Its significance at the heart of the Benedictine vocation is highlighted by its connection – both by means of the cloister and by means of the *horarium* – with the monks' life of prayer. This connection is made visible as the monks make their way along the cloister, moving from the abbey church to the refectory. Each meal follows on from a period of prayer and can be seen as a continuation of that prayer. Breakfast follows *Lauds*, and lunch follows the Midday Office, while supper follows the half-hour period of private prayer after *Vespers*. The use of the refectory as a ritual space reflects the use of the abbey church in a number of respects. Like the abbey church, the refectory is treated as a space of silence and prayer and, as in the choir stalls, monks are seated in a specific order, reflecting their place in the community; novices and juniors are seated at one table and the rest of the community sits along the tables in the order in which they received the habit, with the exception of the abbot, prior, and sub-prior, who are seated together at the end of the room.

Prayers are chanted before Lunch and Supper (at Breakfast the monks individually say grace in silence before eating). The hebdomadary (the monk appointed to intone prayers for that week in both the abbey church and the refectory) begins by chanting *Benedicite* (Blessing), with the community chanting *Benedicite* in response. The hebdomadary then intones the grace (I give the grace before lunch for ordinary time[18] as an example here), with the community joining in after the first two words:

> *Oculi omnium in te sperant, Domine:*
> *et tu das escam illorum in tempore opportuno.*[19]

The doxology is then chanted, with the monks bowing as they sing praise to the Holy Trinity, just as they would at the same point within the Divine Office:

> *Gloria Patri et Filio et Spiritui Sancto:*
> *sicut erat in principio et nunc et semper*
> *et in secula seculorum. Amen.*[20]

The monk who has been appointed for that day to read aloud during the meal then asks the abbot to bless him: all respond *Amen* after the abbot chants the blessing. At this point all sit and a scripture reading for the day, drawn from the Liturgy of the Word at the community Mass, is read out. At supper, the martyrology of saints is also read out, giving brief lives of the saints whose anniversaries fall on the coming day. Only after this is the food served.

It is clear, then, that this was a space within the monastic routine of prayer. It was also a space for the community to serve one another, as well as guests who came to the monastery. All able-bodied monks were obliged to take their turn as reader or server in the monastic refectory according to a rota, and novices in particular were heavily involved in the duties of serving as part of their formation. Here, a common connection is made between the importance of service

---

18 The times of the year that fall outside the seasons of Advent, Christmas, Lent and Easter.
19 'The eyes of all creatures look to you, Lord: and you give them their food in due time' (Psalm 145:15).
20 'Glory be to the Father, and to the Son, and to the Holy Spirit: as it was in the beginning and now and always and for ages of ages. Amen.'

and Christ's example in washing the feet of his followers.[21] Around Maundy Thursday, in conversation with one monk who served as priest for a nearby parish, we discussed the symbolism in the act of washing the feet of his parishioners as part of this Holy Week liturgy. The monk directly linked this act with the importance of serving the rest of the community at mealtimes in the refectory: 'Each mealtime, it's like a little Maundy Thursday ... it's Christian charity as it should be, really. We're all servants of one another, after all.'

Perhaps the most striking feature of the meal is that the monks sit and eat in silence (with the exception of feast days, when the monks are given special permission to talk after grace has been chanted). Food sharing might be seen as an ideal setting for conversation, with such talk considered an ingredient of the meal as important as the food itself in its capacity to create and maintain social relationships. Commensality is clearly central to the life of the monastery, yet the community is brought together in the act of sharing food without any accompanying exchange of words. (There is, in fact, a sign language which the monks occasionally use when, for example, they wish someone to pass the butter; see Irvine 2011b: 230-231.)

While the monks eat in silence, one of the community, seated at the lectern, begins to read from the book chosen by the abbot or prior. The books to be read are not necessarily of an overtly 'religious' character. Some selections are indeed chosen for their spiritual value, such as *What is the Point of Being a Christian?* by Timothy Radcliffe, a former student at the monastery school, who went on to become head of the Dominican order; however, this is not always the case. Books are read continuously over the course of months, with the reader picking up each day where he left off the last time. As a result, the books became part of the everyday life of the monastery, creating a shared focus during the meal and generating remarks and conversations outside of mealtimes. They could also occasionally become a source of humour within the community: the selection of Jonathan Fenby's *Penguin History of Modern China* as a reading led to various jokes around the monastery about liturgical innovations representing a 'great leap forward'

---

21 John 13: 1–15

or 'cultural revolution'. On another occasion, listening to Andrew Marr's *A History of Modern Britain*, the reader had reached a point where Marr explains how Ian Fleming's loving description of American food in the James Bond novel *Live and Let Die* – hamburgers, fries, salads with Thousand Island dressing, ice cream! – would have excited the British readership, who were still on postwar rations. As the community and guests listened to the words and contemplated the distance between the delights being described and what they found on their own plates, the monks began to laugh. The reader, unable to suppress his own amusement, had to stop, and Andrew Marr's words about the culinary fantasies of ration-time England were met with an understanding which he had probably not anticipated.

So, throughout the meal, the monks share a common focus: they listen to a common text. The importance of remaining silent is made clear in this setting. Community does not emerge from small talk; the monks cannot rely on the back and forth of chatter as a way of building up social connections. They do not break up into pairs or small groups in order to talk to one another, and they do not dwell on what they have to say themselves. Together, as a family, they focus on hearing what the reader is saying. They share in the act of listening.

Monastic stability in a world of non-places

I have focused on the life of the refectory at some length here because it represents a key element of the monastery as an architecture of stability: the desire to create a shared home. The monastery's identity as a household is based, in large part, on sharing food, a process which it grants sacred significance.

Insomuch as commensality might be central to the identity of the household in England, it is often invoked as a thing of the past (Murcott 1997; Yates and Ward 2017); something very much associated with the nuclear family, and part of a narrative of 'crisis' and fragmentation of that family unit, belonging to a 'golden age' now departed. True to their commitment to the ideal of the household, monks sometimes locate their own meals within this narrative. Over tea I asked one of the members of the community who had used the term 'household' in conversation what it was that made the monastery a household, 'Oh, you know, little things, obviously living together and sharing but little things, like don't let the sun go down on your anger, that's Paul[22] of course, but it's good household advice.' At this point the monk explained that sometimes, after a disagreement, the monks would push little notes under one another's door during the *summum silentium*[23] to try and explain themselves and show that they still cared about the person. He continued, 'eating together, taking the time to eat together, that's very important ... it's such a shame that so few families do now, with pressures of work and television. So the real question for me is, is a family a true household if it doesn't eat together? And families are breaking up ... no home life, of course.'

As another monk, at the time a teacher in the school run by the monastery, explained to me: 'I think what we demonstrate is the value of staying put. Modern society is so full of people rushing from one place to the next, one job to the next, even one family to the next. But we're able to stay put, and I think there's something that's attractive about that because so many people are rootless.'

Here, he reflects the message offered by a 1970s commission of monks and nuns from throughout the English Benedictine Congregation, who emphasised what they saw as the 'witness value' of stability: 'Through the vow of stability Benedictines bear witness, in a torn and individualistic world, to Christian unity which knows how to overcome barriers. To live in community is to make the approach to Christ more clearly visible ... In an unstable world where life is characterized by mobility and fragmentation, a Benedictine community can be a centre where life is deeply experienced and where others come not only to share in silence and prayer, but also to discuss the social realities of the present time ... Stable monastic

22 Ephesians 4: 26
23 The 'great silence' or 'total silence' that falls over the monastery through the night between Compline and breakfast the next day.

life confronts the fleeting character of human experience, so evident today, and seeks an understanding of the meaning of life itself' (Rees et al. 1978: 142–3).

As we saw at the start of this chapter when the abbot spoke of the cloister as a garden of contemplation 'in a world dominated by noise and too much busyness', these are presented as counter-cultural values. As he elaborated later that day in a discussion on vocations, 'What we are doing here seems so obviously out of fashion. Having to choose one thing and stick to it, routine rather than the search for novelty. But being rooted in place when so much of the world is rootless. Living together when things seem so fragmented. There are people out there asking whether there is another way and we have to be there for them.' In asserting these counter-cultural values, the monks harken back to another invented tradition – that of the stable family unit – but do so as a critique of the ubiquity of forms of life that deny stability; where ties of care and responsibility to others are eroded by the fact that people do not have the opportunity to settle, to build community and develop a sense of belonging or long-term connection with others who share the same place. The 'witness value' of stability, from this perspective, is that it forces reflection on whether conditions of contemporary life mean that our life cycles move from one fleeting interaction to the next without being able to grab hold of the stability that would allow us to develop enduring bonds.

What forms of architecture form the backdrop to this social life of instability and disconnection? Marc Augé (1995: 78) describes such a lived environment: 'A world where people are born in the clinic and die in the hospital, where transit points and temporary abodes are proliferating under luxurious or inhuman conditions … a world thus surrendered to solitary individuality, to the fleeting, the temporary and ephemeral, offers the anthropologist (and others) a new object.' He describes such spaces as 'non-places': 'If a place can be defined as relational, historical and concerned with identity, then a space which cannot be defined as relational, or historical, or concerned with identity will be a non-place' (1995: 77–8). Supermarkets, airports, hotels and motorways, 'these crowded places where thousands of individual itineraries converged for a moment, unaware of one another' (1995: 3), which replicate in predictable forms with little or no reference to local history or geography, are examples of these 'non-places', through which individuals pass as isolated individuals with minimal social interaction. You could be anywhere; and why would it matter, seeing as you're only on your way to somewhere else? You're certainly not here to build a lasting connection.

It is in such a context that the counterfactual architecture of the monastery comes again into its own. As a longed-for home in which the monks could live as a family – rather than a temporary dwelling before being transferred elsewhere – the architecture materialises the debates and reforms that placed the emphasis on stability as the great essential of Benedictine life. As a visible monument to endurance within the landscape, the grand designs sought to witness to this desire more generally: a 'What if?' question challenging the proliferation of non-places with its insistence on household, stability, and place.

CHAPTER 3

The rhythm of stability

The call to prayer

In the depth of the first lockdown during the COVID pandemic, the monks shared on their Instagram a video of the bell tower of the abbey, its single 5¼-ton bell Great Bede announcing the call to prayer. With public church services suspended across the country and the doors of the monastery closed to visitors, the booming bell sounded out a reminder for miles around that a rhythm persisted behind the walls; a rhythm drawing the monks six times a day to the abbey church. Shared on social media, it carried the reminder even further, witnessing to the Benedictine structure of time as a movement through points of prayer.

Through that period of lockdown, a key element of the monks' outreach[1] was to emphasise the value of routine and share this sense of structured time. With a whole population finding themselves constrained in circumstances of separation, daily lives replaced by a repetition of days stuck within the same confines, the monks were particularly attuned to the impact of lockdown's temporal distortion. The bleak reality was articulated during a healing service broadcast online from the monastery: 'Routines have gone, needs have accelerated ... despondency and a feeling of aimlessness has settled almost nationally ... because the consequences of our present situation seem, as it were, to be almost indefinite as well as unlimited.'

---

1   See Irvine (2021a) for an ethnographic account of the monks' digital outreach at this time.

Around this time, one of the monks of the community who had been teaching at Sant'Anselmo, the Benedictine College in Rome, emailed me describing the sharp shifts in emotion as Italy struggled with the wave of COVID-19 infection. The sudden decision to close places of learning feeling almost like an unexpected holiday; excitement quickly engulfed by the fear and uncertainty about the situation, anxiety of risk from the infection and grief amidst the rising deathtoll. And then lockdown. 'Now, inevitably, it has begun to shift to a kind of stale boredom. Cassian of course had just the word for it – acedia. Yesterday I just went to the end of the drive, simply to look outside and enjoy (really enjoy) the sight of the wisteria in the road. That is the real pity – to miss the spring colours and smells.' In giving the name *acedia* to this 'stale boredom' which so many of us had been confronted with, what was particularly striking was the way in which he reached back into the history of the monastic experience. John Cassian, born around 360 A.D., compiled and digested the teachings of those 'desert monks' who had withdrawn from society to live lives of prayer on the Nile Delta. In his *Institutes* he describes the dejection and weariness that was a frequent foe of the monks, and was denoted by the Greek word 'acedia', a word that might roughly be translated as 'lack of care'. Crucially, acedia was seen to have a temporal dimension, a kind of torpor when time seems motionless. This is made clear in its association (referred to by Cassian and commonly discussed among the monks) with the 'noonday demon' of the 90th psalm – the despondency of that point of the day when the sun seems stationary in the sky and the monk wonders whether the day will ever come to an end.

Yet it was here that the monks felt that they had something particular to offer that a wider public could find valuable. The struggle with acedia had a long history, and the time discipline of the *horarium* served as a way of giving structure to time that might otherwise drift into aimlessness. Everyone had had to adapt to lockdown, but for monks there was a sense that they had the benefit of having been trained for these kinds of circumstances; a certain expertise in 'social distancing'. After all, monks have 'always spent most of our time working from home'. This became a key motif in the content the monks posted across their social media platforms, which burst into life providing daily content from the start of lockdown.

As was explained in one YouTube video, where the prior of the community offered lessons from monastic life for social distancing: 'It might be tempting to stay in bed all morning if you have nothing particular to get up for, or so it seems. But actually, in the long run you'll probably find that you feel much worse.' It is important to have a plan to your day which gives it shape, and to have a consistency of routine. The pattern of monastic living is one of structured time, a structure which emphasises 'the right amount of sleep, food, prayer, work' and moderation in all things – 'try not to be obsessive, but do a bit of everything that is important', and have regularity in doing it (significantly, another of these 'thought for the day' videos stressed the indispensable nature of recreation as part of this routine).

In this moment when the monks wanted to speak from a distinctive position of contemporary relevance, it is striking that they sought to share the contours of a schedule. This concern with the rhythm of the day reflected my experience of fieldwork in the monastery a decade before: here was a life underpinned by time discipline.

The common rhythm

'We are a human clock,' pronounced the monastic librarian, starting to make his way to the abbey church in response to the ringing of the bell. The books and papers remained spread out on the desk, his chair pushed back; whatever he had been doing was to be suspended for now. His statement was evocative, although any attempt to draw further elaboration was stymied by the fact that the monk now clearly had somewhere else to be.

The daily rhythm of the call to prayer and its response – this 'human clock' – can be characterised as both a mechanical action and a personal reaction. It is a *mechanical action* in the sense that the ringing of the bells is controlled by an electronic timer, which triggers the striking mechanism at preset points in the day. The tower of the abbey church does not have a clock face[2] and does not contain a clock mechanism, other than the timer triggering the ringing of the bell. It is the bell that publicly announces time in the monastery, shaped around the 'hours' of the Divine Office, announced automatically according to a predetermined pattern. The rhythm of the call to prayer is also a *personal reaction*, in the sense that the day is marked by the movement of the monks to the abbey church in response to the chiming of the bell (unless, as we shall note later, work or infirmity prevents them from attending at that particular time) and by the monks joining their own prayer to that of the rest of the community. As one monk explained, 'The thing about the Divine Office being central to monastic life isn't so much about spending all your time in the abbey church. We spend more time sleeping for one thing. It's more about how you respond when the bell rings. Being ready to put the work of God first.' The monks are therefore *active* participants in a *rigidly timed* system directed according to the hours, minutes, and seconds of Greenwich Mean Time (or British Summer Time) and signalled by the bell, which is then acted upon through ritual prayer.

The *horarium* is one of the key means by which monastic stability as a specific vow of Benedictine life is secured. The shapelessness of the day as 24 empty hours to fill is countered by the structure of the liturgy of the hours. The indeterminate nature of the day is countered by a specific routine, recurring in time, around which shared activity in the monastery is anchored. In other words, if stability as an ideal means that monks have a place to be, a lifetime to grow there, and a constant family within which they grow, it is the *horarium* which structures that lifetime and co-ordinates activity within that place such

---

2 A clock was part of the earliest design for the abbey church by Dunn and Hansom and, when they completed the lower part of the tower in 1884, they left three round openings for the clock faces (James 1961: 21). However, no clock mechanism was installed, and so clock dials never materialised on the tower; when Giles Gilbert Scott completed the tower in 1938, he inserted tracery into these circular openings, artfully disguising their original purpose (James 1961: 100).

that the community develops its strong sense of togetherness as family.

In the first chapter of his sixth-century *Rule*, discussing the different kinds of monks, St Benedict is particularly vicious in his condemnation of what he terms 'gyrovagues' – wandering monks who flit from place to place; entirely self-interested and without the discipline which comes from the mutual support of the monastery, they 'indulge their own wills and succumb to the allurements of gluttony'.

In their self-presentation, the monks would frequently employ this contrast between the *cenobite* – monks living, eating, and praying together in community – and the *gyrovague* to emphasise the importance of stability in the dimension of space: it is through commitment to living with others in a particular place that the monk's will is shaped beyond himself and ultimately towards God. Yet the temporal dimension, which co-ordinates the shared life of the community, is also crucial, and here the monks would employ a different contrast between *cenobitic* and *idiorhythmic* ways of life.

The term is borrowed from the Greek Orthodox setting; Marios Sarris, who carried out ethnographic fieldwork on Mount Athos[3], explains that the word *idiorhythmic* is derived from a combination of the Greek words for 'private or personal' and 'manner, way, routine, order of life', and describes the idiorhythmic life thus: 'Idiorhythmic monks could possess private property, were not obliged to attend the services in the main church, and had separate meals. In general, each monk was allowed his own "rhythm", or manner of life' (Sarris 2004: 116). In my fieldsite, the sense of a common 'rhythm' to monastic life was particularly important, as shown in the definition of idiorhythmic that I was offered the first time I heard the term used in conversation: 'monks who follow their own timetable'.

When the monks at Downside cautioned against idiorhythmic

3 While Sarris is remarking on idiorhythmic monasticism as a type, his fieldwork was carried out in a *cenobium* rather than an idiorhythmic monastery, and in fact he suggested that the tendency on Mount Athos has been towards the abolition of the idiorhythmic system in favour of the *cenobitic* (Sarris 2004: 133).

tendencies, they were flagging up the danger that monastic life could be undermined by people always having somewhere else to be when the bell rings. Even when a monk is drawn away from the common timetable to do something which might be seen as good in and of itself (for example, work responsibilities at the time of the liturgical hours), it can still undermine the foundation of Benedictine life: it is the sense of shared movement within time which is the living pulse of the monastery's architecture of stability. As one monk explained, 'you can convince yourself that you can make your own timetable, if you have to pray separately, eat separately, but do you really have the discipline to do it? There are a lot of temptations in the world, and sometimes we can find very good excuses when what we're actually doing is giving in to temptation.' Recalling difficulties experienced during time spent living away from the monastery to serve as a parish priest, he continued, 'that's why I prefer being in earshot of the bell [to working away from the monastery].' It wasn't that he needed it to keep time – 'I have a watch for that!' – but that it reminded him 'what the time is for'.

In the ethnographic reflection on the *horarium* that follows, what I want to convey is this sense of being encompassed by the time structure of the monastery: a schedule as the condition of life, giving shape to the day. The philosopher Byung-Chul Han (2020: 3) writes that 'Today, time lacks a solid structure ... It disintegrates into a mere sequence of pointlike presences; it rushes off. There is nothing to provide time with any hold [Halt]. Time that rushes off is not habitable.'[4] Han's approach here is particularly relevant because he writes from a position of loss, presuming an erasure of the ritual elements that might structure and give rhythm to time. This oppositional stance reflects the contrast we saw in the previous chapter between the rootedness of the monastery and the perceived instability of the contemporary world. If, then, unstructured time has become uninhabitable, the call to prayer within the monastery resists this uninhabitability. As Han goes on to explain, 'Rituals stabilize life.' So,

4 See also El Guindi (2008: 124) in her anthropological account of the significance of daily prayer in Islam: 'Without rhythm, Muslim life becomes clinical, routine, prescriptive, and dry.'

just as the architecture of stability roots the monk in space, so too the *horarium* roots the monk in time.

Marking the hours

Through the night the monastery is wrapped in silence – the *summum silentium*, or great silence, which follows the last point of prayer of the day, stilling the enclosure as a space of quiet and solitude until breakfast. Within this silence, a bell rings at 5.40am: the signal to rise and prepare for *Vigils*, the first Office of the day. A postulant or novice lights the candles on the altar as another bell sounds at 5.55am. One by one, the monks emerge from the cloister, dip their hands in the holy water font, mark the sign of the cross on themselves and make their way to the choir stalls to kneel in prayer. Some are punctual; one or two will shuffle in late. As was pointed out to me by the novice master – who was used to newcomers adjusting themselves to the struggle of rising early – Chapter 43 of the *Rule* of St Benedict appears to show a slight leniency by noting while monks must do penance if they are late, at Vigils they should be given a little time to show up, specifying that monks must have arrived before the chanting of 'Glory Be to the Father' at the end of the first psalm. Accordingly, it instructs that the first psalm is meant to be chanted especially slowly, to give people time to get in place. For the novice master, this was a sign of the all-important moderation and mercy of the *Rule*, 'written with ordinary human beings in mind, who might sometimes find themselves having slightly overslept'. But, all the same, he warned, 'one shouldn't make a habit of it!'

On the hour, the abbot raps his knuckles on the stall in front of him, giving the signal to stand and turn westwards to face the altar. Unaccompanied by the organ, the *hebdomadary*[5] (often abbreviated to just 'hebdom') intones 'O Lord, open our lips,' to which the monks respond 'And we shall praise your name.' The first psalm of the day's liturgy is known as the *invitatory*, described to me by the novice master

---

5   The monk appointed for that week to officiate during the Divine Office and at mealtimes in the refectory.

as 'a summons to worship, you've been in your cell through the night, now we're moving from the cell to the oratory, this is the call'.

At the core of the Divine Office is a sequence of psalms and canticles, all chanted antiphonally (the cantor sings one verse, then all sing the next verse, and so on, with the cantors and the community singing alternate verses), each ending with the Gloria Patri, sung as two verses. Throughout the Divine Office, the monks bow as the first verse of the Gloria Patri is being sung. At Vigils, following the *invitatory*, the psalms and canticles are grouped into 'nocturns' that each conclude with a reading (from scripture or from the church fathers) and a period of silent prayer, ending only when the abbot knocks on the stalls to give the signal to proceed. These lengthy periods of listening and silence were especially characteristic of *Vigils*, a deliberate punctuation of personal meditation and contemplation within the collective prayer. This creates a strong sense of continuity between *Vigils* and the period of private prayer which follows it.

After the concluding prayers – 'May God's help be with us always', to which all respond 'And with our absent brethren'; 'Let us praise the Lord', to which all respond 'Thanks be to God' – the abbot raps his knuckles on the stalls to signal that the service has ended, and the first part of the day specifically set out for private prayer begins. For this half hour, a few of the monks would remain in the stalls, kneeling or sitting. Others left the stalls and went to sit in the nave, perhaps, as one monk suggested I might do, looking up at the eastern window as the sun rose outside. Still others returned to the monastery wing and to their cells. Here, we see the deeply individual impulse of contemplative prayer (which will be the focus of Chapter 5), the monks' drift to different parts of the church and enclosure reflecting the personal nature of their desire to be with God at this moment – a desire nonetheless housed within the common purpose of the day's collective rhythm.

The monks return from private to public prayer for the second Office of the day, *Lauds*, which begins at 7.10am.[6] During the winter

---

6 Lauds was moved from 7.05am to 7.10am in 2006 during my fieldwork to ensure that the *horarium* did not impinge on the half hour of private prayer in the morning, as discussed in Chapter 5.

months, at this time the sun was in the process of rising and illuminating the abbey church. In the late spring and summer, by Lauds the sun has risen, light pouring through the great east windows, soaking the body of the church in blues and yellows. We are praying as the day opens around us. The significance of this was repeated to me on numerous occasions. Early on in my fieldwork I heard one of the senior monks explain to the guests present at tea that Lauds was an opportunity to come together and give thanks for the new day, making an 'offering of the day ahead. Everything is a sweet and fragrant offering to God, even sufferings, even the nice day out with friends you're hoping to have.' Not everyone around the table was wholly comfortable with this as it was phrased. Another monk pondered whether we should be so proud as to assume that 'everything' we might offer in our sinful state is worthy, and whether we should instead ask humbly that our offerings are acceptable to God, directly quoting Psalm 51, as chanted in Lauds that morning: *burnt offering from me you would refuse, my sacrifice, a contrite spirit, a humbled heart you will not spurn*. The community's sole novice at the time, who had been sitting listening to the debate, chimed in that such humility was exactly the point: 'if we only had perfect things to offer, we wouldn't have much, so we must be prepared to offer flawed things'.

When I met with the monastic choir master to discuss the recent history of the liturgy of the hours at Downside, and how the community arrived at the pattern of worship it uses now (a series of liturgical shifts discussed in Chapter 4), he explained that the key guiding principle of the monastery's current use of the psalter is that it reflects a desire to 'consecrate time' by reflecting the character of different points in time as distinct moments through which the day is offered in prayer. 'The central question is, how do we encounter God in that specific moment? How do we hallow *that* time as prayer? ... At Lauds, and then again at Vespers in the evening, we are consecrating these turning points of the day.' This then shaped the use of psalms at each point of prayer. Some psalms had the character of reflection, meditation, or lament and seemed to speak within the 'stillness of the hours of darkness'. Lauds was specifically prayer at daybreak: 'praise and thanksgiving at dawn, a new song for the new day ... Each day is a little Easter really. As the sun rises, we rise to new life once again, and we celebrate this with psalms that have a specific character of praise.'

In particular, this sense of the dawn as a 'little Easter' was reflected in the final psalm of Lauds always being one of the *hallel* psalms – psalms that begin with the exclamation of praise 'Alleluia!', whose frequent and prominent use is particularly associated in the Catholic liturgical context with Eastertide and the celebration of Christ rising from the dead. Following this final psalm, the monks turn to the altar to the sing the *Benedictus*, Zechariah's canticle from the Gospel of Luke,[7] which again reflects the theme of praise and contains the symbolism of the sun rising in darkness:

> The loving-kindness of the heart of our God
> Who visits us like the dawn from on high.
> He will give light to those in darkness
> Those who dwell in the shadow of death

After the chanting of the Lord's Prayer and the concluding prayers of Lauds, on the abbot's signal the monks proceed from the choir stalls to breakfast. Although the monks first need to return the cowls which are ceremonially worn over their habits at Lauds, a couple of the monks move more directly to the refectory, leaving their cowls on any convenient surface as they pass by, to be retrieved later.

Here, as noted in the previous chapter, we see the close link between the time of prayer and mealtimes as the monks move from abbey church to refectory and from praying as a community to eating as a community – each activity with its appointed place in the monastic timetable. Once the monks have taken their breakfast, this marks the end of the *summum silentium*, the transition from the quiet and solitude of the night to the communal business of the day complete.

At 8.35am, there is a *Conventual Mass*. This is a Mass attended by the whole community, and was generally concelebrated[8] by

---

7 Luke 1: 68–79.

8 In Masses which are concelebrated, several priests say Mass together, all partici-

several of the monks who are priests. A rota informs the community of who is to be the principal celebrant for that day, leading the prayers and giving a short homily. The Mass is typically served by one of the monks who has not yet been ordained as a priest, usually a postulant or novice.

The monks then turn to their particular work duties for the morning, gathering again at 12.30pm for the *Midday Office*, the shortest of the hours. In conversation with the choir master about the liturgy, he pointed out that, while canonically it was only required to celebrate one of the 'little hours' of *Terce*, *Sext* and *None*, and as such they might appear secondary to the pivotal 'major hours' of Vigils, Lauds, and Vespers, he nevertheless considered prayer at this time 'fundamental to the shape of the day'. He explained that when, at an earlier point during his monastic life, he started teaching in the school, he quickly found himself missing the Midday Office due to the pressure of other time commitments, 'which seemed a small sacrifice but in fact was a warning sign of the loss of monastic discipline, drifting away from community life and the *Rule*'. Here he alluded to the problem of acedia (as discussed earlier), explaining that it was little wonder that the desert monks complained of the 'noonday demon' – it was precisely at this time that the day seems to be dragging on monotonously and you 'lose sight of the purpose of things'.

If the opportunity to come together in prayer gives monks a structure to brace themselves against the noonday demon, so too does the opportunity to eat as a family, and once again monks move directly from Midday Office to the refectory for lunch. The mealtime is a continuation of the cycle of prayer, beginning with the chanting of the grace before meals, and reflecting on the liturgy of the day through the reading of scripture from the conventual Mass before

---

pating in the consecration of the bread and the wine. There is no requirement that monks should concelebrate, as monks may choose to celebrate Mass separately. In addition, due to the canonical restriction on bination (the celebration of Mass twice on the same day), there were often a number of priests celebrating Mass elsewhere that day who would nevertheless attend the Mass without concelebrating.

The rhythm of stability

food is served. After this, the monks sit eating in silence while the lector appointed for that week reads aloud from a book chosen by the prior (often a work of history or biography).

The afternoon is again taken up with work duties, though those who can will often gather at the timetabled moment for tea, 4.15pm – a more relaxed occasion than the other points in the day when the monks come together in the refectory, with speaking allowed and the opportunity to meet guests currently staying in the monastery. The monks then return to the west wing for a daily chapter meeting, at which the abbot reads from and reflects on the *Rule*, and any community matters are discussed.

At 5.40pm, Great Bede rings out again, summoning the monks for *Vespers*. The monks arrive from different directions, some moving slowly and deliberately, hoods already up in recollection; others who have had to hurry upon hearing the bell throwing their cowls on over their habits in an effort not to be late. One by one, they gather, standing in the archways of the cloister in a moment of reflection (*statio*) before the cloister bell rings at 5.45pm and the monks, lined up in order of seniority (primarily, the order in which they were clothed as monks), process in pairs into the body of the church. The monks bow in turn as they reach the altar, then immediately turn and bow to the monk they are processing alongside, honouring the presence of Christ in their brother, before taking their place in the stalls.

Vespers was repeatedly described to me as a service of thanksgiving. In the account of the shape of the liturgy given by the monastic choir master, emphasising the symmetry with the salvific symbolism of the dawn as in Lauds, the other 'pivotal hour', this thanksgiving directly connected the monks' own movement through the day with the time of salvation history. 'We give thanks for the day just passed, and for God's providence in the incarnation' – themes expressed in the selection of psalms, and in the chanting of the Magnificat, the Canticle of Mary from the Gospel of Luke.[9] Before the concluding prayers, the gathered monks call to mind the community beyond the immediate time and place as the necrology is read, listing and recalling in prayer all monks and nuns of the

---

9 Luke 1: 46–55.

English Benedictine Congregation who died on that day in previous years.

A further half-hour period of private prayer immediately follows Vespers, before the monks make their way to the refectory for supper, which again begins with the chanting of grace before meals and a scripture reading from the day's Mass, followed by the Martyrology, giving brief accounts of the lives of the saints whose commemorations fall on the following day. The monks once more eat in silence while a book is read to them. Following the chanting of grace after supper, the community moves to the calefactory to take coffee and spend some time in recreation with one another.

Compline, the last Office of the day, is at 8.00pm. Once the monks have taken their places in the stalls, the abbot goes to the lectern and reads a chapter from the *Rule* of St Benedict. As he turns, bows to the altar, and returns to the stalls, the lights illuminating the lectern are switched off and the choir is left in darkness, the only light coming from the candles on the altar. A hymn is sung:

> *Before the light of evening fades,*
> *we pray O Lord of all;*
> *That by your love we may be saved,*
> *from every grievous fall.*
>
> *Repel the terrors of the night,*
> *and Satan's power of guile.*
> *Impose a calm and restful sleep,*
> *that nothing may defile.*

At Compline the same three psalms are used every day, unlike the psalmody for the other hours, which changes from day to day on a two-week cycle. The focus is on the darkness of night as a realm of temptation and sin, and the power of God to overcome this darkness. Compline concludes with the Nunc Dimittis, the canticle of Simeon from the Gospel of Luke.[10] Finally, all process from the stalls and past the altar, where they turn to a statue of the Blessed Virgin Mary

---

10 Luke 2: 29–32.

and, as the final collective act of the day, chant an anthem in her honour. As a blessing to end the day, the abbot sprinkles the community, and any guests sitting in the nave, with holy water, before returning to his position, pausing, and bowing towards the statue. The rest of the community joins him in bowing. The monks then raise their hoods, return to their cells, and the *summum silentium* of night time begins.

The segmentation of time

This intensely routinised pattern to the day reflects the *Rule* of St Benedict's central concern with the organisation of time. While it takes a particular form shaped by the seventeenth-century restoration of the English Benedictine Congregation, the nineteenth-century return of the monasteries to England and the monastery's own liturgical reforms of 1968 in the wake of the Second Vatican Council (see Chapter 4), it nevertheless bears the imprint of the key idea that the *opus Dei* (the work of God, that is, the liturgy) should give shape to the whole day and that all the monks' waking and sleeping moments should be accounted for within this structure.

Returning to the theme of the 'human clock', the historic significance of monasticism as a force shaping contemporary time discipline has been a source of some debate. I want to discuss this debate before returning directly to the perspective of the monks for two reasons. Firstly, because, as we will see, the role of monasticism in the history of timekeeping is something that has been a source of interest to the community. But secondly, because an examination of the particular relationship between the *Rule* and the clock highlights a specific irony around the *abstraction* of time. While monastic timekeeping has been seen as a driving force enabling a mechanised approach to time, what we see in the ethnographic account above is that the *horarium* is understood as a grounding for stability, not only in its capacity to enable social co-ordination but also as a means of 'hallowing time' in a way that resists treating time as an abstract quantity.

The importance of routine within the *Rule* – and timekeeping in the service of that routine – has long attracted the attention of those seeking to trace the development of the 'clock time' that conditions contemporary life back to a point of origin. For Agamben (2013: 18) the 'chronometric scansion of human time', which we associate with the division of labour in the factory, has a precedent in the segmentation of time in the *Rule*. Temporal organisation is central to Agamben's understanding of how monks' lives become one with the *Rule*. The division of the day such that 'the whole life of the monk is modelled according to an implacable and incessant temporal articulation' (2013: 21) is 'a sanctification of life by means of time' (2013: 24): it is in this way, Agamben suggests, that monks come to view their lives liturgically, such that the whole of life becomes the Divine Office and an embodiment of the aspiration to pray constantly. But, in casting his eyes from the 'strict absoluteness' (2013: 19) of the hours of the liturgy to the factory and the conditions of industrial time, Agamben stumbles into a debate which is of some significance.

In *Technics and Civilization*, Lewis Mumford famously made the connection between the *Rule* of St Benedict, with its need for timekeeping, and the emergence of the clock – suggesting that in this way the monastery laid a fundamental groundwork for the development of the modern industrial age: 'monasteries ... helped to give human enterprise the regular collective beat and rhythm of the machine; for the clock is not merely a means of keeping track of the hours, but of synchronizing the actions of men' (Mumford 1934: 13–14). The clock is here viewed to be an inevitable product of the organisation of time around points of prayer that fall at specific points of the day: 'some means of keeping count [of the hours] and ensuring their regular repetition become necessary' (1934: 13). This rhythm of time radiates out from the monastery, not least through the sounding of the bell, which impacts on the time-consciousness of a wider population.

Such a mode of timekeeping is grounded in a concept of a time that moves regularly and steadily, independent of human activity and observation: what the clock materialises is an *abstract time*, an independent world of sequences in which time has its own measurable and consistent regular motion. It is through our naturalised belief in this consistency and regularity that we act when prompted, and this allows us to co-ordinate social and economic life in a precise way. For this, suggests Mumford, we have the monks to thank.

This sense of abstract time relies on a disconnection of time from its social and natural markers. But does this take us too far from the intentions of the *Rule*? Dohrn-van Rossum (1996: 33) argues that Mumford's mechanistic image is erroneous, failing to reflect the *elasticity* of time within the *Rule* and misrepresenting it on two key scores.

Firstly, timekeeping as envisaged in the *Rule* of St Benedict was bound to natural rhythms: daylight and the seasons. As the daylight became more plentiful during the summer months, the Offices of the day could be spread out; in the winter months, the hours needed to be closer together so that Vespers and Compline would be said while there was still sufficient daylight, Compline itself marking the passage into darkness (Dohrn-van Rossum 1996: 36). The shifting light of seasons also shaped the timetable of meals, with Benedict prescribing different arrangements for summer and winter months. It is unthinkable that such a system could have been rigidly timed: 'Between post-midnight vigils and sunset stretched a fixed sequence with times that were, to a certain extent, movable' (1996: 37).

Secondly, the sense of the rhythm of time within the monastery being automated understates the human involvement in shaping and marking this rhythm. The *Rule* and its predecessors emphasise the importance of the individuals tasked with the role of signalling the time (Dohrn-van Rossum 1996: 56; see also Agamben 2013: 20, who notes 'their importance cannot be exaggerated'). The social response is to their call, rather than the time itself, and early monastic time-measurement devices such as marked candles and water outflow clocks (Dohrn-van Rossum 1996: 57–63) were an aid to these role holders. This serves to recalibrate our idea of the envisaged time discipline. Punctuality was certainly important; however, 'the required punctuality was not related to abstract points in time, but to points in the sequence of the rhythm of collective conduct' (1996: 37).

This leads us back to the social dynamics of time in the monastery. The sociologist Eviatar Zerubavel develops Mumford's theme by tracing the historic significance of medieval monasticism's 'spirit of scheduling' with its 'sanctification of punctuality' (1981: 35), but he is particularly attentive to how these temporal norms are an integral dimension of the relationship between the individual and the collective. The *horarium* is considered to be a boundary, distinguishing its group members from the rhythms of the world beyond, and generating a 'temporal symmetry' (1980: 168), by which the monk's own specific activity at any given moment (rising, praying, eating, working, sleeping) is reflected in the bodies of others around him; through this simultaneity individual actions become communal actions. Here we see the interplay of constraint and freedom in the monks' temporal regularity: in the face of the coercive force (1980: 160) of the timetable, there is a loss of spontaneity of action; a reconstitution of the self through the stripping of individuality (1980: 167). Yet there is also the freedom of being relieved from scheduling and the decision of what to do, when, such that the monks' moment to moment can be redirected towards what is deemed most meaningful: the eternal relationship with the eternal God. Here (calling to mind Great Bede ringing out beyond the monastery, over the valley and over the internet) we should be cautious about treating the boundary of the *horarium* as an overly rigid one, marking an absolute distinction between the monk and the universe beyond. (See also Pryce (2018: 244) on the 'permeability' of the monks' cell.) Containment within the schedule not only builds community, but expands it outwards in space and time.

Returning to Downside, the affinity between monks and the history of timekeeping formed part of the fabric of everyday life in the monastery. Clocks of various shapes and sizes were dotted around the enclosure; many of these were part of the personal collection of a deceased member of the community, Augustine James. A keen horologist and collector of historic clocks, he sold off much of his collection upon entering the monastery; the remains of his collection became part of the property of the monastic community, and he retained an interest in the maintenance and repair of clocks throughout his life. A caricature by a contemporary, Hubert van Zeller, shows him encased within a grandfather clock while winding up another clock.

The monastic library, where I would spend much of my mornings – and which itself bore an uncanny resemblance to a sundial – contained one of Britain's most substantial collections of historic texts on sundials and timekeeping, a by-product of the pioneering antiquarian research by the monk Ethelbert Horne on 'scratch dials' carved into the walls of medieval churches. More recently, the monk Leo Maidlow Davis designed, carved, and installed a sundial as a memorial to one of his deceased brethren: he was subsequently invited to give the annual lecture to the British Sundial Society, taking as his topic timekeeping in the *Rule* of St Benedict.[11] In his lecture he gave an account of significance of the *horarium* not only in organising time, but also in giving meaning to time.

> The Rule gives us a detailed programme that enables monks to live such a careful and attentive life as will bring them closer to God and to eternal life. Integral to this life was the careful measurement of time both by day and by night. We owe much to the monks whose sense of time and structure has flowed over into the complex organisation of time upon which we so heavily depend. However, time without eternity is wearisome and deadening. Reflecting on St Benedict's vision of time may help to restore an awareness that time matters, not for its own sake, but because it can remind us that every moment of our lives is infinitely precious.

In these words we see a recognition – and even a sense of pride – that Benedictine monasticism has made a key contribution to the development of a scientific understanding of time. Yet the task of looking to history is also part of locating the monks' own identity. It is also worth remembering that whatever the timekeeping basis of monks at the time of the *Rule*, the contemporary life of the

---

11 I am grateful to Dom Leo Maidlow Davis for providing me with the notes of his lecture.

monastery is shaped by a more recent imagination. The building of the abbey church (complete with its bell tower) at the end of the nineteenth and into the twentieth century reflected a new desire to restore the prominence of monastic life in England, and to accomplish this by elevating the standard of monastic observance in the Congregation – shifting away from the idiorhythmic habits of isolated priests on the mission towards, and anchoring stability in the shared life orientated around the liturgy of the hours.

Of course, if the monastic *horarium* of the sixth century is understood and restored through the lens of the late nineteenth and early twentieth centuries, then it should be no surprise that English Benedictine monastic timetabling is infused with the time capitalism of the industrial era, with its quantification and commodification of time (Thompson 1967). The indispensability of the precision of the clock to contemporary monastic life and its management is witness to this. Yet (noting the call above that we need to 'restore an awareness that time matters') this is a form of life that also contains misgivings about that pulverised notion of time.

So there is an irony here: as we saw, the *horarium* in its regularity has been treated as an engine towards an 'abstract' conception of time, but the danger is that abstraction of time empties it out in ways that leave it 'wearisome and deadening'.[12] Zerubavel (1981: 62), highlighting the abstraction of the clock, argues that 'clock time is a symbolic system whose elementary units, like words, have no intrinsic value of their own'. But the monastic emphasis on stability in time as well as space contains a caution about the drift that can occur when the abstraction of time causes it to lose meaning.

One of the effects of the *horarium* is that it shapes other activities – such as work – in relationship to the points of the day where the monks gather for collective prayer. (A similar point has been made by El Guindi (2008: 129) in her discussion of the shape

---

12 In this context, the passing remark by Bourdieu (1963: 58) that the Kabyle in Algeria sometimes refer to the clock as 'the devil's mill' is striking – detaching people from 'submission to the passage of time scanned in the rhythms of nature' (1963: 57), the rigidity of the clock is seen as eroding the relational basis of time that gives it its moral character.

given by the rhythm of prayer in Islam: 'Daily prayer interweaves intervals of sacred and ordinary and so integrates spheres of lived experience' (2008: 153)). Working in the carpentry shop in the afternoon, I was often struck by the start-stop nature that this imposed on our tasks there: we were conscious of the hands of the clock that hung above our heads amidst the religious pictures and memorial cards, and we timed our own departure from the workshop with some precision. It was perhaps with this in mind – the fact that we had to leave off work sometimes at an inconvenient moment – that one day, as we packed away, I asked the monk who had been teaching me how to use a spokeshave whether the intensely timetabled nature of monastic life wasn't sometimes something of a nuisance. 'Well, of course you can pray at any time. I think if you take away the hours [of the Divine Office] the day seems shapeless though. We pray at a given time and each hour hallows that particular time, it makes the activity around that particular time prayerful. Prayer after rising, prayer before eating. There's a rhythm to it and it's that rhythm that gives the day its character.'

Universal prayer

Returning, then, to the sound of Great Bede marking the hours: what is announced is not abstract time, but time as a relationship. And, crucially, this is not just an internal relationship but one that expands outwards.

This idea of an expansive relationship was explained during a retreat in the monastery for young men considering their vocations. Sitting in the guest wing, drinking tea and joking about the need for caffeine to adjust to the early morning rising, the young retreatants were addressed by one of the senior monks of the community: 'The most powerful thing about the Divine Office is the idea that you are praying the same prayer as so many other people. And you will come in at the same time next day, and the next day, and next week you will say the same prayers. Sounds tedious, no? Well, you know what they say, the first 50 years are the hardest ... But no, really, it's not tedious when you think about it as something shared by everyone, if you imagine that at that moment in time you are joined in prayer with people the whole world over, and that you are doing what monks and other faithful have done for generations. You're sharing their timetable too. I'm not going to say that makes it easier to get up in the morning, but it certainly makes the idea of a fixed timetable of prayer seem expansive and liberating, and not oppressive.'

This is a sense of time which is not just on your own terms. Indeed, the Divine Office was described to me repeatedly as the 'prayer of the whole church' and, in shaping the day through this cycle of prayer, the monks are able to imagine themselves not only as part of a monastic household, but beyond that, as part of a church at prayer, a wider universe in which voice is added to voice.[13]

The sense conveyed to me was that the liturgy of the hours offered an expanded sense of perspective beyond the individual; a consciousness of the deeply social nature of prayer. This came through particularly clearly in my conversation with the monastic choir master, where we had been discussing the development of the liturgy in the past 50 years (see Chapter 4). He was particularly keen to stress how the importance of collectivity motivated liturgical reform. We had been talking about attempts to ensure that the Divine Office was a vehicle for collective experience, such as choosing hymns that address prayer to God in the first person plural, when he explained, 'You might have your own concerns which you have been struggling with in private prayer, but when you are called to prayer in the Office, these concerns are subsumed, in a way they are objectified, you have your subjective concerns in life but the business of the Divine Office is not your concerns, not your business

---

13 This is poetically expressed by Cuthbert Hedley, an English Benedictine monk and bishop of the nineteenth and early twentieth centuries who wrote a book of meditations for priests on retreat. 'Joining my poor and unworthy voice with this grave symphony of worship and petition, my feeble breath becomes a part of that which is mighty and divine' (Hedley 1894: 160), even 'a part and a voice in that grand universal choir in which Jesus presides' (1894: 167).

but the business, the prayer of everyone, of the whole church as a unity.'

Such an approach is reinforced by the way the psalms are understood. The psalms as texts possess a deep subjectivity, reflective of the mind of a particular individual praying to God (some psalms might express despair, some joy, and so on). But in the fact that this subjectivity does not neatly map onto our own, chanting psalms encourages a heightened perception – or at least a recognition – that in prayer we are in the presence of the subjectivity of others beyond ourselves. You are not simply chanting psalms that are reflective of your own personal state of mind. Rather, the psalms follow a set order over a two-week cycle in which the whole psalter is recited. One monk, who entered the monastery in the 1990s and often serves as a cantor, explained that when chanting the psalms, he imagines himself to be joining with those people who are experiencing the emotional states set out in the psalm, even (or, he suggests, especially) if he finds himself in a very different state of mind. You might have arrived very despondent, but the psalmody is full of praise and joy; you might have arrived in a good mood, but find yourself chanting a cursing psalm. 'The psalms are the prayers of an individual, so of course they are ideal as the prayers of individuals. But we're not chanting them individually ... and we don't necessarily share the mindset of the psalmist.' The monk chants these words with the understanding that they are the common prayer of the church, and in doing so 'we stand alongside and represent those in that state of mind, we stand alongside them in Christ.'

This movement of the individual beyond himself is well illustrated by the practice of *statio* before Vespers. The monks assemble in the cloister as the bell rings; they stand in line along the walls like statues in niches, their hoods up and heads bowed in a moment of collection before the signal to process into the Church. This can be seen as a gathering, both in the sense of the monks gathering together in one place before the procession, but also in the sense that it gave individuals an opportunity to gather their thoughts. The gathering and focus on the task ahead are part of the process through which the monk is removed from his personal circumstance.

He is removed from his immediate concerns and activities, and called by the bell to the abbey church to be part of something universal.

Absent brethren

The *horarium* applies the Benedictine vow of stability to time itself. As a key element of the *cenobitic* life, it casts into relief what are perceived to be the problematic dimensions of spiritual individualism, drifting from the community by 'following your own timetable' or losing a sense of the moderation of the *Rule* in balancing the day's activities. Routine, structure, and repetition are not just the seeds of abstract time, but of relationships: in relationship with the day, with the community, and as part of an expansive universal rhythm of praise, *in saecula saeculorum*.

Yet it would be wrong to treat this as a form of de-individuation. Even incorporated into a human clock, the self does not disappear and can experience the *horarium*'s demarcation of time as an intrusion.

In among the archival papers of one of the monastery's key advocates of liturgical reform is a printed label with hours marked at intervals along the edge, purportedly to be stuck to a candle:

> Directions for use – just before going to sleep, instead of placing the candle in the candle stick, stick it up your   to the mark indicating the number of hours you wish to sleep, then lie on your face, light the candle and go to sleep.

At the top of the label, in block capitals, the monk had written LITURGICAL ALARM CLOCK. Something of a literal intrusion, but the point of the joke – especially for the monk compelled to rise for Vigils – is clear.

As a means of shaping the relationship between the individual and the community, the apparent expansion of monastic time beyond the self could also be experienced as a form of constraint. As one of the senior monks in the community explained to me,

The rhythm of stability

'When the bell rings, I could be peeing or trying to write a poem or anything and I have to think, I've got to finish and get to the church ... The bell marks the limits of individual creativity.' Little wonder, then, that apparent 'idiorhythmic' tendencies emerge at the interface of individual roles and needs with the routine of the community.

Attending the hours of the Divine Office some days, the empty seats in the stalls were themselves notable presences; absences that showed visible cracks in the collective routine, signs of the demands of other routines and other pressures upon community life. The monks would shuffle up along the stalls to close the gaps and get on with things. Then, at the end of each hour, the recognition that prayer expands beyond the small number in the stalls, calling to mind those beyond the gathered community: 'May God's help be with us always.' 'And with our absent brethren.'

PART II

Prayer, private and public

CHAPTER 4

Liturgical prayer and the limits of participation

'Unless we get it, our monastic churches will become museums'

In April 1964, a telling exchange appeared on the pages of *The Tablet*, a weekly Catholic newspaper. As the Catholic Church prepared for a reform of its liturgy in the wake of the Second Vatican Council, a layperson wrote a letter suggesting that – for the time being at least – English Benedictine monasteries should act as guardians of the Church's heritage and 'keep alive' the traditional forms and language of the sacred liturgy.[1] The immediate response from one monk of the community, Gregory Murray (who, as we shall see, played an important role in reshaping Downside's monastic liturgy), was a vigorous rejection of the idea that Downside should become 'a liturgical National Trust'. Instead, he insisted on the need for reform. 'Unless we get it, our monastic churches will become museums in which visitors will be able to witness a liturgical worship which the Church will have discarded elsewhere as ineffectual and obsolete … it seems to me that, instead of lagging behind, we Benedictines should take a leading part in the liturgical reform. Does not our greater liturgical experience entitle us to do so?'[2]

This exchange came at a time when monastic communities were

---

1 Letter to *The Tablet*, 11 April 1964, 416–7.
2 Letter to *The Tablet*, 18 April 1964, 443–4.

considering how they should engage with and respond to change. Examining what is at stake here, we see how in a Benedictine context any question of reform is infused with reflection on the meaning and importance of stability.

Earlier chapters have considered different dimensions of this stability. Chapter 2 explored how monasteries embody continuity within the landscape and in history; a continuity that connects generations through time through a sense of repetition and return. Do significant changes to the liturgy rupture this continuity? Chapter 3 examined the rhythms that shape the daily routine; debates around reform bring into focus the extent to which this *horarium* serves as shared prayer, grounding community life and deepening family relationships. A further consideration – the point of contention in the exchange above – is how a world beyond the cloister relates to this rhythm of prayer and what it means to be in time with the Church.

This chapter examines the process of liturgical change within the monastery. *Sacrosanctum Concilium*, the first constitution emerging from the Second Vatican Council and promulgated on 4 December 1964, focused specifically on the renewal of the liturgy, including the Divine Office. Benedictine communities responded in diverse ways to this call for renewal (Lynch 2017; Guarino 2018), and at Downside the possibilities of reform were already a subject of ongoing debate. On 17 October 1967, in response to a request from the Congregation, the Consilium for the Implementation of the Constitution on the Liturgy granted English Benedictine monasteries permission to adapt and modify the form of the Divine Office to meet the specific requirements of each community.[3] Here I focus on the nature of the changes, the underpinning principles they express, and the dynamics around these shifts.

At Downside, the changes made possible by this permission were implemented from Easter 1968: a reduction of the number of hours of the Divine Office to three (Matins, Midday Prayer, and Vespers), with the course of psalms to be completed over two weeks, and a shift of language from Latin to English. This

---

3 Consilium for the Implementation of the Constitution on the Sacred Liturgy Rescript Prot 2919/67.

substantial transformation of the daily rhythm of monastic stability was followed by disruption of the architectural grounding in response to the changes to the liturgy of the Mass in 1970; the main altar in the abbey church was moved and the sanctuary and choir reorganised to reflect the revised rite. This process took nearly two years and, during that time, much of the daily liturgy had to be celebrated elsewhere in the monastery buildings.

The central question at this time of change is *what it means to participate*. Recent anthropological scholarship (Pina-Cabral 2018; Kelty 2019) considers the nature of participation in ways that help bring this question into focus. I argue that many of the key arguments shaping liturgical reform were grounded in an idea of participation that emphasised the 'contributory autonomy' (Kelty 2019: 14) of the individual entering into collective prayer. Such an approach looks to the sincerity of the participant (Keane 2007) and is suspicious of anything that might appear to strip individuals of their agency to consciously and sincerely engage – a mode of suspicion not entirely dissimilar to the argument of Maurice Bloch (1974, 1986) that the performative elements of ritual restrict freedom of engagement as participants are coerced by language or actions whose origin is outside themselves. Yet at the same time we hear voices urging caution about the erosion of what might be called the liminal qualities of ritual (Turner 1969, 1976) that enable participation in something that transcends the self. Looking at how these positions were articulated offers a microhistory of the crucial questions facing the wider Church.

Making sense of the liturgy

The community were not passive recipients of change, and indeed some monks were in the vanguard as advocates and even campaigners for liturgical reform. 'Agitate for better things – yes, agitate; it is the laity's business to insist on being given a form of worship which they can follow and in which they can take their proper part.'[4] This was

---

4 Illtyd Trethowan, 'The Christian Mystery', 105, File 3659, Downside Archives.

the advice given by Illtyd Trethowan, a monk of the community, as part of a series of talks to laypeople during an Easter retreat at Downside in 1956, and subsequently prepared for publication.[5] More outspoken was Gregory Murray, whose letter we saw at the start of this chapter. His campaigning even took him on an intensive speaking tour of the USA between June and August of 1959, visiting places of 'strategic importance to the lay participation movement'[6] – there, his advocacy of a liturgy in the language spoken by the people led to him being dubbed 'Dom Vernacular' on the cover of the December 1959 newsletter of the Vernacular Society, *Amen*, with a headline summarising his claim: 'People Reduced to Silence'.

In following the arguments presented for a Churchwide reform of the Mass that would better enable lay participation, we see some of the key principles that would also inform community discussions about the monastic liturgy. A central theme is the importance of intentionality to participation, and that this intentionality is demonstrated by active engagement. Such engagement is obstructed when it is difficult to understand what is going on; there needs to be, as Trethowan puts it, a 'determination to make sense of the liturgy'.[7]

'Liturgy is meant to be intelligible … we are supposed to understand the words of the liturgy',[8] and this intelligibility is a requirement if we are to 'bring our minds fully to bear'[9] on the

---

5 The manuscript, entitled 'The Christian Mystery', was subsequently rejected by the Diocesan Censor on the grounds that reference was made to unapproved translations of the Bible, and that the explanations of moral issues and the limits of a purely 'mechanical' view of religion might be misunderstood by those without a theological training. As a result of this rejection, Trethowan was temporarily restricted from leading retreats. Given the theme of this chapter, it is worth noting that the advocacy for liturgical renewal and the call for laity to agitate for reform were not themselves part of the grounds for rejection.

6 Notes on the itinerary of the USA Tour Summer 1959, Gregory Murray Box 4/7, Downside Archives.

7 Trethowan, 'The Christian Mystery', 104, File 3659, Downside Archives.

8 Trethowan, 'The Christian Mystery', 92, File 3659, Downside Archives.

9 Trethowan, 'The Christian Mystery', 105, File 3659, Downside Archives.

words. Without this capacity for comprehension, Trethowan argues, there is a risk that we treat liturgical participation as a purely *mechanical* process, rather than something we enter into with conscious understanding. It is a misunderstanding to think that 'if you pay in your cheques in the manner prescribed, go through the motions according to the book, then you will be all right'.[10] 'The Mass isn't magic'[11] – it doesn't work simply as a mechanism operated following the rules of attendance and leaving everything else up to the priest, whether we understand him or not. Rather, the Mass is the point at which we enter into Christ's sacrifice and victory, and we must take that opportunity by making a personal effort of attentiveness in mind and will. It is therefore right for the laity to adopt a sense of 'propriety, of ownership and responsibility'[12] by calling for a form of the liturgy that makes this possible. Yet the situation he saw around him was far from this: 'Congregations often seem to take no part in what is going on and to take no interest in it. How, indeed, should they, in view of the meaninglessness of most of it?' (Trethowan 1952: 107).

For Murray (1977: 76), the right of the people 'to hear and understand all the words' had a number of implications. The first was the need for a fully vernacular liturgy, as the use of an archaic language was a barrier to participation: 'the congregation (most of whom know no Latin) will either listen without understanding or else not listen but read the English [translation] in their books. So why sing the Latin? Just nostalgia, I suppose.'[13] And one should not assume that monasteries were exempt from this need: 'The crucial question of the language of the liturgy presents just as great a problem for many monks as for others ... I gather from discussions here and elsewhere that the majority find the Latin a real hindrance (some indeed an insuperable barrier) to the

---

10 Trethowan, 'The Christian Mystery', 3, File 3659, Downside Archives.
11 Trethowan, 'The Christian Mystery', 55, File 3659, Downside Archives.
12 Trethowan, 'The Christian Mystery', 106, File 3659, Downside Archives.
13 Handwritten note by Gregory Murray following notes for 'Plainsong and the vernacular – Lecture at Royal School of Church Music 1968', Gregory Murray Box 4/7, Downside Archives.

conscious prayerful understanding of what they are actually singing, saying, and hearing during the performance of the liturgy.'[14]

This was not simply a matter of understanding the language but was also about being able to attentively hear and follow what was going on. Murray saw it as absurd that priests should be 'muttering inaudibly' (Murray 1977: 69); the prayers of the Mass should be 'proclaimed in a loud voice so that all will pay attention' (1977: 49). To this end, Murray wrote several notes for himself and papers for the community (as well as letters to *The Times*[15]) on practical points of projection, enunciation, and pronunciation, including the correct speed and accentuation of public speech. One monk, casting his mind back to his time as a newly ordained priest, recalled to me Murray's 'helpful' (said somewhat sarcastically) presence lurking at the back of the church offering advice. Another monk confirmed, 'you'd hear him shouting things like "I can't hear you" and "stop mumbling!" It was frankly terrifying.'

But, in Murray's view, the relationship between performance and content could also be a source of danger. 'The problem is a perennial one. Once the liturgy is consciously adorned with beauty, there is always the danger that its beautiful externals may come to be mistaken for the liturgy itself. So that what begins as a praiseworthy attempt to emphasize the holiness of the act of worship can in fact defeat its object by distracting attention from that act of worship.'[16] His zeal here was noteworthy. Murray was a celebrated musician; having trained in church music from a young age as a chorister at Westminster Cathedral, he had gone on to become a well-known organ recitalist. It was therefore from a position of authority that he

---

14 Letter to *The Tablet*, 18 April 1964, 443.
15 From a letter to *The Times* written in February 1970, copy in Box 4/7, Downside Archives: 'Can anything be done to preserve the English tongue from the ravages of the intrusive "r"? "The idear of" has been in currency for a long time and is quite common, alas, among those who otherwise speak well ... Recent weeks have brought a veritable plague of "lore and order" from BBC announcers and news readers.'
16 'Music and the Mass', notes for a Lecture given to the Bristol Newman Association 21 November 1966, 12, Gregory Murray Box 4/7, Downside Archives.

took aim at the ways in which church music had come to restrict understanding and participation. 'As one who has spent years singing such music, I must also confess how seldom I have been able to give the words my attention, in view of the absorbing demands of the music' (Murray 1977: 24). The line of critique here is anthropologically significant; a suspicion of ritual performance's capacity to *conceal* meaning (Bloch 1974) – this is a point we shall return to later. Accordingly, emphasis is placed not on performance but on communicative function: 'we must never forget that music began its liturgical life with a purely functional purpose – to carry words' (Murray 1977: 75).

The principles outlined so far show an emphasis on the individual's ability to understand the meaning of the liturgy: comprehension as a grounding for the participant's intentionality in prayer. But as an account of participation, this only gets us so far, as the liturgy is the prayer of the Church, not simply of individuals. This communal dimension was of critical importance to the positions being argued above. 'We must make it obvious when we meet in church ... that we meet as members of a family. By a full participation in the liturgy we do express and convey this truth (Trethowan 1942: 8).

'The Church comprises the People of God, a community. When the Church gathers for Mass it is not as an assembly of isolated and individual worshippers ... but a community united in an act of community worship.'[17] Again, for those advocating reform, there was a frustration that the liturgy in its existing form obstructed this unity. As Murray described it, 'The Mass action itself was manifestly the action of the priest at the altar. He had his back to us and only occasionally turned to face us. Even then, he was advised to do so with downcast eyes, lest he be distracted from his personal recollection – so that even he was regarded as engaged on an individualistic duty ... the vast majority of the congregation said their own prayers ... Whatever form their prayer took, they were not necessarily connected directly with the Mass itself ... In other words, although we had all assembled to "hear" Mass, we did it in our own

---

17 'Introducing the new Ordo Missae', June 1969, 1, Gregory Murray Box 1/7, Downside Archives.

Liturgical prayer and the limits of participation

individualistic way, with no sense of community worship.'[18] By highlighting its absence, this account makes clear the importance of *shared attention*. In the situation described, the congregation are a distraction to the attention of the priest; meanwhile the congregation, unable to follow what is going on, turn their attention inwardly to their personal devotions. Where music was added to the mix, it threatened to be yet another pole of attention, congregations leaving the business of liturgical music to those performers able to grapple with its technical demands, while the priest had to block his ears to the choir and the organ while he gets on with saying the Mass (Murray 1977: 43). Following liturgical reform, Murray argued, shared attention would enable communal participation in place of such disconnection: 'we can all join together with full attention to every part of the Mass in orderly succession.'[19]

The reason for outlining these arguments in some detail is partly to show how some monks were active in public debates within the Church at large, but also because they give us insight into some of the principles that influenced reform of the liturgy within the monastery itself. What they express is a particular sense of what it means to be a participant: a mode of participation that Chris Kelty (2019) terms *contributory autonomy*.

Kelty (2019: 35) sees the Second Vatican Council and the liturgical reforms that followed it as one part of a wider story in which participation emerges – politically, economically, and socially – as the normative mode of engagement in the twentieth century. Yet crucially, this understanding of participation is grounded in a particular ideology: 'Only by virtue of becoming an individual, possessing liberty and an autonomous moral and political conscience, do we become capable of freely contributing to the creation or maintenance of a collective' (2019: 14). What I am arguing is that the principles above reflect this ideology of contributory autonomy. Calls for the liturgy to be *meaningful* place the emphasis on individual understanding as a necessary basis for intentional participation. This

---

18 'Musings on the Mass', undated notes, Gregory Murray Box 4/7, Downside Archives.
19 Letter to *The Tablet*, 8 November 1975, 1,088–9.

precedes and is considered necessary for the emergence of a collective, with shared attention drawing the intentionality towards a common goal. That is not to say the views above are representative of the community as a whole, and a little later we will turn to debates within the monastery that potentially reveal the limits of this perspective. But they do express an understanding of participation that shaped the reforms at this moment in the history of the monastery and the Church.

Not turning the church into a concert hall

It was early November in 2006 when I played the organ in the abbey church for the first time. I'd been invited over supper on All Saints' Day. In contrast to the collective silence of mealtimes on ordinary days, on solemnities the community and guests are allowed to talk during the meal, with a little wine helping the conversation along. After the grace before meals and the scripture reading, the intonation of the reader gives way to chats at different ends of the table. Varied individual voices are heard, and personal interests and enthusiasms are shared – from sports, to conjuring, to engineering. It was on such an occasion that I was talking with the monk who provided the organ accompaniment for the chant at Conventual Mass and Vespers. After chatting about our shared interest as musicians, he asked if I'd like to play the organ the following afternoon.

    I was intimidated by the instrument itself and the acoustic, but improvised a little before playing some rather muted interludes. After I'd finished, the monk who had invited me expressed surprise (and I suspect disappointment) that I hadn't played any 'loud French music'. But then he continued: 'quite right, of course. That was a very important thing, not to turn the church into a concert hall.' He recalled a time as a young monk when the abbot told him off – in a friendly, but nevertheless firm, way – for accompanying a visiting tenor in an impromptu performance of some extracts from Handel's *Messiah* in the abbey church. 'That was a lesson in humility for me of course, but it also relates to a more general point, something that was very important then.' The organ was primarily an instrument for the liturgy. 'So the idea that the performance of the music was distracting from the meaning of the liturgy, that the externals were getting in the way of the prayer, this idea not to turn the church into a concert hall was very important.'

He went on to show me the simple underlying harmonies he used when accompanying the set of psalm tones used in the monastic liturgy. 'Nothing too obtrusive. And the tones themselves are very simple' – just a reciting note and a three-note cadence. These nine tones, written by Gregory Murray for use following the reform of the office in Easter 1968, made deeply familiar by their repetition throughout the whole Divine Office, continue to be used for the psalmody to the present day. '"Tones not tunes" was how he [Murray] described them. The idea being that they allowed you to focus on the words of the psalms, rather than the performance of the music.'

It was somewhat ironic to be having this conversation at the console of the grand abbey church organ with its four manuals and 142 stops, built in 1932 and widely recognised as one of the finest instruments produced by the organ builder John Compton (more usually associated with theatre and cinema organs). It was an organ well suited for performance, and Gregory Murray had been the performer who brought it to life. So frequent were the broadcasts of organ recitals from the abbey church at this time, the monks joked that the organ must have been wired up to the BBC. But over the course of his monastic career, he grew increasingly uncomfortable with the place of the virtuosic in the church, and his hostility towards performance protruding into the liturgy was unmatched. 'In the Roman Martyrology for April 5th there is a story of a cantor who was shot in the throat with an arrow aimed by an Arian heretic as he was singing Alleluia on Easter Day. There have been occasions when I would have welcomed the intrusion of an Arian who was a good marksman' (Murray 1977: 12).

The functional simplicity of the 'tones not tunes' was presented in contrast to the Gregorian chant, medieval melodic forms developed for use in the Mass and the Divine Office and first notated in the tenth century. The study, revival, and codification of this chant was a particular focus of the restoration of monasticism in nineteenth-century France, with Prosper Guéranger's efforts to return to a Benedictine way of life at the Abbaye Saint-Pierre de Solesmes half a century after the French Revolution driving an active rediscovery and energetic dissemination of the Gregorian tradition as 'the soul of the monastery, the echo of history' (Bergeron 1998: 24). Such an attempt to bring the past into the present resonates with Downside's own architectural medievalism (see Chapter 2) and the role that tradition plays in asserting continuity (Hobsbawm 1983). Yet in this historic moment of critique, the concern is that form might obscure function – drawing attention away from the meaning itself, especially in the melismatic elements that draw a single syllable over many notes. So the adoption of a new functional set of psalm tones to serve as 'word-carrying formulae' following the 1968 reforms to the Divine Office[20] was with the hope that the community could 'give more attention to what we are singing than how we are singing it'.[21] Here, as discussed above, attention to meaning grounds intentionality.

After my somewhat faltering introduction to the abbey church organ, the conversations with the organist nevertheless continued. He went on to explain the frustration that he and others of his generation felt about the mechanical nature of a liturgy that had become a routinised duty, the very form of which seemed to undermine any possibility of the monks' minds being in tune with their voices. (An interview with the abbot at the time, Christopher Butler, reflects precisely this atmosphere (Granfield 1967: 51), saying of the younger monks 'I think that they have a horror … for anything that is phony – anything that is hypocritical, unauthentic. They feel that we are preserving the present structure of the monastic Office just for the sake of preserving.') The organist told me that the 'unthinking' state of the liturgy led him and a friend to go so far as to formulate a 'modest proposal' for the community: in the interests of efficiency, perhaps they needed only to chant the telephone directory. At the appointed time for each liturgical hour, the bell would ring and

---

20 'Report on the Office at Downside Abbey, September 1969', Gregory Murray Box 4/7, Downside Archives.
21 'Plainsong and the Vernacular', Gregory Murray Box 4/7, Downside Archives.

the monks would file into the choir stalls. They should then open the telephone directory and begin chanting its contents. An alarm clock would be set to go off after an appropriate length of time (to be calculated according to the level of solemnity expected for that particular point of prayer). The monks would then stop and pack up, resuming the next hour where they left off.

Such a parody of monastic worship probes the place of liturgy in community life. It satirises both a perceived disconnection of ritual action from meaning (it may as well be the telephone directory for all the attention the words can be paid), and the relationship between routine and intention (are the monks just going through the motions?). That the conventionalised nature of ritual distances it from individual intention is a classic theme in anthropological theory (Tambiah 1981), and indeed at various points in history this very point has led to Catholic ritual formalism being treated as an object of suspicion. (See, for example, Duffy (1992) on the increasing suspicion of ritualism in post-Reformation England, where reformers associated repeated actions with lack of knowledge, understanding, and intention.) An excellent ethnographic elaboration of such misgiving is provided by Keane (2007: 187), who describes the criticism of Catholic prayer by a Sumbanese Calvinist minister: 'there are often formulae. Can't skip over or go contrary to the way of praying. Have to follow exactly ... We on the other hand are not taught like this.' As a result, the Catholics come to be compared with Sumbanese ancestral ritualists, who are seen to approach prayer in a similarly formalistic manner. For the Calvinists, any such speech acts lack sincerity because of their 'fetishistic displacement of agency onto objectified verbal formulae' (2007: 193). Does the pray-er *know* and *mean* what it is they pray? What is striking here is that in a time of reform, such concerns come to be expressed within Catholicism as well as against it. Indeed, the telephone-directory proposal pushes the point even further (as good satire should): so detached is form from intention that the semantic content has become effectively arbitrary.

As I tried to bring these themes up in conversation with other monks at teatime, the librarian introduced me to a further joke highlighting concerns about formalism and intentionality. In the days of persecution, several monks are seated together in secret, reciting the Divine Office. Suddenly, they hear soldiers bursting through the door and realise that they are about to be arrested and put to death. 'We had better stop what we are doing,' says one, 'and pray.'[22] Like most good comedians, the librarian would rarely elaborate for risk of dissecting the joke. But the question posed by the punchline is clear enough – when the liturgy becomes a mechanical duty, has it ceased to be prayer?

Genuine family prayer

The principle that the monastery should grasp this moment of change is clear in an article published in the monastery's scholarly journal, the *Downside Review* – but tellingly, that article is immediately followed by a note of caution. First, in favour of renewal, Cyprian Stockford (1964: 317) insists that 'it is still necessary, if there is to be genuine communal participation, to provide a meaningful and relevant form of prayer. This would mean, in the first place, a vernacular Office – in any case a practical necessity if monastic vocations are to flourish in a Church whose life is to be centred on a vernacular liturgy. Benedictine monachism, if it is to survive as a living force in a renewed Catholic Church, cannot remain as a sort of repository for irrelevant medievalism. We cannot be mere traditionalists.' Archaism in language and form is not only a barrier to understanding and conscious engagement but also risks disconnection from contemporary life.

But this problem of relevance, meaning, and intention is also linked to the problem of shared attention. What possibility can there be for 'genuine family prayer' if 'the majority of the community is unable to attend most of the choir office' (1964: 315)? As a fixed pattern

---

22 The joke has clearly survived as part of the oral culture of the monastery for a while; a variant of the same joke can be found in Gregory Murray's papers. 'Priests out in the country sitting under a tree – saying Matins for tomorrow at 2pm – thunderstorms getting nearer etc. – "My God, we'd better say some prayers."' The Divine Office, talk for Maidenhead Newman Circle, 16 February 1977, Gregory Murray Box 1/7.

of prayer unyielding to the realities of the monks' everyday lives, all too often the liturgy fails to draw the community together – attention is fragmented. So, in place of the 'exclusivist' emphasis on tradition, Stockford advocates an 'incarnational' approach 'centred round the common and the communal'. What this meant in practical terms was that, given the commitments that monks have beyond the choir stalls, a reduction in the number of hours was desirable to create a shape of daily prayer that would allow the whole community to gather as a family. If monasticism is to express the 'solidarity' of communal life, 'we must be prepared to sacrifice whatever is secondary – the letter of the Rule, traditional language and music, the eight hours – ... in order that monastic worship should fulfil its essential function as the communal prayer of each monastic family' (1964: 323).

These views clearly pre-empt the core features of the 1968 reform. However, the editorial response that immediately follows makes it clear that Stockford's view did not represent a settled consensus within the community. That the editor at the time was none other than Illtyd Trethowan – whose advocacy for a fully participatory liturgy was discussed earlier – shows that this was no simple matter dividing monks along neat party lines; for many it was a space of ambivalence. The central concern expressed in the editorial is whether an accommodation with the everyday loses sight of the need for transcendence (1964: 326). The desirability of a wholly vernacular Office is questioned:[23] 'I should be sorry to see the complete disappearance of the Latin liturgy and should therefore

---

23 This ambivalence around the use of the vernacular was evident in *Christ in the Liturgy* (Trethowan 1952). On the one hand, use of the vernacular might aid comprehension and participation; 'I must confess that in recent years a rooted objection on my part to vernacular liturgy in any form has been slowly undermined by what has seemed to be the logic of facts' (1952: 116). Nevertheless, Trethowan warned not to underestimate how far the Church's 'spiritual roots' are embedded in the Latin which had been the expression of its liturgical tradition for so long (1952: 117), and in particular retained a hesitation about whether it was appropriate to translate the Divine Office, noting the particular difficulty of translating Old Testament texts into a '"timeless" English ... intelligible but not undignified' (1952: 134).

regard it as proper for it to be retained in monasteries where Latin is understood (and I see no reason why novices should not learn Latin)' (1964: 324). The question of language and meaning is, of course, an important one; debates around the value or hazard of retaining apparently archaic language in ritual highlight the interplay between intelligibility and mystification (Tomlinson and Engelke 2006: 21) that becomes a source of tension in times of reform. But note that Trethowan is not rejecting intelligibility here – he expects that Latin *should* be intelligible to monks. Rather, the point is about whether, if the liturgy has the possibility to transcend the everyday, the sacred language should be distinct from ordinary language (see also Tambiah 1968, reflecting the point that a sacred language is a feature of most religions, the notable exception being some forms of Christianity). In this sense, the question of language is but a point of detail within a wider reservation: is the monastic liturgy at risk of becoming too worldly? In asking how much can be sacrificed in the interests of relevance and practicality without losing sight of the principal end of prayer – union with God – Trethowan looks to the liturgy's potential to transcend, and not simply reflect, the world.

Seeing this divergence of views laid out on the page gives some sense of the debate taking place at the time; a debate that would become the focus of formal discussions involving the whole community and finally a full chapter vote. A majority voted to implement the reform, but other dissenting voices were present. As one monk who was involved in these discussions explained, some of the key concerns were around authority and historical continuity. 'There were certainly some who asked, is this too far removed from what Benedict writes in the *Rule* ... is it too far from what we had been taught in the novitiate?' Alongside such disquiet, even among some who recognised the case for reform there was a question of whether the pursuit of purely functional forms and an accommodation with everyday patterns of living and expression would undermine the numinous character of the liturgy.

Notwithstanding monastic obedience, such concerns do not simply evaporate following the result of a majority vote and its implementation by the abbot. A strong supporter of the reforms recognised that several of his friends had been hurt by the result of the vote, but nevertheless told me in such a context it would be a mistake to think of this as something imposed upon the community. In such circumstances, the role of the abbot is not simply to compel, but to care for the whole family, to listen and even to console: 'he was very considerate over the minority, granting exemption to the few among them for whom it was the last straw.'

It is jarring that a reform seeking a pattern of family prayer leads to individual divergences from the common life, with exempted monks allowed to continue with the old Office in whole or part. For those monks, the monastic liturgy became a private practice at least to some degree. Here changes intended to allow for increased participation generate partial fragmentation – an added irony of which, it was suggested to me, was that even the participation of those it was meant to benefit was not always assured: 'I remember one of the old monks who had struggled with the reform, I told him "well, it's meant to allow more of the school fathers [monks with teaching duties] to attend." "But they never do attend!" he replied.' Elements of the community become separated from one another. This separation was poignantly expressed by the handful of monks who gathered to continue chanting Compline at the end of the day, even though it had been 'scrapped' – meeting in the crypt, apart from the main body of the church and apart from the rest of their community.

Ritual reversion

In the following decades, we see a continuing strand of critical reflection on the limits of reform.[24] Indeed, the story since has been one of gradual (though far from total) ritual reversion.

During the early days of my fieldwork, meeting with the abbot to

---

24 See, for example, seven years after the reform, the publication of an article in the *Downside Review* by one of the younger monks of the community questioning whether a monastery had any authority to depart from the *Rule* by reducing the number of hours, which should always be said at their proper time (Yeo 1975).

discuss the history of Downside's liturgy, he explained that he had experienced something of a 'crisis' while working in Rome as secretary to the Abbot Primate in the 1980s – seeing other congregations, it became apparent how different the practice of the English Benedictines was. 'The large majority of Benedictine monasteries, founded or reformed since the French Revolution, have imbibed the spirituality of Solesmes and Guéranger.' Here Prosper Guéranger's work restoring monasticism in France stands as an iconic demonstration of the role of the liturgy as the source of a historical Benedictine identity (Winthrop 1985; Bergeron 1998) and the embodiment of a golden age of monasticism. By contrast, the English Benedictines remained grounded in what seemed to the abbot a 'spirituality for solitaries'[25] – a focus on personal prayer rather than shared liturgical life (see Chapter 5) – and the influence of Guéranger never took root. This led him to ask: to what extent was this apparent departure from a wider Benedictine emphasis on the liturgy as the 'centre and source' of monastic prayer desirable or sustainable? Here, we have some indication of the approach of leadership at Downside at the end of the twentieth and beginning of the twenty-first century, increasingly influenced by the emphasis on liturgical tradition and restoration elsewhere in the Benedictine world, and revisiting aspects of Downside's own reform on the grounds of both continuity with tradition and its relationship with global patterns of Benedictine life.

The reform of 1968 has subsequently been reshaped by a series of alterations that reveal different dynamics within the community (and the Church more generally), illuminating tensions at the heart of ritual reform. This reshaping can be considered in four key areas.

A principal change came in 1995, when the liturgy of the hours shifted from a 'sequential' course of psalms (that is, one that

---

25 One indication of this is the observation that while the community's superior Christopher Butler had played a prominent role in the Second Vatican Council as Abbot President, he had little enthusiasm for discussions about the liturgy (Phillips 2024). As one of the monks recalled, 'he never moved from his conviction that personal religion, above all prayer, counted for more, and the corporate expression of our faith can so easily become formalism' (2024: 300).

proceeds numerically through the psalms over the course of the week) to a 'distributed' course of psalms reflecting both the shape of the day (as described in Chapter 3) and the shape of the week, 'helping monks to pray at particular times, and so help them make prayer the rest of the time' in the words of the choir master. This implies a selection based on 'exegetical criteria': what is the particular character of the *hours* within the daily cycle and the days within the weekly cycle, and looking at the content and character of each psalm, what selection of psalms would be most fitting for prayer at that time? Significantly, by taking as its basis a scheme offered in the *Thesaurus Liturgiae Horarum Monasticae*[26], published in 1977 by the Abbot Primate for use across the Benedictine Confederation, this change reflects a renewed emphasis on consistency with wider Benedictine tradition. At the same time, the all-important link between the intention of prayer and attention to the meaning of words might be said to follow the guiding principles of reform discussed above. Subsequent changes, however, are clearer instances of ritual reversion.

In 1998, a further shift restored the chanting of the *Gloria Patri* at the conclusion of each psalm. The frequent repetition of this prayer is a feature of the *Rule* and, prior to the reforms of 1968, it was chanted at the end of every psalm during the Divine Office (and so, repeated hundreds of times over the course of the week). However, as a feature of the 1968 reforms, this was replaced with a single *Gloria Patri* (in English) after all the psalms had been chanted. One of the monks who had been part of the discussions in the 1960s joked that this was part of a 'war on vain repetitions'[27] and that such frequent repetition of the same words had been deemed 'redundant'. Here again is the tension between the intentionality of prayer and the apparently mechanical use of repeated words. For Tambiah (1981: 161–2), the frequent repetition of specific

26 The pattern adopted for use in Downside Abbey is a local adaptation of Scheme B, as presented in the *Thesaurus Liturgiae Horarum Monasticae*.
27 A reference to the words of Jesus as represented in the King James translation of Matthew 6:7: 'But when ye pray, use not vain repetitions, as the heathen do: for they think that they shall be heard for their much speaking.'

formula is indicative of 'ritual involution'; such a condensation can indicate 'meaning intensification' but is also vulnerable to 'meaning atrophy' (1981: 163). As Bloch (1974: 76) has argued, repetition as a characteristic of 'frozen' ritual language marks its difference from everyday language (in which repetition might be deemed 'mere redundancy'); so, at a moment where emphasis is placed on the link between meaning and intentionality, and where the distance between ritual and the everyday world comes under scrutiny, it is striking to note this excision of 'vain repetitions'. Yet the apparent redundancy of repetition can also be a vehicle for intensity (Bazzanella 2011). Coleman (2019: 176), drawing on his research with Swedish Pentecostals, remarks that, even in Protestant contexts explicitly characterised by an emphasis on sincerity in language, repetition nonetheless offers intensification through the accumulation of a 'weight of words', entering into an excess that transcends the normal.[28] So restoring the repetition of the *Gloria Patri* points to a wider re-evaluation of the potential within those elements that had seemed atrophied.

A third key area of revision was the *horarium* itself: from a compression of the liturgy of the hours into three occasions of public prayer to the present arrangement of the Divine Office across five points of prayer. In fact, a first reversion here took place as early as 1985 when Compline – the removal of which had been particularly divisive, as we saw above – was restored. A further re-expansion (and with it, an earlier rising time) occurred in 1999, when Vigils and Lauds were restored as separate Offices in place of the single Morning Office.[29] While not a restoration according to the legal basis of the *Rule* of St Benedict (Yeo 1975), this does go some way towards restoring the traditional shape of the liturgy as

---

28 See also Yelle (2003: 103) on the use of repetition as augmentation in Hindu mantras, an 'accumulation of motivation' which intensifies the directional force of the discourse.

29 An earlier initiative prior to their restoration at separate times was the introduction of a hymn marking a transition between the prayers of Vigils and those of Lauds within the combined Morning Office. This occurred in 1998 along with the restoration of the repeated *Gloria Patri*.

prayer distributed throughout the day. In my conversation with the abbot about the place of the liturgy in the English Benedictine Congregation, he stressed the importance of St Paul's call that we should 'pray without ceasing'[30], understood in the specific context of St Benedict's instruction in Chapter 43 of the *Rule* that 'nothing is to be preferred to the work of God'. Loaning me a copy of a book by a Dutch Trappist monk (Vermeiren 1999), which had impressed him during his time working in Rome and which he had subsequently translated into English, the abbot explained that it had helped him to understand how the Benedictine call to pray at specific times underpins a general call to continuous prayer, shaping the monk's disposition of the heart as he moves through the day: an interweaving of prayer and life. The reduction of the number of hours was therefore not only a departure from the intention and the authority of St Benedict but a loss of this structure, in which prayer flowed into the rest of the activity of the day (the significance of 'prayer after rising, prayer before eating', discussed at length in Chapter 3). Here the importance of restoring shared prayer at the beginning and the end of each day reflects this sense of the whole of the monks' waking and sleeping hours becoming shaped by the rhythm of prayer.

A fourth area of change, again with the character of ritual reversion, was emerging during my fieldwork in 2006. New books arrived in the choir stalls – the first volume of the latest edition of the *Antiphonale Monasticum*[31], which had just been published by Solesmes Abbey. The provenance of these books was itself significant: a suggestion of convergence with wider practice of liturgy in the Church, with Solesmes and their nineteenth-century liturgical revival as exemplars not only historically (Bergeron 1998) but also as a hub for the contemporary dissemination of Gregorian chant. This arrival was accompanied by some disruption to the normal order of things. Unfamiliar sounds could be heard at unfamiliar times as

---

30 1 Thessalonians 5:17.

31 The three volumes of the *Antiphonale Monasticum*, updated from the pre-Second Vatican Council editions, contain the complete Gregorian chant for the cycle of the Liturgy of the Hours.

additional choir practices were inserted into the rhythm of the weekly cycle. As it was already used in the Mass, Gregorian chant was certainly not new to the monks; but its use in the Divine Office was unfamiliar, and the chants themselves required some rehearsal, with less confident singers following the lead of the more experienced until they found their voice. In this first phase of the introduction of the *Antiphonale Monasticum*, antiphons (a sentence, usually from scripture, set to a melodic chant) were added to Vespers on feast days, to be sung before and after each psalm, as well as the Magnificat. In those initial uses, the novelty of the introduction was particularly apparent, with some fumbling around the new books and a couple of uncertain starts. Over time (and with the arrival in 2007 of the third volume of the *Antiphonale*), the antiphons were phased into the liturgy more and more, gradually becoming part of Vespers on all days of the year. I was told during my fieldwork – pretty much unanimously – that there was 'no appetite' for a fully Latin Vespers within the daily *horarium*. In fact, since 2019 a full Latin Vespers is sung on feasts and solemnities. However, for most days the arrangement that persists is one in which Latin Gregorian chant is inserted before and after English psalms, which are still sung to the 'tones not tunes' of the 1968 reforms that serve as 'word-carrying formulae'.

Again, these developments were not immune to critique within the community. The organist, for example, remained loyal to Gregory Murray and retained many of his reforming principles. Responding to another monk's somewhat tongue-in-cheek description of Murray as a 'liturgical fascist', he said that such a description 'could all be considered good clean fun, said in the right tone and context. It's true he would express his views in a forceful style. But to speak of the force by which reform was imposed on the community is a big joke, compared with what has been imposed on the community more recently.' One of his key concerns was the apparent centralising impulse of recent changes, contrary to the spirit of the autonomy of each Benedictine family. 'I've spoken in the last two visitations of creeping centralisation, only to be met by the expression of disbelief, "What centralisation?"' In addition to this, not only to his ear did the chants from the *Antiphonale* fit badly with the 1968 psalm tones – the intonation suitable for Latin being different from that suitable for English – but he was also concerned by the 'tinkering' that risked undoing of some of the key principles of the reform. Indeed, reflecting on the history described in this chapter, the juxtaposition of these two elements might seem odd when we consider how the composer of the psalm tones viewed liturgical excess: 'The abuses began, not with Mozart and Haydn, but with those over-enthusiastic medieval musicians who developed the elaborate and flamboyant Gregorian Chant ... it is most difficult for the hearers to know what [the words] are when the syllables are separated by long melismata or musical flourishes' (Murray 1977: 24). What we hear today, then, reflects reform and reversion, revision and tradition: a composite that draws into proximity different poles of debate over the past sixty or so years.

Young fogeys and the future of the past

'So are you one of these young fogeys?'

The question took me by surprise and it was only after a few moments that I grasped the context. The Latin Mass Society[32] were coming to the abbey church to celebrate the Tridentine Mass – the form of the Mass that had been celebrated prior to liturgical reform. Preparations were under way, new candles had been brought and were being put into place, boxes of missals were being unpacked and guests could be heard discussing how to navigate the re-ordered liturgical space. The monk who had asked whether I was a young fogey was already in his forties at the time of the Second Vatican Council; raised Catholic and having entered the monastery straight from school, his whole life to that point had been shaped by the traditional liturgical forms. Yet he had enthusiastically embraced the Council as a challenge impelling him to open up his own theological ideas and their expression. Crucially, both his experience of the rhythms of community and his work as priest in an inner-city parish

---

32 A national Catholic organisation which promotes the use of the liturgical rites published following the sixteenth-century Council of Trent.

caused him to see the urgent need to 'bind prayer and living together' at the points where they might have become detached. Now, nearing his 90th birthday, he wanted to know whether I was part of a generation set on smothering the spirit of that moment.

This was one of several occasions where the monks' experience navigating reform within their own community and its rhythm of stability shone a light on the dynamic of participation within the wider Church. The principles of reform themselves become the subject of critical reflection.

The community's relationship with this particular Mass might best be described as semidetached. On the one hand, the celebrant was a monk of the community, and the fact that permission was given for the Latin Mass Society to organise a Mass in the abbey church suggests some implicit approval. This became an annual event; and indeed Downside hosted other Latin Mass Society activities, including in 2010 a training conference for Priests who wished to celebrate this form of the Mass. On the other hand, the fact that the abbey church was being used by an outside group did not make it a community event: the Mass was celebrated at a time when the church was otherwise unused, not as part of the monastic family's own pattern of prayer. Moreover, reaction to the Mass within the community was decidedly mixed. Some were supportive, some were curious (in one case remarking, 'I might just pop in and see what they're up to') and a few monks sat in the nave as part of the congregation. Others made it quite clear that they intended to keep away.

The concern about 'young fogeys' was quickly followed by the same monk remarking on 'pathological nostalgia', and the danger that those coming from far and wide were stoking a 'two-church syndrome, a sense that this is the real thing and what is happening in their parishes is not'. But, at the same time, he said he found himself 'strangely fascinated, because there is clearly a sense for them that something is missing'. This returns us to the crucial sense of meaning as a basis of participation; what are the dimensions that render the liturgy meaningful beyond comprehensibility? Again, the continued process of reflection and revision within the community described above points to a wider reconsideration of ritual efficacy beyond the purely functional. This current of thought can already be discerned at the time of reform. Illtyd Trethowan, having argued determinedly (if reflectively) for significant renewal and the principle of participation, nevertheless met the reforms once they arrived with a more muted and critical tone: 'The recent changes in the Roman Liturgy have been misapplied in so far as the "numinous" character of the Eucharist has become obscured in some parts of the world (a disregard for the dignity and beauty of the liturgy has much to do with this)' (Trethowan 1971: 207–8). The question of ritual concealment is flipped. Whereas earlier we saw a concern that the form of the liturgy might obscure its meaning, here we see a different emphasis: a consciousness that a purely functional approach might obscure the potential of the liturgy to open up a sense of presence beyond the everyday.

To reflect on this, the most proximate anthropological analysis is that of Victor Turner (1972a; 1972b; 1976). In a series of articles in the journal *Worship*, published by the Benedictine monks at St John's Abbey in the USA, Turner reflected on how, as a convert to Catholicism, he could 'hardly remain unmoved' (1976: 506) by the impact of liturgical reform, standing in sympathy with those who, in the wake of change, 'sorrow as widows do for the death of someone beloved' (1972a: 392). This makes him ethnographically interesting as a witness to this moment of change in the Catholic Church, as well as theoretically interesting in how he applies his understanding of the ritual process to it. For Turner, the effect of the reform was to undermine the anti-structural character of the liturgy, based on an erroneous assumption that ritual should reflect social structure, rather than open up an opportunity to stand apart from everyday social life. This, of course, reflects his wider sense of ritual's potential to generate a 'time and place of withdrawal from normal modes of social action' (Turner 1969: 167), in which everyday identity, roles, and status might be dissolved in order for new forms of 'comradeship' (1969: 96) to emerge.

A crucial element of Turner's personal frustration emerges from the fact that his own movement towards the Church was, in large part, associated with his learning in the field to recognise ritual's substance in its own right.[33] 'After many years as an agnostic and monistic materialist I learned from the Ndembu that ritual and its symbolism are not merely epiphenomena or disguises of deeper social and psychological processes, but have ontological value' (Turner 1975: 31). One gets a sense of the alarm, then, felt by Turner as he sees within the Catholic Church's liturgical reforms the 'clear influence' of the structural-functionalist model (1972a: 392) and the consequent assumption that the liturgy 'should change in response to social structural changes'.

So far in this chapter we have seen the arguments articulated within the monastery and the wider Church for a meaningful liturgy as a grounding for participation. What Turner emphasises is a different dimension to participation: the liturgy cannot be 'merely a reflection of secular social life' (1972a: 391), but should instead be a 'stripping and levelling of man before the transcendental', in which we 'confront eternity, which is equidistant from all ages' (1976: 524). As such, the liturgy cannot be in flux to reflect changing times and changing locales, but must strive to be 'a place that is not a place, and a time that is not a time' (1972a: 399). Of course, from a different theoretical perspective, here we return to the power of the invention of tradition (Hobsbawm 1983), and the legitimation of authority through appeal to an unchanging order that transcends the vicissitudes of time (Bloch 1986). Clearly, that which Turner presents as outside of time and beyond pragmatic worldly considerations nonetheless bears the marks of a particular political moment in the Church: the Council of Trent, convened between 1545 and 1563. Its codification was an act of centralisation which provided a 'steel brace' (Klauser 1969: 127) to the Church, at the cost of local liturgical variations. The circumstances of this 'bracing' are, of course, the Protestant Reformation and its challenge to the legitimacy of Catholic ritual practice (Reid 2004: 40), ushering in an 'epoch of rubricism' (Klauser 1969: 119), which came under scrutiny in the wake of the Second Vatican Council. From this perspective, social and political change – whether mid-sixteenth or mid-twentieth century

---

33 For discussion of the interrelationship between Turner's anthropological work and his conversion to Catholicism, see Deflem (1991); Larsen (2014).

– inflects the form of the liturgy, and the experience of prayer sits in relation to historical forces that themselves become objects of critique.

Returning to Downside, we see this in action as critique of these historical transformations probes what it means to participate. A month after the visit of the Latin Mass Society, the English Benedictine Congregation's Liturgy Commission met in the monastery for its annual symposium, taking as its theme 'Liturgical Renewal: Reform of the Reform?' The day's academic discussions slotted into the day around the rhythm of prayer in the abbey church. Monks and nuns from the Congregation and beyond moved between the choir stalls and the more sterile conference space in the monastery's east wing to scrutinise the very liturgical forms they had just used for worship.

This year, the invitation to Alcuin Reid, at the time a monk of Farnborough in the Subiaco Congregation,[34] provided a catalyst for debate. His critique of the reforms as a rupture in the historic development of the liturgy (Reid 2004) had been published with a preface and recommendation from Joseph Ratzinger, who had since gone on to become Pope Benedict XVI. Inevitably, this meant Reid's views were not only a source of discussion in their own right but also invited speculation on what might be happening at this moment in the history of the Church.

Central to Reid's argument was a view that the growing popularity of Masses such as the Latin Mass Society event held the previous month was 'due to the frustration of their desire for a numinous, God-centred liturgy which bespeaks transcendence', in contrast to the apparent 'artificiality' of new forms 'laden with pop-culture idioms' that seem to approach liturgy in the manner of a 'DIY kit'. The lines of debate that emerged in reaction to this are ethnographically instructive. The principle of participation remains central: debate arises from the question of what participation is and what it involves. On the one hand, in the arguments that shaped liturgical

---

34 Reid subsequently was involved in the foundation of the Monastère Saint Benoît in Provence, France, a community living according to the *Rule* of St Benedict and placing especial emphasis on liturgical traditionalism.

reform, participation is understood as a convergence of individual intentionality – the mode of participation that Kelty (2019) describes as 'contributory autonomy'. Yet, as Kelty notes, this models collectivity as secondary to individual agency and, for Pina-Cabral (2018: 446), this sense of participation as 'coordination between individuals' stands in ambivalent relation to an understanding of collectivity as primary, the fundamental reality within which we recognise ourselves.

A key theme in the symposium was that of continuity: to what extent did the reforms constitute a radical departure from what had been shared by generations of the faithful? On the one hand, those who spoke of discontinuity, or even rupture,[35] highlighted not only the loss of historical tradition, but what this loss implied: a disconnection from the body of the Church through time and space. Here the idea of 'archaism' took on very different connotations. For some, an obsession with the archaic showed all too clearly a 'museum mentality', an emphasis on preservation that leads to worship becoming stuck in time. This can lead to a different kind of temporal rupture – a rupture from the action taking place in the present and even a risk of irrelevance. But, for others, apparently 'archaic' forms were to be treasured precisely because of this distance they provided from the action of the world; and this had practical implications for the relationship between monasteries and wider society – 'people come from far and wide to avoid the dark clouds'.

What, then, is at stake in talk about the 'artificiality' of the liturgy? In asking whether we needed a 'reform of the reform', one monk summarised the problem as he saw it in this way: 'Do we have unedited access to tradition, or are we speaking words that reflect only the world we see around us, products of our own culture and limited perception?': a point that was immediately recognised even by one of the monks who was generally an enthusiastic defender of reform: 'The hand of man, you see the hand of man too much in it.' Considering this in the light of anthropological theory, this connects with Turner's defence of the traditional liturgy as a liminal reality by

---

35 Robbins (2007) shows the interplay between continuity and rupture to be a key dynamic for an anthropology of Christianity – albeit accepting that he reflects a Protestant ideal type in his particular focus on discontinuity.

which people were carried beyond the immediacy of the time and place in which they lived and 'incorporated into the universal Ecclesia' (1976: 512). Yet this seemingly evades the critical question of intentionality: a ritual dynamic which Maurice Bloch considers from another angle, focusing on the relationship between tradition, authority, and power. Bloch (2004) examines ritual forms as a mode of deference: it is not *my* intentionality that is important, but the intentionality indexed by the source of the words (and such a source is often a generalised entity not amenable to interrogation, such as 'tradition', 'the ancestors as a group', or 'God'). This is a development of his long-standing argument that ritual language is a performance which communicates and enforces authority through the loss of individual creativity and the appeal to a transcendental force as the source of tradition. (Bloch (1974: 58) tells us that the Merina of Madagascar describe the formalised speechmaking of the elders as 'speaking the words of the ancestors'.) This way of approaching ritual – as a form of deliberately restricted communication in which the individual *defers* the right to speak their own words, instead allowing themselves to become the vessels for 'traditional' words and actions – can be construed as a 'self-attack by participants, an attack on their own intentionality so that it may be replaced' (Bloch 2004: 76).

And yet it is precisely this displacement of intentionality that becomes an object of scrutiny at times of reform,[36] when – as we

---

[36] Indeed, a deeper examination of a key example in Bloch's analysis reveals reconfigurations around intentionality at times of historic change. Bloch uses an account of the role of memorisation in Islamic learning (Eickelman 1978) to demonstrate the importance of quotation and repetition by the individual learning the Koran: 'The student should, ideally, learn the Koran perfectly by heart and so become a totally transparent medium just like Mohamed himself. He should become a sort of tape recorder' (Bloch 2004: 72). But it is perhaps telling that Bloch's use of Eickelman here is somewhat restricted. Elsewhere, for example, Eickelman (1992) describes how mass education in Oman has created a 'new religious imagination', which emphasises the process of finding meaning and understanding in the text being memorised; here, the displacement of intentionality cannot fully account for the process of learning, and the reader

have seen – an emphasis on sincerity and agency calls into question the apparently mechanical actions of ritual (Keane 2007). At the Liturgy Symposium, the common criticism of the Tridentine Mass was aired: 'Are the laity aware of what the priests are doing while they have their back to them? … To what extent is someone truly part of the celebration of the Mass if they can neither hear the priest nor understand him?' Similarly, when discussion turned to the use of the vernacular and the simple tones in the Divine Office, these were defended as allowing the monks 'to truly hear the psalms, not simply to recite them'.

Guarino (2018: 83), in her ethnography of the Benedictine community at Weston Priory, Vermont, highlights the deep link between understanding and authenticity that motivated the monks' use of the vernacular in the liturgy. She quotes one of the community: 'if you are really using your own language, prayer becomes authentic. You are the author of it. Then it has author-ity … If you use somebody else's language … it will always be somebody else's.' This inversion of Bloch's emphasis on ritual as deference to tradition, instead grounding authority in sincerity and individual intentionality, shows one of the pivot points of ritual change. But the rooting of meaning in the culturally proximate and personally comprehensible in turn becomes an object of critique: does it close off the possibility of transcending the everyday – an experience that 'adds up to a divine-human meaning beyond any individual's experience' (Turner 1976: 517)?

Here, the question of how far we are 'aware of what is happening' becomes misleading – a point that was raised in the liturgical symposium. 'If the emphasis is on making it understandable, even to the youngest child, then we may be missing the point.' Where the liturgy comes to be seen as a series of messages to be received and understood, 'the danger is that you end up thinking that you can comprehend the liturgy', rather than 'contemplating the transcendence of God, the awesomeness of God's presence that passes all understanding'.

---

is certainly more than a 'tape recorder'. So my point is that it is worth paying attention to these moments where a previously deferred intentionality becomes a source of active attention.

Liturgical prayer and the limits of participation

The nature of participation

Having considered the *horarium* as an expression of the monks' stability in time, this chapter has focused on the recent history of Downside's liturgy to understand the form and shape of the *horarium* today. A core principle here has been the importance of participation – the liturgy as the expression of a family joined in prayer. What is at stake, then, is not only how participation is enabled or inhibited, but the very nature of that participation.

The ideal of participation that underpinned liturgical reform within the monastery in the 1960s placed the emphasis on the need for a *meaningful* liturgy, relevant and accessible to individual understanding as a basis for intentionality in prayer. Accordingly, we see a wariness towards elements of performance that conceal meaning, and rejection of a merely mechanical understanding of prayer. The co-ordination of the attention and intentions of participants expresses the collective nature of the liturgy as 'genuine family prayer'.

I follow Kelty in describing this understanding of participation as 'contributory autonomy'; but he goes on to note that this mode of intentional and procedural contribution is often at the expense of the affective dimension by which we recognise ourselves immersed in something greater (Kelty 2019: 97) – understanding ourselves not simply as individuals, but as instances of a collective (2019: 251). Indeed, subsequent developments at Downside, including successive instances of ritual reversion, probe the limits of this understanding of participation. Elements that had appeared archaic or redundant are re-evaluated; the sense that performance *conceals* meaning gives way to a consideration of how to express meaning beyond the purely functional. The monks' reconsideration of the need for the numinous points to a different understanding of participation as a relation that transcends the everyday.

In contrast to a sense that collectivity emerges as a co-ordination of the intentionality of the individual, Pina-Cabral (2018: 440) considers a different mode of participation: 'how the person confronts the social within themselves, how persons come to be collective'. This brings to the fore 'the more transcendent or mystical aspects of the relations that participation describes' (2018: 438). The sense that this mode of participation might be undermined by contributory autonomy lies at the heart of Turner's critique that to join with the 'throng of believers' requires 'a collective vehicle' (Turner 1976: 516–17) by which the individual moves beyond the limitations of their own time and place, beyond their own thoughts and intentions; we are *isolated* by the focus on individual intentionality.

The contemporary shape of the liturgy bears the marks of these considerations and reflections over time – shaped by a desire to 'bring our minds in accord with our voices',[37] but also a desire to recognise those minds and voices as expressions of something that transcends the self. In this way, the question of what it means to participate brings us back to the challenge of stability: the incorporation of a life cycle within an enduring family, the place of a voice of prayer within the eternal praise of God.

---

37 *Rule* of St Benedict, Chapter 19; but this is also taken by Gregory Murray as a basis for his call to reform the monastic liturgy such that monks can focus on the meanings of the words. See 'The Divine Office, talk for Maidenhead Newman Circle', 16 February 1977, Gregory Murray Box 1/7, Downside Archives.

CHAPTER 5

Contemplative prayer and the problem of other people

The pulse of prayer

Early morning, between Vigils and Lauds. I am sitting in the nave and I can see my breath. It is the first part of the day dedicated to personal prayer, and inevitably my mind is starting to wander. Following the advice I had been given, I call all my attention to the stained glass above the altar – not as an object of reflection, but as a focus to centre my prayer when the thoughts chatter away. Christ. Light. Candlemas has passed and the light is coming through the window earlier now. My mind is wandering again, and I end up thinking about the routine ahead and how I was settling into the stability of the day's rhythm.

Great Bede rings in the tower above. No movement. It is only several minutes later, when the cloister bell rings, that the monks start to make their way unhurriedly to the choir stalls, and several minutes later again that the abbot raps his knuckles on the stalls to begin Lauds. Clearly, I have missed something. After breakfast I discover what has happened. Pinned to the noticeboard by the entrance to the monastery's west wing, the *ordo*[1] for the week contains a note: from this day on, Lauds will start at 7.10am and not 7.05am. Although by this stage the significance of time-discipline seemed clear, this still came across as rather pedantic. Why adjust the timetable by a mere five minutes?

1 The community's liturgical calendar.

Later, in the carpentry workshop, it was explained to me that the shift was to protect the time for personal prayer. On days when Vigils ran longer it was feared that monks were not getting their full half hour's worth, and so the simple solution agreed by the monks in chapter was to push Lauds back slightly. On that first day, the bells had rung at the old time, but would catch up in due course.

This reflects the importance of the 'two half hours' in the English Benedictine tradition. As one senior monk explained to me – a monk whose commitment to the local parishes well into his later years often kept him away from the monastery's collective prayer, and whose sense of total distance when his hood was raised seemed quite at odds with his highly personable manner at other times – the place of those two half hours dedicated to personal prayer in the timetable was fundamental to preserving the integral element of English Benedictine life. 'If you were a kind of ornithologist of monks, whatever that would be, then our tradition of contemplative prayer is how you'd spot us and pick us out. That's our identifying mark.'

These periods of time are visible expressions of the pulse of individual prayer shaping monastic life in the spaces opened up by the *horarium* of shared prayer: a pulse felt in these moments of solitude between Vigils and Lauds, and between Vespers and supper, but also in the pronounced silences between nocturns at Vigils, and in the great silence of night at the end of the collective routine of the day. Here, the spirit of the two half hours spills over into a possibility of prayer infusing the whole of the day, working and resting – and it is precisely for this reason that a collective intention to put private prayer before other activities at specific points was to be protected from encroachment.

Located within the contours of the monks' daily routine, what does this tradition of contemplative prayer reveal about monastic stability? In the chapters so far, the ethnographic emphasis has been on the way that collective practices root the monks in shared space and time. And, as we have seen, the practice of contemplative prayer is part of this rhythm (see also Irvine 2020). Yet at the heart of this chapter are social dynamics that apparently sit in tension with this purely *institutionalised* understanding of the vow of stability. Ernst Troeltsch (1931), in a sustained attempt to work through the distinctive sociological implications of mysticism – which he defines in its most general sense as the 'insistence upon a direct inward and present religious experience' (1931: 730) – emphasises the *immediacy* of such a pursuit, apparently untethered from the mediation of institutional religion, of authority, and shared practice. The pursuit of a 'direct and personal religious life' (1931: 738) can therefore, Troeltsch argues, leaves the mystic 'indifferent towards every kind of religious fellowship' (1931: 734) and disengaged from the very elements that serve as the rallying point of institutional relations. The conclusion he draws from this is that 'Mysticism is a radical individualism' (1931: 743). We do not have to follow Troeltsch all the way to this conclusion to recognise it as an important provocation: it forces us to reflect on the distinctive social impact of the practice of contemplative prayer as *personal* prayer (frequently, and tellingly, referred to as 'private' prayer) and the kind of relationship it orients the monks towards. Key to this understanding of prayer was the remarkable space of freedom that it afforded. Yet, insomuch as this freedom was experienced as a space beyond mediation, this followed on from an insistence that prayer pushed at the very limits of communicability. Reaching the point where I have nothing to say, I am forced to confront not only the limits of the concepts I have at my disposal, but the very limits of my finite mind and body – in other words, the limits of the self that operates in and is mediated by the everyday social world. I am left speechless and empty-handed in the face of the universe. How, then, does this emptiness in the solitude of prayer figure in the stability of a life lived with others?

From 'God as we picture him' to 'God the unknown'

It was striking that, while several of the monks were interested in whether I was drawn to this form of prayer, encouraging my study of it and asking how I was getting along, they were nevertheless reluctant to offer specific guidance. As one monk explained to me, 'one offers encouragement, but that is not the same as giving an instruction manual, because no instruction manual can exist. I don't want to sound prescriptive, because I don't think this is an area within which one can be prescriptive.' My friend the organist declared himself 'agnostic' on such matters – of course, he had his own ideas, but he was very wary of speaking in absolutes and wanted to allow for variety.

What was often emphasised was the importance of silence; as was explained to me by the novice master, prayer is 'getting used to silence', and silence was both the 'condition for prayer' and was 'itself prayer'. Passing through the enclosure door with its stark call for SILENCE, I would consciously remind myself that being there to learn did not necessarily mean I was there to talk, and I would try to sink into this silence, especially during the 'two half hours'.

The question remained of what to do within the silence. At first I filled it up with my own thoughts and reflections but this seemed only to obliterate it. So I tried to meet the silence with my own silence. But the more I waited, the more I listened, and the more I read the literature on prayer that the monks directed me to, the more I felt a discomfort within this silence, a sense of stripping away that left me restless and increasingly adrift. I became increasingly sensitive to the theme of *failure* that seemed to recur in what was being shared. Such a usage might have come as a surprise given the pejorative sense of the term. But this failure had a specific essence: a sense that what the mind was trying to do was no longer fit for purpose. Such failure was not about giving up on prayer, but nevertheless its recognition *as* failure remained crucial as a point of confrontation where the limits of the self were laid bare.

Such a recognition was key to the account given by the community's librarian. Listening to him share his experiences, the autobiographical character of his understanding of prayer became clear: an expression of the universal core that led him to the Catholic Church as a young Welshman in the RAF, as well as the monastic spirituality and history that had drawn him to the Benedictine life in his student days, and a condensation of the formation he had received as a young monk.[2] He started by remarking on how many people find that they have trouble praying, and this makes perseverance in prayer difficult: 'They may well have found their experience of trying to make progress in prayer on the face of it a time-wasting exercise. These days, if you don't get instant results in anything, to give up seems the obvious answer. Life is too short. You think, surely there are more useful things I can be getting on with.' Here, he said, it is useful to have a 'road map' of prayer, 'the experiences of those who have gone before … This map of prayer does not gloss over the fact that in the way ahead there will be some rough patches, dark nights of the soul, but they are not the end, there is life beyond them.'

What does this 'road map' consist of? For the librarian, it started with people's experiences of 'discursive prayer', which he defined as 'prayerful pondering on episodes in the life of Christ, using the imagination and the sense to reconstruct the scene, reflecting upon it with the reason, summoning up with appropriate emotions … I don't need to tell you this is the "Ignatian" model' [that is, the model associated with St Ignatius of Loyola and his Spiritual Exercises; I will discuss this in more detail later].

But, for many, this discursive approach to prayer becomes increasingly difficult. 'They can't concentrate anymore. They have nothing to report back on … There is a great temptation to give up praying altogether.' This resonated with my own sense of unease in the silence, which – when I brought it up – was met with a quotation from scripture, 'He must increase, I must decrease' (John 3: 30). Indeed, according to the road map that the librarian was laying out, these rough patches were seen to have had a purpose: 'To change our means of praying, to develop our spiritual faculties … to focus us on God the unknown, rather than the ways we picture him.'

2 Others in the community have noted how the librarian's account here is infused with certain phrasings of Christopher Butler, abbot at the time when he was received into the monastery (see Butler 1961 for an outline of his approach to prayer), suggestive of how the 'road map' that follows might be considered something passed through the generations.

Contemplative prayer and the problem of other people

In this way, the failure of focus in discursive meditation, and the inability to bring imagination, sense, reason and emotion to bear, was a crucial threshold. Here was the point at which we move into a new means of praying, open to God itself rather than representations of God.[3] However, the librarian went on, it is precisely at this stage that people find their prayer grows restless. The ways of describing the experience of prayer, and the ways of describing the God that one is praying to, take on the language of absence: 'nothing', 'a void', 'a blank' – conceptualisations that point to the absence of concepts. We seem at a loss. Nevertheless, what the individual is 'doing or suffering has been well and truly prayer. The reason why it is is because the essence of prayer, like everything moral and spiritual, lies in the intention ... If you intend to pray, then you are praying, whether you are conscious of it or not. If you want to pray, then you are praying, even if there are no signs of success in doing so'. In this sense, prayer was a 'humbling' experience, 'seemingly the reverse of other human accomplishments ... a case of moving from complexity towards simplicity, from a state of being in control to one of passing over the controls to another'.

The idea of prayer being grounded in its intention is a crucial one, as it recognises that prayer is ongoing even when the mind and body no longer appear to be following. A specific demonstration of this was in the notion that prayer might continue even having fallen asleep.[4] The monk with whom I worked in the carpentry workshop suggested that I try taking a short passage from scripture as 'food through the night', with the idea not just that I would meditate on it at bedtime but that, moving beyond reflection to longing, it would remain my prayer while I sleep. Later, hearing him offer this practice to a group of young men making their retreat in

---

3 A process resonant with the 'active cultivation of the awareness of ignorance' Mair (2015: 252) described in the context of Inner Mongolian Buddhism.

4 Thinking in terms of the tradition of prayer in the monastery, this suggestion also occurs in the letters of John Chapman (1935: 117), Fourth Abbot of Downside: 'I have come to the conclusion that one can remain united to God even when one goes to sleep in time of prayer. Don't laugh!'

the monastery, he suggested the words of Samuel: 'Speak, Lord, your servant is listening.'[5]

Those words carried a particular edge for me following the librarian's account of prayer; as he explained, 'We instinctively twist Samuel's cry "Speak, Lord, your servant is listening" into "Listen, Lord, your servant is speaking."' The road map of prayer, with its emphasis on the potential of silence beyond the limits of our speech, suggested that apparent difficulties were opportunities to move past this focus on the self. While one is focused on one's own mental and emotional processes, the self is prominent in prayer. The failure of these forms of attention to the self is therefore key to reaching a state of attentiveness to God.

How far am I justified in placing this analytical emphasis upon failure? From one perspective, the very fact that there is recognition of 'life beyond' such a point shows that it is clearly understood as a crucial step in the transformation of the one who prays. But life is not experienced backwards from the vantage point of a future destination; to insist after the fact that this confrontation with the limit of our human capacities was a welcome transformation would not do justice to the stark accounts of disorientation, discomfort, and even the sense of God's absence at the point where such a threshold is reached. 'God dropped out of my life one night in Oxford', as one of monks of the community begins an account of the philosophical framework of contemplative prayer (Foster 2015: 1). 'In the bitter cold, a gap yawned. A bit of solid ground I had counted on just crumbled away.' So to acknowledge failure is to be honest about this sense that something integral has broken down. But additionally, engaging with failure matters because the recognition of *what* has failed upon reaching this threshold becomes a crucial part of learning what needs to be let go. To unpack this further, I want to consider how the 'road map' above resonates with two key sources to which I was introduced in the monastery: Augustine Baker (1575–1641) and John Chapman (1865–1933) – historic sources that are nevertheless ethnographically crucial, because referencing them was the primary means

5   1 Samuel 3: 9–10

through which monks sought to give me a sense of the terrain I was venturing into.

Failing to think about God

Augustine Baker[6] was himself a Welsh convert to Catholicism, joining the English Benedictine Congregation at the point in history when monks were entering monasteries on the European continent and, following their formation and ordination as priests, sent as missionaries to their post-Reformation homeland. Although Baker would eventually be sent on the mission to England himself, dying of the plague in London, his primary influence on English Benedictine mystical teaching comes from his time as spiritual director to the English nuns at Cambrai. The voluminous writings he produced during this time to aid the nuns on their way were circulated in manuscript form,[7] but for most subsequent English Benedictine monks, understanding of Baker's teaching comes primarily from *Sancta Sophia*, or *Holy Wisdom* (Baker 1657). This posthumous distillation of Baker's work under the editorship of another seventeenth-century monk, Serenus Cressy,[8] has become a staple reading in English Benedictine novitiates.

The essence of Baker's teaching, and its influence shaping the 'road map of prayer', came through clearly in an encounter one day in the library. Having seen a reference in an archival manuscript to

---

6 For discussion of Augustine Baker's life and teaching in the context of the history of the English Benedictine Congregation, see Lunn (1975); Clark (2004); Temple (2017, 2019).

7 In recent decades, critical editions of many of these manuscripts have been published under the editorship of John Clark. These were appearing on the shelves of the library during my fieldwork in the monastery.

8 Significantly, Temple (2017: 224–5) argues that the publication of this compendium could be considered an attempt to contain Baker's influence, owing to anxiety about unofficial copying of his manuscripts, presenting his teaching in a way that stripped it of much of the context of controversy in Baker's source writings.

'Fr B. and his S. S.' (which I did not yet understand to mean 'Father Baker and his *Sancta Sophia*'), I asked the librarian if he could help me decode this. His response was to declaim some lines by Leander Normanton, a seventeenth-century monk of the community, that had been written to accompany an engraving of Baker:

> In sable lines o're a silver ground
> The face of that mysterious Man is found,
> Whose secret life and published Writings prove,
> To Pray is not to talke, or thinke, but Love.

The vision of prayer contained in this last line offers a succinct summary of what has been carried through from the influence of Baker into the contemporary prayer life of the community. What we see in Baker's teaching is a model of passage from meditation to contemplation. We start out with 'discourse of the understanding' (Baker 1657: III, 86), mental reflection on elements of the faith. Yet, where someone finds they are reaching the limits of this understanding, it is no good for them to be 'kepd all their lives in Meditation, repeating over and over againe the same toylesome Methods, without any progresse in Spirit, to their great anguish and disquietnes' (1657: III, 105). Instead, the 'cure' is in 'ascending to the Internal Exercises of the will'.

For Baker, this passage from prayer of the intellect to prayer of the will consists at first of what he describes as 'forced immediate acts' (1657: III, 138). These are deliberate expressions of desire which focus the will upon God without seeking comprehension through reason. The individual who prays in this way passes from the representation of a mystery of faith, or an expression of the greatness or perfection of God, to 'acts' by which the self is directed to God, through expressions of adoration, glorification, resignation in 'Contradiction to selfe Love & interest', and 'pure melting Love to God, (in which all Images of creatures, yea all direct representations of God are excluded)' (1657: III, 166).

Crucially, the role of language in prayer is here recast. Such 'acts' may well consist of words and, as such, contain a representational element; but this element is downplayed in the transition from 'discourse of the mind' to 'act of the will'. Words used in prayer are thus an act of deliberately directing the will and offering oneself to God, not a focus for reflection and scrutiny in their own right. Indeed, Baker envisages that the use of representations will come to diminish, with contemplation growing more and more 'pure' as the need for mental images lessens; thus, beyond these 'forced acts' are 'aspirations', where 'the soule hath no other use of the understanding but only antecedently to propose an object, which is no other but only a generall, obscure, confused notion of God ... the maine busines being to Elevate the will, and unite it to God so presented' (1657: III, 246). The ultimate fruition of this shift is contemplation, 'That is, the Union of the soule, which is no where corporally; that hath no Images nor Affections to Creatures in her; yea that hath lost the free disposall of her owne faculties, actuating by a portion of the Spirit above all the faculties, and according to the Actuall Touches of the Divine Spirit; and apprehending God with an exclusion of all conceptions and apprehensions: Thus it is that the soule being no where corporally or sensibly, is every where spiritually and immediately united to God this Infinite Nothing' (1657: III, 304).

Aside from the fact that the practice of the 'two half hours' is itself attributed to Baker's teaching (see Butler 1919: 108), the principal thread from Baker to the contemporary community is the emphasis placed on prayer becoming an act of the will rather than the exercise of representations of the mind.[9] And it is also worth noting there is a social dynamic to this: not only Baker's emphasis on solitude, but his emphasis on God as the true guide over and beyond that of spiritual directors and their external authority. Here we see the immediacy that Troeltsch (1931) treats as characteristic of mystical prayer, and start to probe some of its implications: to what extent do one's roots in the institutional life of the church become merely incidental – or even a distraction – in a state of contemplation? As Temple (2017: 217) notes, 'Baker's mysticism was

---

9 Here it is worth noting Baker's distinction between the 'scholastic' path, with its intellectual operations, and the 'mystical' path, with its spiritual operations (see Temple 2019: 29).

… rooted in a suspicion of both worldly knowledge and worldly authority' – later I will discuss how this made his teaching an object of suspicion.

Returning to the librarian's 'road map', another key theme is *restlessness*. This resonates with the advice of John Chapman, abbot of the community from 1929 until his death in 1933,[10] from which time on his approach was increasingly grafted onto the existing tradition of personal prayer. I had been introduced to Chapman in my earliest days visiting Downside, when I was gifted a copy of his *Spiritual Letters* (Chapman 1935). Handed to me during a chat over a glass of whisky, the gift represented the giver's curiosity about whether I myself was drawn to this way of prayer.

Chapman had followed a call to the Anglican priesthood following his university studies, but converted to Catholicism before he was ordained, and subsequently became a monk of Maredsous Abbey in Belgium, at that time a house of the Beuronese Congregation,[11] making his solemn profession at its foundation at Erdington Priory, near Birmingham. He had largely developed a 'theory' of prayer[12] before the circumstances of the First World War had caused the closure of the community at Erdington and led him to transfer his stability to Downside Abbey. His *Spiritual Letters* – a posthumous compilation of advice given in letters to laypeople, priests, and religious – draw the reader with the practical and grounded nature of the advice: 'Pray as you can, and do not try to pray as you can't' (1935: 109). Also noteworthy – and in accord with Baker – was his recognition that 'mysticism' was not the domain of only a select few specialists, but an ordinary path all people may find themselves on.

---

10 For details of the life of Chapman, see Hudleston's memoir, which prefaces his edition of the *Spiritual Letters* (Chapman 1935). For discussion of his approach to prayer, see Butler (1959); Coakley (2002: 40–54).

11 Now an abbey of the Congregation of the Annunciation.

12 In a letter to a Canoness Regular of the Lateran, in which he outlines his approach, he writes, 'I really had no theory worked out until last November [1912]' (Chapman 1935: 119). The text of this letter was then subsequently reprinted in *Pax*, the journal of the Caldey Benedictine community he was temporary superior of at that time, and subsequently issued as a leaflet.

But, above all, I was struck by the encouragement Chapman offered to those experiencing failure, for whom prayer has become 'a dry land where no water is' (1935: 46). Indeed, a recurrent theme in Chapman's letters is guidance for those who come to experience this dryness. Whereas at one stage it was possible to pass the time with thoughts on a religious subject, the individual in the act of prayer now finds himself unable to think, and the language of prayer seems to have no meaning. Where one might once have summoned emotions through meditative reflection, now 'affections, instead of coming easily, won't come at all' (1935: 283). The value of this dryness is that it leads us to change our way of prayer. 'All those who find it impossible to meditate … and find they cannot fix their thoughts on a subject, or understand the meaning of the words, unless they cease to feel they are praying, are meant to cease all thinking, and only make acts of the will' (1935: 119).

What is being described is a kind of desire that meets with silence: to sit and want God, but not to be able to summon up ways of thinking about God that respond to this desire; to sit in a state of aridity, seemingly incapable of an emotional expression of this desire. What is being taught is that this silence places us at the limits of the self. In one sense – a sense that the monks do not shy away from – we are hitting a wall. God is beyond any finite concepts and images at our disposal, and what we desire is God, not those concepts. But here David Foster (2015: 27), a contemporary monk of the community, argues that reaching these limits 'can be a threshold to a different kind of awareness', a point at which 'There needs to be a shift in the centre of gravity of our attention, away from us to the object of our attention.' This involves a 'suspension of thought, a kind of blankness in what we bring to experience or rather openness to it' (2015: 96–7).

The trouble is, writes Chapman (1935: 137), that this can feel like you're not doing much: 'The soul itself often feels rather idiotic, and wonders whether it is not wasting time, knowing that, if it described its state to any sensible person, it would be told to go and do something useful, and not moon.' In fact, in this state of emptying oneself out to be with God, our imagination may wander, finding itself unoccupied. But this is because openness to God as He is, rather than as we imagine Him, is an openness that must go beyond thought or feeling; Chapman therefore maintains that this 'simple prayer' 'is absolutely easy, if only you realise that it is a prayer of the will, not of the intellect, or the imagination, or of the emotions' (1935: 45–6). We must therefore deal with what Chapman terms a 'divided consciousness' (1935: 255); a recognition that the 'real me' is expressed in the will that seeks God, and that we cannot come to identify the 'self' with our thoughts and feelings.

It is therefore possible to be in a state of prayer even when the imagination 'runs off as it pleases' (1935: 255); involuntary reflections and worries during this state may be something you 'can't help' (1935: 89). For this reason, it is useful to repeat a phrase of prayer as a way of 'throwing a bone to the dog' (1935: 73), so as not to end up worried or allow our will to be distracted by our emotions or thought processes. Ultimately, these are incidental to our prayer, so much so that they can be disowned: 'The real "I" is the will which gives itself to God, (the emotions and imaginations are not me, they are in me, but they are not under my control)' (1935: 175).

This idea of throwing a bone to the dog became characteristic of how I spent the half hours of personal prayer, and beyond. The arrival of thought other than prayer was expected: my mind was a little gossip and I could hear it chattering away. But what I was being taught was that I didn't always have to engage it in conversation. In various ways, I was directed to find a focus, typically adopting a single, short, piercing word to call my attention away from that chattering of the mind and back towards the intention to be with God. Of course, this point of focus did not have to be a word. In my early explorations of *where* to spend the two half hours, noting the dispersal of the monks through the monastery, the idea of taking the stained glass above the altar as my focus was put to me, and many mornings were spent looking up at the image of Christ, Ruler of the Universe. A candle could also be a point of focus, although this suggestion came with a note of caution; one monk told me about a contemporary of his who had used a candle as a focus for prayer in his cell and 'almost burned the whole monastery down' when he fell asleep: 'a very dangerous business, all this piety!' Again, variety was emphasised, which – alongside a desire for solitude –

was one of the reasons the monks dispersed in these times of prayer. But these times were not spent smothering the thoughts – the more you think about the thoughts, even if you're thinking about how you wished they weren't there, the more you're drawn in by the distraction – but refusing to follow them; making an act drawing the will elsewhere, understanding that there is a 'real I' that cannot be reduced to thoughts and feelings, and which remains seeking God.

Kataphatic and *apophatic* forms of prayer: why the distinction matters

What are the implications of this model of divided consciousness? Here, it is helpful to consider such an understanding of prayer in comparative context. One of the key things I want to argue is that we need to take seriously the distinction between *kataphatic* and *apophatic* forms of prayer – a distinction that has also been highlighted as analytically significant by Luhrmann (2012: 161).

By kataphatic I mean, essentially, approaches that allow the person at prayer to be led by words, images, and concepts; thought and sense are heavily involved in what can be considered a process of mental, and often emotional, engagement. Apophatic forms of prayer, by contrast, deny that words and images can adequately reflect the nature of God – God is beyond our understanding and narrow sensory capabilities. That which can be imagined or comprehended in our finite minds holds us apart from the infinite God, and the failure of mind and sense is thus the start of contemplation.

The Jesuit Harvey Egan (1978) illustrates the difference between these two approaches by reflecting on two 'paradigmatic cases': the Spiritual Exercises of Ignatius Loyola, sixteenth-century founder of the Jesuits, and the fourteenth-century mystical text *The Cloud of Unknowing*. The kataphatic way of the Spiritual Exercises is that form of discursive prayer that the librarian termed 'prayerful pondering'; but, as Luhrmann (2012: 172–84) has described in some detail, this is a path which involves not only active reflection but the cultivation of the senses, stirring the imagination to vividly immerse the mind and body in prayer. *The Cloud of Unknowing*, by contrast, 'provides an excellent illustration of orthodox Christian, apophatic mysticism. It urges forgetting and unknowing in the service of a blind, silent love beyond all images, thoughts, and feelings' (Egan 1978: 413). In advising the use of a simple, one-syllable word (such as 'God' or 'Love') in prayer as a dart of longing beyond the limits of our finitude, the word is valued 'not for its meaning (for he must not advert to its meaning) but for its simplicity. This one word helps his spirit to be poised at its fine point, to eliminate distractions' (1978: 407). Prayer here is a process of emptying oneself. It is worth noting that the paradigmatic example that Egan draws upon here is seen as particularly important within the tradition of the English Benedictine Congregation, not only as part of the heritage of pre-Reformation English spirituality with which English Benedictines are keen to stress their continuity, but also more specifically because the *Cloud* was a key influence on Augustine Baker, who was involved in the transmission of the text and wrote a commentary on it.[13]

Why is this distinction between *apophatic* and *kataphatic* modes of prayer important? Firstly, I think it helps us recognise a significant gap in the ethnographic record. A great deal of recent ethnographic attention has been paid to the *kataphatic* form. Tanya Luhrmann especially has shown 'inner sense cultivation' (Luhrmann and Morgan 2012) as key to the way in which American Evangelical Protestants in the Vineyard churches build up their capacity to sense God as a vivid auditory and emotional presence, and imagine God as an interlocutor (Luhrmann 2004, 2012). This emphasis has been shared by recent studies of religious communities. In her ethnography of the Franciscan Sisters in the United States, Corwin (2021: 99) describes how prayer facilitates an embodied 'experience of the divine through the remarkable power of language'; Lester (2005: 200) examines prayer as an opportunity for 'conscious reflection and meditation'

---

13 Benedictine scholars have debated the nature of the link between the *Cloud* and Augustine Baker. Spearritt (1974) argues that in Baker's teaching, what we see is a post-Reformation survival of the spirituality of the *Cloud*; Lunn (1975), however, is more cautious, pointing to a wider pool of influences on Baker than just English pre-Reformation sources.

among Mexican nuns; while Naumescu (2012: 240) examines how Ukrainian Eastern Rite Catholic monks train in a 'science of feelings', which he describes as 'the development of specific bodily and mental skills, conceptual acquisition, imaginal conditioning, and the cultivation and mastery of powerful emotions'. These are important accounts, offering rich illustration of the practice of prayer in contemporary Christian life. Nevertheless, it is important that we do not come to see the focus on imagination and sense as the full picture; we need to pay close attention to when and why thought and sense are made *central* to prayer, and when and why they are seen as something to *move beyond*.

But this is not just about the importance of recognising different 'flavours' of prayer (as important as that may be). The distinction also matters a great deal because it points to different kinds of social and institutional relationships in the life of prayer; in particular, it makes visible important differences in the relationship with authority.

Both Lester (2005) and Naumescu (2012) focus on the formation of novices, whose training in prayer is linked to the cultivation of discipline in relation to a spiritual director.[14] We see self-scrutiny and sense awareness within the framework of institutional authority. To be trained in kataphatic prayer is to learn a set of skills, and one can assess whether those skills meet up with institutional expectations; here, not only does one open oneself to evaluation by others, but one also comes to evaluate one's own success. As the experience of prayer is communicable, consisting of describable images and feelings, there is a possibility of sharing this experience in such a way that progress in prayer can be evaluated by others, including those in positions of authority. It can be articulated, shared, monitored, and made subject to the template of Church expectations.

Apophatic prayer makes such guidance, and such evaluation, difficult. Not only is there a silence about what the experience of contemplative prayer is like – a silence made necessary by the fact

---

14 For a similar approach within a Theravada Buddhist context, see Cook (2010) on self-formation among practitioners of vipassana meditation in Thailand.

that it is beyond thought and sense – but we also see a resistance to anything that might be seen as 'prescriptive'. This is noteworthy, as it reflects the freedom associated with the practice of prayer.

Here we return to the provocation offered by Troeltsch (1931) in reflecting on where the mystical impulse leaves the mediation of religious institutions. What became clear over the course of fieldwork in the monastery was that contemplative prayer possessed the radical potential to insist upon a domain of activity that was held apart from communication. While the circulation of texts provided a framework to speak about the preconditions of contemplative prayer – the 'road map' that leads there – there was not only a reluctance to describe contemplative prayer itself, but an insistence that its nonimagistic and nonconceptual nature rendered such a description impossible. Indeed, relating to God in ways that are distinct from the conventional means of self-awareness and how the self conventionally communicates with others in the world, there is limited scope for external authority structures (within the monastery, as well as beyond the cloister walls) to guide and shape the self in prayer: each monk is left *solus cum solo*, 'alone with the alone'. Whereas the discussion of stability in previous chapters of this ethnography has placed the emphasis on the monks' shared grounding within the household through the structures of institutional life, something distinct is happening here.

To explore in more detail this social significance of the ineffable nature of contemplation, let us return to the 'divided consciousness' discussed above: 'O God, You know these thoughts are against my will, I don't want them, they are not ME' (Chapman 1935: 90).

It is interesting to compare this 'disowning' – what Faubion (2013) describes as the mystical exercise of desubjectivation – with the approach described by Lester in her ethnography of a Mexican Catholic convent (she does not identify the order because of concerns over confidentiality): 'There will be times, Mother Veronica said, when postulants will experience a "dryness" … when they will feel that the Lord is not with them and will feel nothing in prayer. When this happens, there is an absence of the comfort that the soul usually feels in the spiritual life' (Lester 2005: 201). So far, such a description follows Chapman's account of the 'night of the senses' (he takes the term and the analysis from St John of the Cross), in which feeling and discursive reason cease to operate. Yet the contrast between Chapman's approach and the Mexican convent that emerges in the next sentences is startling: 'But you must remember that you are to blame for this … It is produced by your infidelity. The will of God has become weak within you and you have to reinforce it … When you feel that God is missing, it's because you've been unfaithful and you need more discipline' (Lester 2005: 201–2). The differences in the approach taken are noteworthy. Firstly, the failure of sense is seen by Chapman as the beginning of the contemplative path, rather than a sign of unfaithfulness: thinking about God in order to stir up emotion is no longer sufficient – the soul desires to love rather than to imagine. Secondly, whereas Chapman says that reflections on the absence of God are to be treated as 'not ME' and therefore disowned, not fought, this divided consciousness is not apparent in the community which Lester describes, where the sensation of absence calls for 'a detailed critique of your relationship with Him in all domains … a genuine connection with God is predicated on a stark and relentless self-evaluation' (Lester 2005: 201).

For the nuns being described by Lester, prayer, self-awareness, and reflection are closely related, and the appropriate response to such reflections and worries is self-examination, with a view to correction. Chapman continually advises against such an approach. His understanding is that while the mind may be restless, the will is focused on God. It would be a mistake, then, to pull yourself away from attention to God in order to focus on the restlessness of the mind.

What do we learn from the difference in approach between Chapman's advice (which I treat here as representative of a certain tendency in the English Benedictine tradition) and the advice given to the Mexican nuns described by Lester? In Lester's ethnography, the practice of prayer can be understood as a means of self-formation in relation to authority. But if we take the claims outlined by Chapman and articulated in the English Benedictine context seriously, we require a different kind of analysis: one which asks what happens when what would conventionally be understood as 'the self' is treated as 'not ME', and within the act of prayer is disowned.

Talal Asad sees Christian monasticism as a space within which 'obedient wills are created' (Asad 1993: 125). He imagines monasticism as a way of life containing a 'programme of disciplinary practices' in which desire, humility, and remorse are 'constructed and reorganized' (1993: 134). The monk is given a new vocabulary to reconstruct the language of secular desire in the context of the demands of a new way of life (1993: 144), while the identification and correction of faults (1993: 161–5) leads the monk to humility (understood by Asad as self-abasement), and in place of pride the self is reconstituted as something servile. However, my argument is precisely that we need to think seriously about apophatic mysticism because it flags up a rather different relationship with authority: a domain which, by virtue of its ineffable nature, stands apart from this work of reconstitution. Here is the contrast between the approach described by Chapman and what we see in Lester's ethnography: while Chapman treats the finite world of sense with indifference (in the time of prayer at least), the Mexican nuns in Lester's ethnography treat the world of sense as significant; for Chapman it is to be disowned but, for the nuns Lester describes, it is an arena for relentless self-critique, aiding their formation in the Christian life. The model of divided consciousness shifts the action elsewhere. 'The simplest way of making an act of attention to God, is by an act of inattention to everything else' (Chapman 1935: 122).

Resist nothing

I eagerly devoured Chapman's *Spiritual Letters*, but I didn't have an opportunity to speak properly with the monk who gifted me the copy for a while. Still, we would greet one another many mornings before the conventual Mass as he moved along the aisle of the abbey church handing out photocopies of his sonnets to (occasionally rather bemused) congregants. I could see the final form of these would sometimes emerge over breakfast, occasionally breaking the silence of the refectory as he would try to negotiate a word choice or a mental block with one of his fellow monks. These sonnets, often autobiographical, infused with the language of desire and sometimes indicating the site of a struggle, felt like works in progress pointing to something beyond the scope of the poem; words that drew the focus elsewhere. They seemed to serve as breadcrumbs on the trail of the experience of prayer in the night or sitting through the morning's period of contemplative prayer, sometimes rapt, sometimes agitated. There were frequent references to phrases and ideas from Chapman, but also to the New Age writer Eckhart Tolle.

After a while I asked him about this, and he loaned me a copy of Tolle's *The Power of Now*. In particular, he felt that I needed to read the account given by Tolle of the origin of the book, which he said resonated with his own experience. '"I cannot live with myself any longer." This was the thought that kept repeating itself in my mind. Then suddenly I became aware of what a peculiar thought it was. "Am I one or two? If I cannot live with myself, there must be two of me: the 'I' and the 'self' that 'I' cannot live with. Maybe," I thought, "only one of them is real."' (Tolle 1997: 2).

As the monk explained, 'that account by Tolle is one of the most dramatic I know. And I think it's common to a lot of mystics. You have this massive deflation of the self that we build up, and the realisation that there is a different "ME" [he gestures towards himself with both hands], the true self. What he had discovered, his huge discovery, was that you can stop the thinker in you and stay fully conscious. And then he was onto the Chapman gap, you see. And he found himself being sucked into this void, with this inner voice saying "resist nothing!"'

He told me of his own experience in early autumn, 1944. 'I had been putting myself through this torture that they called mental prayer and I was in the darkened church quite fed up and suddenly something in me said "be honest." And I said "this is a bloody bore, this is getting me nowhere, I can't keep doing this." And that pulled the stopper out of the inflatable toy of the ego, that's Tolle's image. And suddenly I realised I was in love and I heard myself say "I'll give you anything you want."' This sense of presence hadn't always stayed with him – he lost it in the 1960s, 'a very angry time, personally and politically of course', and only recovered that willingness to accept the 'drop into the void' in the 1970s. 'That is what Chapman is doing when he says "an act of attention to God is an act of inattention to everything else", he's coaxing us toward that hole. I had to stop paying attention to that part of me that resists God.'

Although it would be fair to say that not all the community shared this enthusiasm for Tolle, his use by this particular monk was nevertheless indicative of the personal freedom for exploration in this area. It had a powerful resonance for him – so much so that, when he died, a friend threw a copy of The Power of Now into his grave at the burial. Here was a fresh means of expressing the dynamics of divided consciousness; an awareness of the sense of being two, allowing us to let go of the part that resists being one in God. But also, for this monk, making the connection between Chapman and Tolle pointed to a wider spiritual awakening, a recognition of general thirst that in turn might lead to 'a Church that comes to know it does not have a monopoly on prayer'. For this reason, he would appreciatively cite the verdict of the theologian Sarah Coakley (2002: 42) that Chapman 'democratized' contemplation, while also noting that Chapman had said of himself – apparently with a tone of approval – 'They call me a Buddhist!'

This democratising and universalising tendency has, in fact, been an important refrain in English Benedictine history. Baker (1657: I, 154) asserted that 'Contemplation is by God denyed to no states [of life],' and Cuthbert Butler (1926: 192), who was greatly influenced by Baker,[15] returns repeatedly to the theme that contemplation is open to all, thinking it a shame that mysticism is 'placed on a sort of pedestal, as a thing to be wondered at and admired respectfully from beneath … Yet it was the standard teaching in the Catholic ages down to modern times that contemplation is the natural term of a spiritual life seriously lived, and is a thing to be desired, aspired to, aimed at, and not infrequently attained.' Here we are far from the 'virtuoso' of prayer set apart from the ordinary layperson, in terrain not easily defined through the hierarchical relations of the Church.[16]

---

15 See Yeo and Maidlow Davis (1982:98–9) on how the influence of Baker shapes Butler's reading of the place of private prayer in the Rule of St Benedict.
16 In the context of Eastern Orthodox contemplative prayer, see Johnson (2010)

Here, adding to my earlier argument that the basis of apophatic prayer in the failure of language and thought insists upon a ground beyond conventional means of social mediation – the crucial challenge of incommunicability – I am now further arguing that an ideology of democratisation presents mysticism as unmediated in yet another sense: a universality that looks beyond the horizon of institutional boundaries and authority.[17] This becomes abundantly clear when we take into account the ways in which, grounded in an understanding of contemplation as a universal potential, monks explore connections with mysticism beyond the Church.

This universality was key to the librarian's understanding of prayer, 'part of man's innate nature, a natural desire ... "Birds fly, fish swim, man prays."'[18] He gave an account from his time with the Congregation's Theology Commission of an episode of monastic dialogue with Tibetan Buddhist monks who had visited the UK: 'On the surface we had little in common in terms of doctrine, of theology in that sense ... But what in fact we had in common was contemplation.' And it is important to note that this understanding long precedes more recent approaches to interreligious dialogue. Baker (1657: I, 11–12) traces the 'propension' to 'Natural Devotion ... even in hereticks, yea Jewes & heathens'; and two abbots of early-twentieth-century Downside take up this point, with Cuthbert Butler (1926) examining examples of mysticism beyond Christianity and, more directly, Chapman (1935: 128–9) stating, 'I believe that Mohammedan (Sufi), Brahmin and Buddhist mystics do arrive at very high states of union with God.' In this sense, the tradition pre-empts interreligious dialogue in the wake of the Second Vatican Council, as well as offering fertile ground for a wider social atmosphere

---

on how the emergence of new forms of authority through the 'democratising' effect of online activity can lead to tensions with the institutional and hierarchical authority of the Church.

17 Again, Troeltsch (1931: 749) suggests that a tendency to universalism – seeing a fundamental basis of the direct experience of God freed from the constraints of a specific tradition – is a potential consequence of the immediacy of mysticism.

18 A saying attributed to St Ephrem the Syrian (c. 306–73).

of globalised spiritual exploration. The monk who had introduced me to both Chapman and Tolle recognised the potential risk of 'spiritual consumerism' here, but nevertheless recalled the excitement of discovery when he was teaching in the United States in the 1970s: 'there was a great sense that people had been seeking technologies for spirituality, the big appetite for the Maharashi through the Beatles, Transcendental Meditation of course, and then we were running prayer sessions, centering, contemplation and then you have these coming to this from Transcendental Meditation and recognising that they were at home in this way of praying.'

Another example of the democratising and universalising approach came from a monk returning from a long period serving as a parish priest away from the monastery, who emphasised the value of silent prayer, not only for his own parishioners but as an 'expression of the ecumenical movement'. He observed that both inside and outside the Church there was increasing consciousness of a desire to reach beyond the point 'where meaning dissolves behind a flood of other thoughts' and the need (as described by Chapman) to find a focus to stop those thoughts drawing the will away from prayer, 'like the tongue being drawn to a sore in the mouth'.

The practical advice he gave to those drawn to this way of praying, in the form of a leaflet, drew directly on the instructions for 'How to Meditate' from the World Council of Christian Meditation: 'Sit down. Sit still and upright. Close your eyes lightly. Sit relaxed but alert. Silently, interiorly begin to say a single word. We recommend the prayer-phrase *maranatha*.[19] Recite it as four syllables of equal length. Listen to it as you say it, gently but continuously. Do not think or imagine anything – spiritual or otherwise. If thoughts or images come, these are distractions at the time of meditation, so keep returning to simply saying the word. Meditate each morning and evening for between twenty and thirty minutes.' This advice reflects the dynamics discussed in this chapter. The World Council of Christian Meditation emerged from the teaching of John Main (1926–82),[20] a monk of Ealing Abbey. Upon rereading Baker's *Sancta*

---

19 From 1 Corinthians 16: 22, an Aramaic phrase meaning 'Come, Lord.'
20 For an account of the life of John Main, see McKenty (1986).

Sophia in the context of the 1960s and the heightened interest in Asian spirituality, Main recognised that the English Benedictine tradition of prayer had much in common with the mantra-based meditation he had learned from a Hindu monk while working with the British Colonial service in Malaya. This led to a reimmersion in that understanding of the potential of mantra. The approach developed (Main 1980) is therefore rooted in a particular understanding of contemplation while making interreligious connections in a way that is entirely consistent with that English Benedictine tradition.

The social significance of all this is that we have already seen the emphasis on the failure of conceptual thought, the breakdown of communication, and the negation of the reflective self within a tradition emphasising the primacy of inner experience (see Temple 2019) as we enter that void. Within this frame, we also see an expansive vision of who may have that experience, including those beyond the bounds of the Church, further probing the limits of authority.

The trouble with mysticism

As Pryce (2018: 108) remarks in her ethnography of American monastic spirituality and contemplative Christianity, 'The language of orthodoxy and orthopraxy is not nearly open enough to describe this movement, even in its monastic guises.' Little wonder, then, that such methods become objects of suspicion. This is well demonstrated by a formal document[21] issued in 1989 by the Congregation for the Doctrine of the Faith, the official body charged by the Holy See for the protection of doctrinal orthodoxy and at this time headed by Joseph Ratzinger, who would go on to become Pope Benedict XVI. The document stresses the dangers of 'erroneous ways of praying' and, in particular, 'the pointed renewal of an attempt, which is not free from dangers and errors, *to fuse Christian meditation with that which is non-Christian*' [emphasis original]. What is clear throughout is that in taking inspiration from sources beyond the

---

21 'Letter to the Bishops of the Catholic Church on some aspects of Christian meditation', 15 October 1989.

Church, as well as moving beyond the conceptual apparatus of Church teaching, the contemplative tradition is considered a source of potential danger. Hence it warns that methods of meditation and contemplation 'must always be offered within the authentic spirit of the Church at prayer, and therefore under its guidance, which can sometimes take a concrete form in terms of a proven spiritual direction'; yet, as we have seen, the apophatic character and universal potential of contemplative prayer pushes at the very limits of this 'proven spiritual direction'.

Over tea one afternoon, a junior monk was discussing (and complaining about) the range of books on the subject of mysticism that needed to be read over the course of his monastic formation. It seemed to him that he was being asked to read a lot of potentially contradictory accounts without getting a sense of the destination. It was in response to this that I first heard the joke attributed to Aiden Gasquet, the nineteenth-century prior of the community: 'the trouble with mysticism is that it begins in mist and ends in schism'. I heard the joke several times after that, and it became something of a theme during my enquiries about prayer – a playful recognition of the cloud of suspicion around contemplative prayer.

What lies at the heart of this suspicion? The statement of the Congregation for the Doctrine of the Faith speaks to a specific anxiety about syncretism, but it has at its heart a more general concern with how a search for immediacy in the relation with God appears to *unroot* itself from the institutional framework.

Such concerns protrude into the history of this tradition of contemplative prayer. Immediately upon being introduced to the *Sancta Sophia,* I was made aware of the atmosphere of suspicion that had surrounded Augustine Baker's teaching. As a spiritual director at Cambrai, Baker's 'insistence on the primacy of inner mystical experience' (Temple 2017: 219) granted considerable autonomy to the nuns under his instruction in ways that seemed to disregard wider structures of authority. After all, if prayer is a personal experience, one's method of prayer should not be subject to external interference (Clark 2004: 219). At the limits of human sense and language, direct experience takes precedence. This led to a formal complaint from the priest (also an English Benedictine monk) who had been sent as confessor to Cambrai, accusing Baker of encouraging the nuns to cultivate a private life of prayer disengaged from the institutional frameworks in which this could be guided by those in authority – in effect, opening up a space of freedom that undermined the capacity of superiors and confessors to direct the moral and spiritual development of the nuns. Consequently, the contemplative manuscripts Baker gave to the nuns were formally examined at a General Chapter of 1633. The subsequent removal of Baker to St Gregory's at Douai did not dispel these suspicions, where concerns about the implications of a mystical teaching that placed inner experience at a remove from the institutional life of the Church were reinforced by accounts of Baker's own disengagement from communal life, wearing plain clothes, spending many hours in his cell, and excusing himself from communal duties (Temple 2019: 41; see also Freeman 2001). While interpersonal conflicts undoubtedly played a central part in the reaction to Baker and the ultimate decision to send him on the mission to England in ill health at the age of 63, the very nature of the suspicions and accusations that surrounded him remain revealing.

The seventeenth century was a time of mounting controversy around mysticism and, specifically, the implications of encouraging an impulse to prayer beyond thought and sense. What has come to be known as the 'Quietist heresy' was the subject of official sanction, beginning with Pope Innocent XI's condemnation[22] of 43 propositions of the Spanish priest Miguel de Molinos. The crucial issue is the extent to which a passive resignation to inner silence in the presence of God renders us indifferent to the external world of mind and sense. The moral panic that prompted such condemnations was the apparent implication in such teachings that external activity (such as devotional practices or good works) was irrelevant to, or even a distraction from, the abandonment of oneself to God. Indeed, at the heart of the condemnations was a concern that the maintenance of inner quiet involved such a disconnection from the active self that any attempt to resist temptation was itself deemed a distraction. As the theologian Bernard McGinn (2021: 7) explains in

---

22 In the papal bull *Coelestis Pater*.

his historical study of Quietism and its condemnation, 'The crucial question is how far passivity extends, and what the relation of passivity to action is, especially the usual activities of the Christian life ... with some justification the Quietists were often accused of denigrating, perhaps even denying, the value of external works,' Some have suggested (for example, Lunn 1975: 270; Kelly 2021: 317) that this cloud of suspicion would have affected the subsequent reception of the teaching presented by Baker, even in the 'sanitised' form of the *Sancta Sophia*.[23] But the significance of this crisis is perhaps more thorough: McGinn has argued that such controversy precipitated a broad loss of confidence in the orthodoxy and respectability of mystical teaching that continues to the present day. More specifically, it led to a reassertion of the role of Church authorities mediating the experience of prayer, ongoing suspicion of those who sought to untether nonconceptual prayer from discursive meditation, and scrutiny of anything that might imply disinterest in the external activity of the person at prayer. That these remained live issues long after the seventeenth century is apparent from the controversy that also accompanied John Chapman's teaching.

Even in the conversation when I was gifted a copy of his *Spiritual Letters*, I was told they had been subject to suspicion of expressing 'Quietist' tendencies, again something that I heard repeated around the monastery (though seemingly never to discourage me from reading him, more highlighting its importance by way of its controversy: 'the Ignatian method was seen as a safeguard to Quietism, so there's a suspicion of those seemingly offering permission to quit it.'). The publication of Chapman's letters was immediately met with comment on their apparent tendency towards this heresy, most notably by Archbishop Alban Goodier (1935), a Jesuit, who made direct comparisons between Chapman's statements and the condemned teachings of Miguel de Molinos, charges which Hudleston (1935) goes to great efforts to rebut. Goodier not only expresses

---

23 Sanitised in the sense that as a digest of Baker's work from manuscript sources, Serenus Cressy's editing avoided that which was polemical and instead emphasised the orthodoxy of what was being taught and its continuity with previous texts on contemplative prayer; see Temple (2017: 224–5).

concerns about the effect of Chapman's apparent indifference to the world of thought and sense, but also sees the letters as encouraging an overly individualistic understanding of prayer, fostering a disinterest in the external life, indifference towards theological teaching, and risking disconnection from the doctrinal authority of the Church.

Returning, then, to the role of stability in monastic life, how should we take account of the 'trouble with mysticism'? The repeated controversy is suggestive of the fact that mysticism offers 'systematic irritation' to the structure and organisation containing it (Faubion 2013: 304). As we have seen, the incommunicable nature of this entry into silence opens up a space of personal freedom. At stake here is whether the silence of contemplative prayer is an unrooting from the institutional frame that gives shape to life in community. During Lent, sitting in the abbey church after everyone else had left, I pondered one of the photocopied reflections handed out before Mass by the monk who had introduced me to Chapman in the first place. This one was in prose form and titled 'Coda to Chapman'. It addressed our generic vocation – in other words, the question of why we are at all. 'Somehow you want this nothing-in-particular ("which is God of course" says Chapman[24] in his cavalier manner). It's as though there were something in you that "knows what it wants" and sees everything, anything, as a distraction from this.' Where was the social life of the monastery in this – part of the want or part of the distraction?

Prayer at the limit

In contemplative prayer we see the crucial interplay of engagement and disengagement that lies at the heart of monasticism. Ineffability has social implications. What does it mean to reach the limit of representation, the limit of mind and sense, to be exposed to the inexpressible? Webb Keane (2006), taking his cue from the challenge of interiority for the Sumbanese Calvinists with whom he

---

24 A reference to the *Spiritual Letters* (Chapman 1935: 58).

worked, draws our attention to a general problem that shapes Christianity's relationship with subjectivity: 'even in its most abstract and transcendent, the human subject cannot free itself from objectification' (2006: 321). The subject that desires transcendence longs 'for a self freed of its body, for meanings freed of semiotic mediation, and for agency freed of the press of other people' (2006: 310). But the means of reaching this transcendence cannot be entirely freed from their socially and materially embedded forms – a body that interacts, words that communicate. This leads to a state of what Keane calls 'anxious transcendence'; the 'irresolvable tension between abstraction and the inescapability of material and social mediations' (2006: 322). Insomuch as the shift from discourse to silence, from thought to 'God the unknown' seeks to negate this tension by disowning the mediations that resist (as Chapman put it, 'they are not ME'), we are certainly brought back to this anxious transcendence by the institutional dynamics and mysticism's awkward tension with authority.

Here the charge of Quietism, with its implication of indifference to the external world, is noteworthy. It indicates the kinds of suspicion that attach to a model of divided consciousness where the very elements of subjectivity that ground presence and action in day-to-day life are peeled away to reveal a 'true self'.

One theologian who has critically engaged with the implications of this divided consciousness is Sarah Coakley (2002), whose reflections on Chapman's *Spiritual Letters* were recommended to me on a number of occasions. Writing as someone who draws spiritual value from Chapman, Coakley nonetheless remarks on the character of a prayer where body, sense and feeling are treated as 'radically disjunct' (2002: 46) to contemplation, and potentially even objects of scorn. Here she sounds a note of caution: 'the profoundest levels of "contemplative" activity do not escape the constraints (sometimes distorting or harmful constraints) of the "frail earthen vessels" in which they are carried' (2002: 54) – a remark that signals alarm about the potential impact of disowning this embodied self. 'If, in that prayer, one is simultaneously courting the release of such unconscious material, and yet also refusing or even repressing it, there may be dangerous psychological consequences' (2002: 52). (In this respect, it is worth noting that the other key context in which a monk of the community recommended the work of Sarah Coakley (2015) to me was in attempting to confront the sources of the tremendous harm caused by clerical sexual abuse, reflecting on the distortion of desire within priestly celibacy.)

Relatedly, Coakley draws attention to the particular way in which Chapman interprets the teaching of the Carmelite mystic St John of the Cross (1542–91), to whom he makes frequent reference in his letters. John of the Cross speaks of the 'night of the senses', a process of purgation such that desire is no longer met with its sensual response, and much of Chapman's advice relates to what to do faced with such aridity. Yet, for John of the Cross, we pass through the night to awaken with God the beloved, and this is expressed through the language of love poetry, often erotically charged. For Coakley (2002: 54), this is a 'startling omission' from Chapman's account. 'Chapman has nothing whatever to tell us about the connection between sexual desire and the desire for God; John of the Cross has – at least implicitly – a great deal.' Chapman's emphasis is on endurance; what Coakley pithily describes as 'sanjuanism with a stiff upper lip'.

This observation certainly resonated with much of the contained atmosphere of personal prayer in the monastery. Shorn of the sensual, and at the limits of communicability, desire was bound up with solitude and silence. An account from one of the monks in the 1960s gives us a vivid sense of how disembedded from life in community this experience could appear. 'There was marked reluctance to say what prayer was actually like from within, to say anything precise or personal about what prayer was for the individual who was advocating it. So our school of prayer was really a do-it-yourself school in which the only principle was that this thing called prayer was all-important' (Harvey 1969: 4). He praises the 'freedom of spirit' this cultivated, but is alert to the way in which it left the individual to fall back on himself: 'one's prayer was not an experience which could be shared or communicated, so there was no sensible touchstone of authenticity' (1969: 5). At the same time the 'formal division' (1969: 3) of the components of life, including a separation of private prayer from liturgical prayer, could lead to a sense that the times of private prayer were 'divorced from other elements' (1969: 4) of life in community. 'The creative aspect of work, and of human relationships, was thus scaled down in favour of the purely or directly spiritual activity of prayer.' What Harvey is at pains to describe is an extraction of prayer from the social: '"How can I cope with the irruption of this person into my otherwise well-ordered spiritual life?" … The resultant private love-world in fact carried with it the same radical constriction as the private prayer-world, stemming from the same fragmentation of consciousness' (1969: 7).

These tensions are expressed by way of introduction to *The Experience of Prayer*, a book co-authored by Downside monks who at the time were living in a parish in inner-city Liverpool (a posting that was taken as an opportunity to explore forms of monastic renewal in the context of wider shifts in the Church, but also explained to me as a convenient way of removing some of the more theologically troublesome monks and limiting the disruption they could cause in the monastery itself). Given the fragmentation described in the introduction, little wonder that later in the book one of the authors states, 'Private prayer is a lonely thing' (Moore and Maguire 1969: 103). But what the book records (again, often in the form of poetry, and, like that of John of the Cross, this poetry is not shorn of erotic components) are experiments that explore the prayer as an expression of desire *with* other people rather than without them – an act of love capable of 'uniting more than two, and therefore able to unite a number on which no limit may be set' (1969: 104). But whatever the hope for a renewal of the relational basis of contemplative prayer, 'such that, to my surprise, I find I can no longer pray most fully when alone', the desire that permeates *The Experience of Prayer* could not be easily contained within English Benedictine life and indeed, of the four Downside monks in Liverpool at the time the book was written, three left the monastic life and priesthood. The other migrated to the USA in the wake of difficulties and struggles with the community and was absent from the life of the monastery until he returned 22 years later.

Recalling (as discussed in Chapter 4) the abbot's depiction of the English Benedictine focus on private prayer as a 'spirituality for solitaries', he historicised this with reference to the influence of

Baker, with his emphasis on individual autonomy in personal prayer, prioritising this over and beyond other aspects of community life – even potentially over the Divine Office, which he seems to have treated 'primarily as a form of mortification'. This emphasis fits with a wider English Benedictine historiography that depicted Baker as a controversial figure warning against 'preoccupation with the details of monastic observance to the detriment of interior prayer' (Spearritt 1974: 292), and living in ways that sat uneasily with the dynamics of community life (Lunn 1975). As the abbot pointed out, any sense that the core of one's prayer life is apart from the collective liturgy sits uncomfortably with St Benedict's exhortation in Chapter 43 of the *Rule*, 'Let nothing be put before the Work of God' [that is, the Divine Office]. At the same time, the abbot recognised this had a particular suitedness for much of English Benedictine history where monks were sent away from their monasteries to live in the relative isolation of the 'mission'[25], a pattern which persisted well beyond the return of the monastic houses to England (see Chapter 7). In that context, the 'Bakerite' approach had tremendous value, equipping the monk to live an individual spiritual life in a state of separation from the community; nevertheless, the question of how to integrate such autonomy into a renewed community and liturgical life remained a live point.

This was reflected in one monk's account of his own formation in prayer trying to find a sense of *shared* silence in a context where 'public and private had become almost completely disconnected … A strange atmosphere. Hugely difficult for a novice to interpret or engage with; I can remember my own mystification … any growth or depth was in the wholly private world of the half hours … it was not in deepening relationships in the community or nourished by the liturgy.'

To what extent, then, is Troeltsch (1931: 743) right in claiming that the immediacy of mysticism with its intense emphasis on 'first-hand experience' implies a 'radical individualism'? There is an untethering from the mediation of the institutional Church as we approach the

---

25 Relatedly, see Kelly (2021) on Baker's polemical call for spiritual formation that fosters the contemplative capacity of priests on the mission, as well as his pessimism about the level of formation provided at the time.

very limits of language, thought, and sense that mediate our experience of the social world. And, as we see in the accounts above, with contemplative prayer marked out as space of freedom, autonomous and incommunicable, this can allow individualism to protrude in ways that complicate the rhythm of stability through community life.

As the theme of individualism is something that comes into prominence in the following chapters, this is an important dynamic to follow. Yet the irony of such an approach is that an emphasis on the *individual* focuses on the very self that contemplative prayer draws the attention away from! For Foster (2015: 98), emphasising the liminality of contemplative experience, the disruption of unknowing does not leave the bounded individual intact: 'in liminality something deeper is going on; some fundamental structure in the way I find meaning is being challenged; and, most profoundly, I am myself put in question.' This resonates with an anthropological understanding of liminality as a *dispossession* of identity and the characteristics of the self (Turner 1969). Stripped in this way, our relationships are reconfigured, and the threshold of contemplative prayer can be a place of transformation: 'it helps me live more deeply in a sense of engagement with others' (Foster 2015: 199).

Indeed, this had been part of the 'road map' of prayer presented to me by the librarian. One shouldn't look for signs of 'success' in prayer in terms of sensations experienced by the self, because prayer operates at the limit of sensation and disrupts the self, but we should see the ways that the openness in prayer reconfigures us. This consists not only of 'a peace and a freedom that are independent of outer circumstances', but also a transformation of the social self. 'A genuine attempt at prayer would leave us disturbed at the presence in our lives of so many elements that cannot co-exist with Christian prayer – unforgiveness, dishonesty, coldness.'

Pryce, in her ethnography of contemplative prayer in the USA, recognising the liminality that arose from a 'capacity to "let go" of the cultural and social norms that separate people' (2018: 182), describes how the monk's cell does not simply symbolise withdrawal and disengagement but 'can become a place of iconic being where a paradoxical relationship of solitude and communion finds its apex in a self with permeable boundaries, a porous self that serves community' (2018: 222). This undoubtedly complicates Troeltsch's emphasis on the individualism of the mystic. But at the same time, we should not lose sight of the monks' own reflections on the how prayer can become disconnected from the life of community, and what I want to get across here are the ways in which the monks drew me back to the nature of this 'paradoxical relationship' and the tensions it generated.

There is an ambivalence here, as indicated by the monk who had gifted me Chapman's letters. The drop into the void is a letting go of that which drags us back into our own egocentricity: a moment where (in a formula he frequently used) 'I want becomes I love'. In this letting go, our desire is no longer hoarded within the constraints of the self. Yet the struggle of dispossession was always recognised in this movement. 'It is no surprise that people can find [prayer] a lonely and thankless task. Yes, I am on the brink of a very forlorn place.'

Perseverance at the edge

Recognising the tradition of contemplative prayer as an 'identifying mark' of the English Benedictine, how does this illuminate our understanding of monastic stability? In the earlier chapters, the emphasis of this book has been on the institutional characteristics of stability. The pulse of contemplative prayer exists within this shared rhythm and grounding but also, as we have seen, exerts tension upon it.

At the core of this institutional understanding of stability is a fundamental sense of stability as perseverance. This is the challenge of standing firm in the faith, a challenge which the *Rule* situates in the collective life of the monastery but which calls on a 'stability of heart' (Rees et al. 1978: 138), keeping the will focused on the search for God in spite of distractions. This personal stability, and its relationship with the monastic household, is articulated (as seen in Chapter 1) in the novice ritually expressing his desire for perseverance before the abbot and community at specific points throughout his probation.

Contemplative prayer clearly expresses such perseverance even as it makes demands upon it. The monk wills an openness to God even as the failure of familiar ways of relating makes it feel like he is hitting a wall. A limit is reached, and contemplative prayer is perseverance at this edge.

This complicates our understanding of monastic stability, because liminality is inherently destabilising! There is a process of defamiliarisation as structures and identities that ground everyday life seem beside the point in the presence of an unknown beyond our finite comprehension. If we follow Victor Turner (1969: 96) and his understanding of liminality's potential, this freedom opens us to the possibility of new ways of relating: liminality 'reveals, however fleetingly, some recognition … of a generalized social bond that has ceased to be and has simultaneously yet to be fragmented into a multiplicity of structural ties'. From this position, contemplative prayer is the perseverance to begin again, having hit the wall of human finitude; listening at the threshold, open to the very relationships that are impossible if we act only within the capacities of our fragmented self. And yet it remains an ungrounding. The possibility of immediacy shifts attention beyond the security of a self mediated by institutional frameworks. Here, of course, is the analytical significance of individualism, expressed ethnographically in concerns about a 'spirituality for solitaries' disinterested in everyday activity, disengaged from others and disembedded from community life.

So this destabilising is important because it clearly operates at a point of tension with institutional stability. But it also returns us to the liminality of monastic life – the monk on the funeral pall, a confrontation of the finitude of a human life with the infinitude of time and space. From this vantage point, stability is not simply the comfort of routine and of familiar places, but a perseverance in a particular time and space at the threshold of the unknowable. It is the openness aspired to in the darkness of the abbey church, before the great silence, as the monks pray Compline together and chant the words of Christ on the cross:[26] 'Into your hands, O Lord, I commend my spirit'.

26 Luke 23: 46

CHAPTER 6

Reading as prayer and learning to listen

Go slow

'Slow, then slower, then slower' was the advice. Shifting in my seat, I look down again at the photocopied page. *'The spirit of the Lord Yahweh has been given to me ... He has sent me to bring good news to the poor.'* I realise I've already skipped over a line. Go back. Slow down.

I had become familiar with *lectio divina* before I started my fieldwork at the monastery. The term *lectio divina* is sometimes translated as Divine Reading or Sacred Reading although, in practice, the Latin form (or the abbreviation *lectio*) was used around the monastery, indicating a particular approach to reading *as* prayer. This form of prayer is something that monastic communities will often share through public talks, retreats for laypeople, books, and so on. It is, in a sense, a product for export, something monks are keen to present publicly. For this reason, it was something that I was expecting to learn more about. I did not have to wait long. During my first week of fieldwork, the monastery hosted a day of recollection for laypeople of the Diocese. The guest master, who was leading the day of recollection, handed out a photocopied page from the Bible (*Jerusalem Bible* translation): a short passage from the Prophet Isaiah 61: 1–6. He asked us to read through it slowly, allowing ample time for this before explaining to us the method of *lectio divina*, which he described as the 'slow, contemplative praying of scripture, through which God talks with a still small voice."[1]

The process, we were told, consists of four 'moments', or stages. The first moment is *lectio* (reading): this involves reading through a short passage, usually a few verses from the Bible, slowly. Then, when you reach the end of the passage, read through it again, and again, several times, each time slowly, reading each word to yourself, 'hearing each word in your mind as though you were reading aloud'. Next, the reader 'comes to rest' on a particular word or phrase in the passage; having read the passage through several times, the reader finds 'a particular resonance' in a part of the text, 'a word or a phrase maybe that seems to speak to you in particular'. Having settled on this word or phrase, you repeat it again and again in your mind, 'considering what it means to you, allowing it to interact with your own hopes and memories'; this is the second 'moment', known as *meditatio* (meditation). This leads into *oratio* (prayer), a 'conversation with God', in which you speak through prayer in response to what scripture has said to you during *meditatio*. Finally, beyond these prayers there is *contemplatio* (contemplation), which was described as 'simply being in the presence of God', resting without having to think or say anything. After this description and explanation of the four moments of *lectio divina*, we were given time to return to the text to read it and pray with it again, while the guest master prepared to celebrate Mass for the group.

Reading – even *personal* reading – is a social process. This is demonstrated not only through the significance of shared familiarity with a set of texts but also, as Eric Livingston (1995) points out, through the learned nature of techniques and conventions. 'Reading is neither in the text nor in the reader. It consists of social phenomena, known through its achievements which lie between the text and the reader's eye, in the reader's implementation of society's ways of reading, in reading what a text says' (Livingston 1995: 16). These cultural mediations not only shape our reading, but also show how

---

[1] The words 'still small voice' are themselves taken from scripture, where they are used in the King James Version of the Bible to describe how the voice of God was heard by Elijah in 1 Kings 19:12.

a text might be read. For this reason, as Jonathan Boyarin (1989) has argued, anthropologists need to pay attention to cultures of readership and to the way that strategies of reading are shaped by the communities of which we are part. This chapter, then, is about the monastery as a community of readers (Irvine 2010c), and the particular context this gives to reading as a way of prayer.

Points of resistance

As noted above, *lectio divina* was a form of 'monastic spirituality' that English Benedictines frequently shared with laypeople through retreats, and one member of the community had written a practical book for beginners on the subject (Foster 2005). So it seemed like a good starting point for participant observation, and I was keen to learn its place in the life of the community. What I had not anticipated, however, was the difficulty it would present to me (Irvine 2021b). The slow, prayerful reading of scripture was physiologically hard. Slowing down the pace of reading required constant effort. My eyes would regularly dart beyond the passage that I was reading; looking around the page for context, skipping ahead to get to the point. Rather than coming to rest in the Word of God, as I was being advised to do, my gaze moved restlessly. A prominent sensation in these early days was that of boredom.

After a number of informal teatime conversations about *lectio*, the novice master, whose responsibility it was to teach the practice to novices as part of their formation, offered to meet with me to provide some further guidance. His own practice, and that which he taught, was guided by the 'four-stage' model outlined above, which is derived from the work of a twelfth-century Carthusian monk, Guigo II. *Lectio divina* as a practice, of course, predates this particular model (for a historic account, see Studzinski 2009). The prayerful reading of scripture was heir to an understanding of transformative encounter through reading as taught by Augustine of Hippo (354–430), and the importance of *lectio* as an integral part of the Benedictine life is grounded in the *Rule* of St Benedict itself, with

Chapter 48 prescribing set times for the monks to engage in sacred reading. Guigo II's work *Scala Claustralium* (*The Monk's Ladder*) is a particular expression of this practice, describing the four rungs of the ladder by which God's lovers ascend to God: reading, meditation, prayer, and contemplation, each of which leads into the next.

The first thing that the novice master explained to me was the difficulty that many experienced when first attempting to practise *lectio*. 'For many of us, especially those who are used to what you might call scholarly reading, *lectio* can be hard to achieve, it's not a kind of reading we're used to.' In particular, attempting to slow down the pace of reading can be a struggle, and even more so for people used to speed reading, or scanning a text to find a particularly useful bit of information.

This was the case for me: having arrived at the monastery directly from university, and specifically from a number of years dominated by the work of essay writing and compiling literature reviews, the culture of readership in which I was immersed was one which valorised quantity of reading and the capacity to shift rapidly within and between texts in search of relevance. Likewise, the novice master recalled the same difficult transition. When he was introduced to *lectio*, before he had entered the monastery, he was a student at university, and was immediately aware of the distance between the kind of reading techniques he had to master in order to get his assignments done and the 'slow, prayerful, deliberate' reading he was encountering through *lectio divina*, a process he likened to 'chewing the cud'. As a result, he too experienced a sense of resistance, which he suggested had also been the case with many he had taught. He needed to make an effort to read slowly. 'For many, repetition of the text is useful; slow, then slower, then slower … and to remember that you don't have to get to the end. That can be very hard, too.'

There could also be resistance at the stage of *meditatio*. 'You have to recognise that we are not talking about exegesis, or Bible study in the sense that's often taken to mean.' An Anglican priest, staying as a guest at the monastery, had asked the novice master about *lectio* after hearing it discussed; having received a description, he asked, 'So it's Bible study, then?' and was told no, that the aim of *lectio* was your own personal reaction to the text, not an interpretation of the text. As it was explained to me, 'you're not trying to mine the text for meaning, as though you were writing an essay, but you're looking for the way God speaks through the text. The text is a catalyst, it's a way of getting to prayer'. Again, for those used to analysing and critically assessing a text as they go, this could be difficult. 'As you read the text, you are listening not just to it, but also to yourself, looking for a resonance, a part that strikes you'; later, he used the term 'echo' to describe this sense of having found something in the text. Settling on this 'echo' and the response to it could be difficult. Sometimes, used to reading through books in one or two sittings, we might experience restlessness, and a wish to move on. I asked about this restlessness: 'like you want to move on in order to get to the point?', to which he responded, 'right, but in *lectio* the personal response we're talking about, that personal response is the point', and it is this response that opens out into prayer and contemplation.

Entering into a new community of practice involved a retraining of the body. Central to this was the recasting of reading as an auditory process. Deliberate subvocalisation – hearing the text as though it was being read to me – radically slowed down the pace of reading while fixing the order of the words, making it difficult to shift around the page at will and restricting the possibility of a 'skim' reading. Repetition encouraged attention to resonances, nurturing a state of absorption (see also Luhrmann 2007) that led to contemplation beyond the text; a movement that reflected an understanding of contemplative prayer's potential (as discussed in Chapter 5) to move beyond words and images, from 'God as we picture him' to 'God the unknown'. Crucially, this retraining was not in isolation, but through immersion in a particular sensory environment. As we have seen, such an approach to reading emerges from the social life of the monastery: listening to scripture within the ritual cycle that structures the day, chanting the psalms morning, noon, and night, alternately listening to a verse being chanted and then making the next verse sound out in response. At mealtimes too, the monks eat in silence while one of the community reads aloud from a book (see Chapter 2). In such an environment, to read is to hear. Repetition also emerges from the institutional structure and timetable of communal life, and especially through the liturgy of the hours in its return to the same words over the cycle of prayer. Here we see the place of *lectio* mediating contemplative and liturgical prayer in the life of the community.

A particularly evocative description of the role of listening in social life comes from Hirschkind (2001), who explored processes of sensory engagement with tape-recorded sermons among Muslims in Egypt. He describes how oratory 'recruits the body of the listener' (Hirschkind 2001: 637), a 'means by which a range of Islamic virtues could be sedimented in their characters' (2001: 627). Relevantly to our understanding of *lectio divina*, such attentive listening is understood as more than mere hearing; it is a process which fosters a new relationship between the listener and God.

One of the monks at Downside, formerly a teacher in school but now retired, offered me the following description emphasising the aural qualities of *lectio*. 'I am searching myself, I'm searching myself for that resonance. But it's also trying to listen to God. God is speaking to me, to where I am right now, and I suppose what we would say is that God's there, he's speaking those words on the page, but a lot of the time they're flying past me. But as you move slowly through the text, you realise that it's not just a voice out there, it's a voice speaking to me, directly. Do you know John Henry Newman's[2] motto, "*Cor ad cor loquitur*"? "Heart speaks to heart"? Well, it's like that.' Another monk, who worked as a parish priest, also drew on the imagery of the heart as he connected *lectio* with liturgical practice. 'How I sometimes explain it is, you know before the Gospel you make a sign of the cross on your forehead, on your lips, and on your heart? I think that demonstrates perfectly what we're seeking. You engage with the text with your mind, you're pondering it. It's on your lips, you're speaking it over to yourself. My lips will often move as I read, in fact. And then you feel the word growing in your heart.' I asked what he meant by 'growing in your heart'. 'I hope we're not going to be deconstructionist about this! Let me

---

2 St John Henry Newman (1801–90), theologian and Anglican convert to Catholicism.

see. It's something simple in experience but doesn't translate well to words. Let me put it this way. When you're reading something, you can read it very superficially. *Lectio* is about going beyond that, it's not just, "oh, that's nice" and then put it away. This is more than that. You are letting it enter you, you are opening yourself to it and yes, you can become very, very moved by it. I've not personally been reduced to tears, but it's definitely something that results in a change within you. Afterwards I will walk around with a warmth, and when I return to that text, that warmth is still there.'

So, in *lectio*, Bible reading was not a search for the objective meaning of the words on the page, but an individual act of prayer, in which 'two people can get two separate things from the same "word of God" and still be both actually hearing God'. For this reason, it was suggested to me by the novice master that not everyone was receptive to *lectio* as a practice; 'not all have the mindset for it'. So the task of reading takes on a different complexion with different goals, as is clearly illustrated if we contrast *lectio* as a style of reading with Bible study involving the 'grammatico-historical method', particularly as described in Vincent Crapanzano's account of American fundamentalist Protestants. When they work through a text, they are searching for God's word to them, but there is a deliberate effort to ensure that the work of discovering meaning works towards a truth independent of the reader. 'There is but one true interpretation' (Crapanzano 2000: 67), and for the fundamentalists Crapanzano (2000: 64) describes, seeking this true interpretation involves working on the 'plain', 'ordinary', 'common sense' value of words. This means taking the approach that 'One should assume a literal interpretation unless there is some indication in the text to do otherwise' (2000: 65); here we are told that the 'literal' reading is opposed to the 'allegorical' reading, and those who attempt to read scripture as though it means something other than that which it appears to say are subject to suspicion. They are looking for God's intention in the text, and there is an acute sense of the danger of reading unintended meaning into a text. This model of textual authority emerges from a community of practice which places a strong emphasis on the absolute authority of Scripture independent of subjectivity (Bielo 2009: 52); that which is in the Bible is '"the Truth", "inerrant", "unswerving"'. This is made clear in the words of a South California seminary student quoted by Crapanzano (2000: 29–30): 'God had spoken to Adam and Eve in clear propositional truth. But the created being the serpent, who was indwelled by Satan himself at that point, came and spoke and caused Eve to question the word of the Creator, the revelation of the Creator. He caused her not to trust the word of God but rather to rely on her own judgement.' Little wonder, then, that *lectio divina* can itself be treated as an object of suspicion in its potential to repeat passages in search of 'echoes' with deeply individual resonances.

Indeed, uncertainty about *lectio* could be found within the community, albeit cutting in a different direction. One of the junior monks, talking about *lectio* with some of the guests at the monastery over tea, shared his concerns about the 'risk of idolatry': 'I don't want to end up worshipping the text, I want to worship God. It's one thing to be learning from the Bible and that's helping you to know God. It's quite another thing to become completely caught up in some kind of obsession with words on a page, rather than the living God. Isn't it meant to be the fundamentalists who are obsessed with the text?' More broadly, the distinction drawn above between *lectio* and reading for study was not as clear-cut among the monks as the descriptions above might suggest. During one conversation in the carpentry workshop, after one of the monks asked how my study of *lectio* was getting on, I took the opportunity to ask him whether he felt there was a real difference between *lectio* and other types of reading. His answer was emphatic: yes, there was a difference, because *lectio divina* was not *just* reading; it was prayer. You might read something in order to find out new information, or in order to broaden your mind, or for pleasure, but during *lectio*, you were reading in order to pray, in order to encounter God; reading was the setting for that encounter, and anything else was secondary to that. Nevertheless, he explained, not all of the community understood *lectio divina* in the same way: some of the monks just considered spiritual reading to mean 'sitting and working through an improving book'.

Tradition and renewal

Attention to the monastery as a community of readers shows how practice of reading is embedded in a daily rhythm of hearing the Word, and how such an ethnography of reading also requires an ethnography of listening (see also Robbins 2001). However, it is also important to see that a culture of reading is not monolithic; rather, we see distinct differences even within a community of practice. This is important because it makes clear that *lectio divina* is not simply an institutional norm into which individuals are inserted, but that we are looking at a dynamic tradition whose adoption and negotiation needs to be historically situated.

The novice master saw it as an important part of formation – not only as a practice in its own right but as a response to the call which begins the *Rule* of St Benedict: 'Listen, my son, to the master's instructions, and incline the ear of your heart.'[3] However, he also noticed that this was a relatively recent development in the life of the monastery. He had encountered *lectio* at university before entering the monastery in the 1970s, but when he asked his novice master for guidance, he found that his novice master knew nothing of *lectio* to teach him. In order to better understand the situation at that time, I was directed to *Consider Your Call* (Rees et al. 1978), the work of the English Benedictine Congregation Theology Commission in the light of the Second Vatican Council, and its call for religious congregations to 'renew themselves'.[4]

We see that '*Lectio divina* may be defined as a "slow meditative reading in search of a personal contact with God rather than mastery of an area of knowledge". But spiritual reading today is often regarded as an activity whose chief value lies outside itself, in its usefulness to some other monastic occupation; it might, for example, provide material or an intelligent direction for prayer or for the apostolate' (Rees et al. 1978: 267). So there is a recognition that

---

3 *Rule* of St Benedict, Prologue.
4 This call is the basis of the decree *Perfectae Caritatis*, promulgated in 1965 by Pope Paul VI after it had been formulated, discussed and voted upon during the Second Vatican Council.

the goal of reading for prayer had to some extent been displaced by the goal of reading as a means to access information,[5] and there is a sense that the reading that St Benedict instructs his monks to attend to daily in the *Rule* was not for the purposes of 'satisfaction of an avid curiosity for knowledge' (Rees et al. 1978: 268), but was considered 'nourishment' for the monks' faith.

There is some discussion in *Consider Your Call* of how to go about renewing the practice of *lectio* within the monasteries at a time when 'for many of us preparations for the academic and pastoral work which has taken the place of manual labour in our lives cannot often be easily distinguished from what we call spiritual reading' (1978: 270). However, the suggestions that more assistance could be offered in the study of scripture, by ensuring that better academic resources were at the monks' disposal, and bringing 'studies and spiritual reading ... into closer relation with one another so that ecclesiastical education could become more spiritual and spiritual reading more theological' does little to suggest how the technique of reading with slow attentiveness as a means of prayer could be developed in monastic life. Interestingly, there is no reference to Guigo II and the model used in his *Ladder of Monks*, even though at the time it was this model that was being increasingly picked up in the monastery as a way of approaching reading anew as a means of prayer. I was told that the message about this approach to *lectio* was disseminated in particular through the teaching of American Trappists (Cistercians of the Strict Observance) who were 'evangelical' about this approach to *lectio*, and 'drove the *lectio* movement' during this time, leading to individual members of the community learning about it and incorporating it into their own practice.

This historical contextualisation leads me to suggest that the rediscovery of *lectio divina* as part of monastic practice might be fruitfully examined in the light of the changes brought by the Second Vatican Council; it was, after all, the consideration of how the

---

5 It was explained to me that this reflected the 1933 constitutions of the Congregation, which took *lectio* to mean theological study. This was changed only following the Second Vatican Council.

monastic life might be renewed which leads to the questioning of the role of reading in the monastery that we can see above. I asked several of the monks what lay behind its revival; many pointed directly to documents of the Council by way of explanation. As one monk explained to me, '*Perfectae Caritatis* [the decree on the adaptation and renewal of religious life] calls for us to return to the sources, to return to the sources of Christian life, and of our particular ways of living the religious life. Well, *lectio* is a double return to the sources if you like. It's a return to the Bible, so the source of revelation, it's paying close attention to what the Bible says. And it's also a return to a deeply monastic tradition, something that is in the Rule and is part of our Benedictine and monastic heritage.'

So *lectio* comes to be seen as particularly appropriate in the context of monastic renewal. Another monk pointed to *Dei Verbum*, the constitution on Divine Revelation,[6] which urges a greater access and attention to scripture from all of the faithful, and more diligence in study and reading of scripture by the clergy: 'I think that call to a new awareness of scripture laid the way for the rediscovery ... of *lectio divina*. It is a call to be inspired by scripture, which is what lectio does.' Christopher Butler, a former abbot of the monastery who is acknowledged as a key contributor to *Dei Verbum*[7] in his role participating in the Second Vatican Council as Abbot President of the Congregation, has stressed that *Dei Verbum* attempted to bring to the foreground the personal aspect of revelation as encountered through scripture. 'God does not simply increase men's store of speculative knowledge; he addresses them as his friends and "holds converse with them" ... In communication between friends or lovers the personal element is always present, and it is often preponderant. Often the truth that my friend imparts to me, like the gift he gives me, is less valuable for its intrinsic content than for its source; and it brings me into an act of communion with this source, my friend' (Butler 1967: 27). As an anthropologist, I find an obvious

---

6 Another document promulgated in 1965 by Pope Paul VI after it had been formulated, discussed and voted upon at the Second Vatican Council.
7 For an account of Christopher Butler's role in the development of *Dei Verbum* see Wells (2002).

'echo' in this appeal to the idea of the gift. As Mauss ([1925] 1954: 10) famously wrote in relation to Maori gift exchange, 'To give something is to give a part of oneself ... to receive something is to receive a part of someone's spiritual essence.' Receiving a gift brings us into contact not only with the thing being given, but also with the person doing the giving, and a gift exchange is a means of forming relationships. If Butler speaks of reading scripture as though he was receiving a gift from a friend, it is because he can see the act of reading as the establishment of a relationship. It is this relational approach to reading that *lectio divina* seeks to cultivate.

Innovation and openness

So *lectio* is grounded in the spirituality of *Rule* and its rhythms of practice, while also being a fresh expression of that tradition whose development is ongoing. We can see this dynamism in the way the approach is open to innovation.

In a reflection that is relevant to Chapter 5's discussion of the relationship between prayer and day-to-day life, and the sense of contemplation as a 'spirituality for solitaries', Foster (2005: 113) notes that while Guigo II's schema ends with *contemplatio*, this may be more suitable for those 'in the enclosure of the hermitage' than for those of us who 'have to come back down the mountain and resume our normal occupations and responsibilities' – in other words, that prayer cannot be an escape but a means through which 'we learn to get back into ourselves'. This leads him to explore further 'moments' in *lectio*: *discretio* 'a consideration of the movement of the spirit in my life'; *deliberatio* 'a wider consideration of what God is doing in the broader circumstances of my life and the world around me' (2005: 130); and, ultimately, *actio* 'living by the word' (2005: 139). These elaborations are part of the approach to *lectio divina* taught by the Jesuit Cardinal and biblical scholar Carlo Maria Martini (1994), linking meditation on the Bible to an ethical commitment to the good. While in the day-to-day life of the monastery this approach did not displace the primacy of the four-stage model, nonetheless an openness to developments such as this is interesting. Firstly, it demonstrates that this is not a static tradition but a dynamic approach; secondly, because it speaks to ongoing reflection on the relationship between contemplation and action; indeed, Martini acknowledges that his approach draws on the insights of Ignatius Loyola's *Spiritual Exercises*, discussed in the previous chapter as an exemplar of the kataphatic approach to prayer.

A more visible demonstration of how *lectio* has the potential to reinvigorate the wider tradition of prayer in the monastery comes from recent development of *lectio* as a collective practice. During a field visit to the monastery in 2015, I was asked if I'd like to take part in 'group *lectio*' in the time between Vigils and Lauds – one of the 'half hours' for private prayer before breakfast has ended the *summum silentium*. A small group of four monks and myself sat around a dining table; the junior monk present lit candles on the table while copies of the Bible were handed out among the group. Following with a shared prayer to the Holy Spirit, and an act of contrition, a short passage from the Bible (taken from the scripture readings for the liturgy of that day) was read aloud. The majority of the time was then spent in periods of rereading and reflection in silence; but rather than the 'echoes' taking rest in the silence of private prayer, within the group dynamic those gathered shared aloud brief 'echoes' where the text had resonated with them, before concluding with the Lord's Prayer, and the sign of peace.

At its core, this experience was not a fundamental departure from *lectio* as I had learned it in my earlier fieldwork in the monastery, following the passage from *lectio* to *meditatio* to *oratio*. But as we took time to read together 'slow, then slower, then slower', the experience was one of listening in a state of shared intimacy; and notably, the move into *contemplatio* was clearly very different in character when there is an expectation of communication with the rest of the group, especially given the tradition of contemplative prayer discussed previously, which places contemplation 'beyond language' and beyond the images and concepts that communication draws upon. This silence was not a step into solitude but a gathering in which the quiet opened vocal expressions of prayer before returning to act within the world in the day to come.

This use of the half hour was an interesting demonstration of openness to innovation and inspiration from new expressions of Benedictine life. The adaptation of *lectio* from an individual to a shared practice – the slow praying of scripture together, sharing the ways in which the text speaks to you, and allowing that to lead the community into prayer – comes from the Manquehue movement,[8] founded in Chile in 1977 by José Manuel Eguiguren as a lay movement inspired by the *Rule* of St Benedict (Barry 2005). Early on in the development of the movement, the founder travelled to England and established a close relationship with the English Benedictine Congregation. This relationship is ongoing, and sees monks travel to Chile to participate in the work of the lay communities there, while at the same time members of the Manquehue movement travel to England to stay in the monasteries there and to participate in the routine of monastic life. While a great deal could be said about the movement which would be an important object of study in its own right, for the benefit of the ethnographic account in this chapter, two things are worth noting. Firstly, the importance of the principle that the Benedictine idea (and, in particular, the English Benedictine model of that idea) can provide an inspiration for lay life. Secondly – and here we return to *lectio divina* – it is interesting to see that the inspiration is two-way traffic; it is not only that the English Benedictines feel that they have inspired the lay movement, but also that they draw upon the life of the lay community within their own spiritual practice.

In conversation after group *lectio*, it was notable that in explaining the structure of their sessions and the practical logistics of how to do this as a group the monks repeatedly referred to lessons learned from the lay community and, in speaking about the value of this relatively new addition to their timetable, they took direct inspiration from the way that visitors from the movement had run group *lectio*

---

8   He himself had learned it from the guest master at the Benedictine monastery of Las Condes in Santiago, Chile, so the vector by which it has passed from monk to layperson and then from lay community back to monastic community is interesting.

with students in the monastery school. Indeed, at a talk given by one of the monks on *lectio* in the monastery visitor centre, it was striking not only that discussion of personal *lectio* (which was the dominant way of describing *lectio* during my main time in the field) opened out into group *lectio*, but that the monk giving the talk, when answering questions, deferred to the experience of a Manquehue community member in the audience, and on several occasions asked if they could add to his answer or answer for him: a demonstration of the community's 'democratising' attitude to prayer as a core value.

Slowness and the social life of reading

What does it mean to go slow? Parkins (2004), pondering the kind of spaces where slowness can exist, asks whether it is possible to prevent the slow being eaten by the fast. The immediate context for Parkins' reflection is the gradual development of the 'slow food' movement, which has grown from its origins as an organisation set up to resist the opening of a McDonald's near the Spanish Steps in Rome, to an international organisation and ideal, attempting to reconnect the consumption of food with the (local) means of production, and to give people 'more time around the table', such that they shift away from cultures of convenience towards a culture in which they are conscious of the act of consumption, the nature of the things being consumed, and their relationship with them (see also Pink 2009). This is a deliberate attempt to re-engage with taken-for-granted acts by *slowing down the pace*.

Pietrykowski (2004) speaks of the modifier 'slow', when placed before the word food in this way, as a means of reconnection, and this modifier has since peeled off to become affixed to wider forms of 'slow living' and 'slow sociality' (Vergunst and Vermehren 2012). This desire to reconnect through slowness is an attempt to find a way of renegotiating the dynamics of a world that leaves us increasingly pressed for time (Wajcman 2014); an active questioning of the way we come to produce and consume in everyday life. It is little wonder, then, monks discerned a wider appetite for *lectio divina*. As an attempt not only to derive nourishment from scripture but to take time to savour the taste, it conjures in the imagination an idealised contrast between a world rushing around and the monastery as a still centre. And indeed it resonated with the desires of many who visited the monastery, looking for just this opportunity for slowness in their lives.

In 2017 BBC Four broadcast a series of films entitled *Retreat: Meditations from a Monastery* answering this hunger. The first of the series was a beautiful film of stillness and prayer at Downside: the absorption in work and contemplation, the peaceful sounds of the gardens, the silence of the abbey broken only by the slow footsteps of a monk making careful preparations for the liturgy ahead. I found it deeply atmospheric. But it was perhaps to be expected that the monks had quite a different experience of things in the presence of the cameras. They recalled the experience of the filming as 'very dull': 'I remember I had to eat lots of bowls of porridge until they got the shot they wanted. Very hard work.' Crucially, one monk pointed to the gap between the idealised representation and the reality. 'It was all part of "slow television" and … it wasn't quite a true version of our life, but that's what they wanted and that's what they gave them, hence it was rather slow, not much talking going on, when we relate to one another very much with talk and laughing and jokes, relating.' Strikingly, slowness here was experienced as *disembedding* – a detachment from the movements, the rhythms, and the sociality of life.

By contrast, slowness and silence in *lectio divina* were understood not as an end in themselves but as the space to listen. You are letting the sound enter you and act upon you. As noted above, I was told to read through the text, 'hearing each word in your mind as though you were reading aloud'; this idea that you should *listen* to the words you were reading, as though they were being spoken, was a recurring theme in the monks' advice. Just as Pink (2009) describes the potential for 'reappropriating the senses' through slowness, it was clear that the increased involvement of the auditory senses was a key element of this slow reading. The text seen on the page becomes a voice to be heard. This embeds reading as a social relationship: 'Perhaps the first step in learning to listen to the scriptures as the word of God is to think of ourselves, as it were, in the synagogue in Nazareth, listening to Jesus read them to us' (Foster 2005: 21). Yet this itself relies on a social life of reading that recasts the written word as a sound to be encountered in daily life; in the books read during the meals shared in the refectory, in the nightly reading of the *Rule*, and in the cycles of the liturgy, such that we are always returning to listen again from the beginning.

PART III

Flight from the world?

CHAPTER 7

Work and pray

The morality of work

What is meant by the word 'work' when it is used in the monastery? In a fundamental sense, the role of work is made clear in Chapter 48 of the *Rule* of St Benedict: 'Idleness is the enemy of the soul. Therefore the brothers should be occupied at certain times in manual labour, and again at fixed hours in sacred reading.' This provides the basis for the understanding that work (or, more specifically, *manual* work) is, along with reading and prayer, a key part of the daily routine and moral framework of the monastery. Of course, in the English Benedictine setting, with the missionary orientation that goes back to its seventeenth-century revival, work has often taken on the more specific connotation of apostolic work in the service of wider Catholic society, with monks in pastoral roles as teachers or parish priests. And there is also a third sense given to the word 'work': the 'work of God' (*opus Dei*), which is the term the *Rule* uses to refer to the praying of the Divine Office as a core occupation of the monastic day. This chapter is concerned with the interaction between these three senses of 'work', and what they reveal about the dynamics of stability and community living.

Each weekday afternoon I would make my way out to the carpentry workshop, a wooden building on the monastery grounds. Sometimes, given his commitments as a parish priest, the monk in charge of the workshop would be called away on parish business, and the door would be locked. But more often the door would open, the smell of sawdust and varnish in the air. As soon as the sound of the bandsaw paused, I would generally be greeted with the words 'Hello, feel free to help yourself to something from the tin' – a tin of chocolate and other sweets sat in the rafters, continuously restocked with gifts from parishioners, and we would eat away at this chocolate as we worked (except during Lent, when the tin was left bare, ready to be filled again at Easter).

In one corner, scrap wood leaned up against the wall, waiting to be repurposed. Along the wall were various table saws, a lathe, and a planing machine, though I mostly moved between the rows of hand tools, handles smoothed to the grip through decades of use. Here too, we were in the presence of past members of the community who had worked in this space; around us were memorial cards requesting prayers for the repose of their souls. And above us always was the crucifix and the clock.

The first task I was given was to cut and shape hangers for vestments – essentially oversized coat hangers, as normal coat hangers might damage the vestments or break under the weight. We would cut the rough shape of the hangers out of reclaimed oak floorboards that had been donated to the monastery. I then planed the surfaces, used a spokeshave to round the edges and sandpaper to smooth the edges and clean the wood. Any remaining marks or unevenness in the rounding were gently brought to my attention so that I could continue the process. It took a couple of months to complete all of the required hangers. Somewhat frustratingly, I subsequently learned that, after my fieldwork, when there had been a change of abbot, whatever need had existed for these hangers was no longer felt, and they were languishing in a sacristy cupboard. Why these hangers were the victim of regime change I will never know, but of course the repetition was also about learning a process and growing in familiarity with the environment of a monastic workshop. I watched and followed the movements of the monk, attempting to see how he stood, how he held the tools, and then to embody for myself what he had done.[1]

1 On the process of learning through movement in woodworking, see Marchand (2010).

I grew comfortable with the tools and with shaping wood, and my hands were suitably roughened for work.

This allowed me to move on to helping with ongoing projects. We repaired chairs for the refectory, built bookshelves for new acquisitions in the library, a footbridge to go over the pond in the garden, a carved memorial cross for the parish cemetery. Generally, I would carry out necessary but basic tasks on these projects, freeing the monk to consider more involved and complex tasks. We sometimes received commissions to work on specific projects. The major project during my time in the field was a lectern of Columbian pine built to be in keeping with the architecture of a church designed by the artist Eric Gill. An important point to make here is that because carpentry was not a primary source of income for the monastery, the workshop was not subject to the basic premises of time capitalism. This meant we could take on orders that would have been economically unviable for commercial firms. The work, having been freed from some of the pressures of the market, could be carried out to exacting standards, the absorbed process an offering to God.

Applebaum (1992: 580–81), reviewing the ways in which Benedictine monasticism has interpreted and shaped the concept of work, draws our attention to the spiritual value of labour: 'the morality of work as a means to combat sin, and work as honorable in the image of God, the master craftsman and architect of the world'. There is clearly an economic aspect to this, in the sense that the monastery as envisaged by the *Rule* is a self-sufficient unit, requiring material sustenance and maintenance; but it is noteworthy that the *Rule* foregrounds the moral dimension. Indeed, Asad (1993: 151), focusing on monastic work as a regime to which one is subjected for the means of reconstituting the self, goes so far as to argue that 'it was precisely humiliation that constituted the point of manual labor, not its economic instrumentality'. But, in a context where God is encountered in the fabric of daily life, this emphasis on the abject quality of labour is surely to miss the point, which lies in work's sacred potential. For Rembert Sorg (1951: 17), a Benedictine monk of the American-Cassinese Congregation, within the framework of the monastic sanctification of life itself, work is 'spiritualized and exceedingly nobled', even a means of participating in the creative act of God: 'Manual labor, which produces, develops, processes and distributes the goods of the earth, continues and completes the work of creation' (1951: 22). From this perspective, it is not that the monk is lowered by work, but that the understanding of work is elevated: that which was considered menial comes to be known as holy.

Certainly, the workshop was a place with a patina of prayer, not only in the accumulation of religious images but in the deliberate and purposeful direction of the body; a care and attention to the work being carried out that echoed the careful movement around the abbey church and the attention to detail of the liturgy.[2] There was an atmosphere of respect as befits a monastic space – if I swore after making a mistake or cutting myself, this was met with a stern rebuke ('Language, Richard ...') – and a meditative sense of absorption through focused repetition. Crucially (and again in a way that pulls against Asad's emphasis on humiliation), this was pleasurable. As Marchand (2022) argues in his ethnography of fine woodworking in England, there is a moral dimension to the pursuit of pleasurable work. To work closely and carefully with materials by hand was an aesthetic pursuit of connection in place of the alienation of work driven by economic motives alone; a desire for meaningful engagement with the world and a purposeful way of living. In the monastery, this pleasure went hand in hand with the reverential character of work: the high degree of attention to the process, the craftsman's respect for his materials and close attention to detail. My attempts to check that I had completed a given task to my own satisfaction

---

2 Strikingly, in his account of artisans and their apprentices in Crete, Herzfeld (2004: 43) quotes a floor maker's remark that in the old days craftsmen 'regarded work as a church'. This respect for the workshop elevates carpentry beyond simple economic activity, and towards a means of what Herzfeld calls 'schooling the body'. By this he appears to mean, along lines similar to Asad, that the individual comes to incorporate within himself the appropriate way in which to behave. This is achieved through a process of repetition and control, which Herzfeld himself suggests is heir 'to long traditions of monastic discipline with a deep concern with the control of bodily movement and desire' (2004: 42).

met with positive reinforcement: 'there is nothing more important than a craftsman's satisfaction with his work', and I was told that 'even if nobody else sees these things [details], the angels will see them'. And, above all, I was reminded to consider what I was doing an offering to God.

However, this manual labour was essentially peripheral to the monastery's main concerns. For the monk I worked with, it was not his principal duty under the vow of obedience; that was his role as a parish priest. Having locked up and gone to the refectory for tea, me with varnish all over my hands and jeans, and the monk still in his blue boiler suit, we would sometimes receive bemused looks and enquiries as to what exactly we had been up to. Other monks, of course, engaged in manual labour. For example, one took on engineering repairs and maintenance around the monastery, while others engaged in gardening. But the general picture was this was secondary to the monastery's focus on apostolic work. For Sorg (1951), the necessary place of manual labour in the Benedictine life is an expression of the Christianisation of that which had been considered servile – even an imitation of the servility of Christ, who washed the feet of his apostles. Sorg writes in the context of a monastic community with a strong agricultural element, a context which more immediately aligns with the call for the monks to 'live by the labour of their hands'[3] than at Downside, where the majority of estate maintenance, cleaning, and the provision of food was outsourced to lay staff, with the monks serving one another in the refectory at the end of this food chain. Such a division of labour implicates monks as the overseers of those who work with their hands, separating those who can devote themselves to spiritual work from those who support them in more material matters (see also Asad 1993: 148–53 on such divisions of labour in medieval monasticism). What can be said, then, of the labour of the monks? In English Benedictine history the impetus towards service remains, but was primarily redirected towards a particular goal: the service of the church through the care of souls.

3 *Rule* of St Benedict, Chapter 48.

Monk and priest

At Downside, the vocation to the monastic life has almost invariably gone hand in hand with a vocation to the priesthood.[4] All monks in the community were either ordained as priests or were undertaking study for the priesthood. This reflected the direction of the Congregation and the expectation that those entering the monastery understood the kinds of priestly work they might be asked to take on.

In June 2007 one of the monks of the community received the sacrament of Holy Orders. He had made his solemn profession prior to my arrival, but he was still studying for the priesthood throughout my fieldwork. I had got used to calling him 'Brother', but now I had to learn to call him 'Father'. As with the solemn profession described in Chapter 1, we can analyse this as a rite of passage with elements of phases of separation, margin, and aggregation (van Gennep 1909; Turner 1969). However, when compared with the solemn profession, the symbolism and direction is different even as core elements are shared.

Before the rite of ordination, the monk is separated from his community. He leaves his monastery in order to spend some days in private retreat, preparing himself for his admission to the priesthood. This time is usually spent at another religious house; in this case, the monk made his retreat at a Cistercian abbey elsewhere in England before returning to his own monastery to be ordained.

The service of ordination is a public occasion, with friends and family in the congregation. The chanting of the monks is at the heart of the liturgy, but participation extends beyond the boundaries of the monastic community. As the congregation sang the entrance hymn to the accompaniment of an organist who was a lay teacher at the school, the monastic community processed into the abbey church, joined by monks of other Benedictine monasteries, members of other religious orders, and diocesan priests. The rite of ordination takes place in the context of a community Mass, concelebrated by

---

4 See Sorg (1951: 53–4) for a discussion of the history of the clericalisation of monastic life and its impact.

all of the priests present as a single body without any distinction of Congregation or Order, each wearing similar vestments. At the rear of the procession followed the abbot, the ordinand, and the bishop of the diocese – invited to the abbey church to perform the sacrament, as only a bishop may ordain someone to the priesthood.

After the Gospel has been read, all remained standing as the candidate was presented to the bishop by the abbot on behalf of the monastic community. Having accepted the candidate, the bishop then addressed a homily to him, reminding all – but the candidate in particular – of the duties of priesthood, and the pastoral responsibilities of the priest within the church: 'to teach, to sanctify, to shepherd'. The bishop then began his ritualised examination. In each question, the focus was on the responsibility of the priest for *the care of others*: is the candidate resolved to carry out the work of the priesthood as a fellow worker with the bishops? Is the candidate resolved to celebrate the mysteries of Christ (the sacraments) 'as the Church has handed them down'? Is the candidate resolved to preach the word of God? Is the candidate resolved to consecrate his life to God 'for the salvation of his people'? Having responded 'I am' to these questions, the candidate knelt before the bishop, who asked him, 'Do you promise respect and obedience to your Ordinary?; Here, it is worth noting that, as priests within the monastery fall under the jurisdiction of their abbot (to whom they vow obedience during their profession), the wording used when ordaining monks is slightly different from the wording used when ordaining diocesan priests, who promise respect and obedience to the bishop. So although the ordination must be carried out by a bishop, after ordination it is the abbot who determines the priest's work.

Following this promise, the candidate prostrated himself on the floor before the altar, as the community chanted a litany in Latin. The saints called upon included several Benedictine saints, two of whom (St John Roberts and St Ambrose Barlow) were members of the monastic community, martyred while serving as missionary priests in England during the seventeenth century.

The candidate then rose from his prostrate position and knelt before the bishop, who laid his hands on the candidate's head in silence. Each of the other priests present came forward in turn to do the same, after which the bishop recited the Prayer of Consecration. The newly ordained priest was presented with the vestments of his new office, the stole and chasuble, and his hands were anointed with the holy oil of Chrism.[5]

As highlighted above, the public nature of the service expresses the expansive connection of the newly ordained monk with the wider world. This is shown not only in the presence of the bishop and many fellow clergy, but also in more intimate ways, such as the inclusion of friends as readers during the liturgy of the word. The offertory also expresses these social connections: as a friend of the monk, I was asked to help by carrying the wine to be offered in the Mass to the altar, alongside a family member carrying the bread. The bishop received the offerings and presented them to the priest he had just ordained, who then receives the kiss of peace from the bishop and each and every one of the other priests present. Meanwhile the girls' choir of the school – a choir which the newly ordained priest helped to direct – sang a piece by Mendelssohn. Mass then continued with the liturgy of the Eucharist: the consecration of the bread and wine by the priests gathered around the altar, to be received by those who have come to the abbey to share in this day.

Once the service was at an end, the gathered congregation continued the festivities. In a hall outside of the enclosure, the monastic community provided a spread of food and a reasonable quantity of wine to aid the celebrations. As the monks, non-monastic clergy, and laity mixed freely around the tables, I approached my friend carrying a medal of St Benedict and asking for it to be blessed – one of many seeking out a 'first blessing' from the newly ordained priest.

The next day in the abbey church, the priest celebrated his first Mass after ordination, offered in thanksgiving for the gift of priesthood. This marks the beginning of the monk's priestly duties and his incorporation into a new social role.

---

5   Chrism is scented olive oil, blessed by the bishop in the cathedral before the gathered priests of the diocese on Holy Thursday.

What do we learn from this ritual? As one of the other monks explained in a sermon shortly after the ordination, the monk who was ordained 'was filled with a special gift – the gift of the dignity of the priesthood. The gift of the priesthood is not a gift for oneself but a gift to enable one to preach the gospel, to bring the good news of Jesus Christ to others, by always being a model of right conduct.' There is clearly an expansion of responsibility and of social engagement, beyond *conversatio morum* and the individual's growth within the community to moral involvement in a wider sphere.

In this regard, it is interesting to return to the solemn profession described in Chapter 1 and, as suggested before, to compare the two. The most notable feature, as highlighted before, is the active involvement of the wider Church in the ritual, especially in the person of the bishop, over and beyond the focus on the monastic family. The fact that the ordination *follows* the separation of the three-day retreat places the rite closer to the re-incorporation of the monk in their new role; whereas the solemn profession *preceding* the monk's 'going to the tomb' locates that rite more closely to the monk's separation from this world. And, of course, it is notable that while the monk lies prostrate in both, the emphasis on elements of death (the funeral pall, going to the tomb) is not present in the ordination; the rite is not funerary in nature, but directed towards life in the world.

So if solemn profession resonates with the monks' funeral, it is interesting to see that, by contrast, monks of the community have pointed out the connection between ordination and marriage. This was made most clear to me when it was recommended I read a guide to courtship (Watkin 1958) by a monk who was, when he wrote the book, headmaster of the school run by the monastery. Monks do not, at first glance, seem the most suitable people to write manuals for romance. But reading of a desire that strives to give itself totally, of the pitfalls of anxiety, insecurity and jealousy, and ultimately of the choice between selfishness and love, it became clear that this was anchored in a sense of the common, though distinct, character of the vocations of priesthood and marriage. As Watkin explains, matrimony is the mutual giving of love by man and woman to one another, while, 'To be ordained is to be a priest of love: not only by imparting love as minister of most of the sacraments of the Church, but by ministering love to all men' (1958: 112). So 'Holy Orders and Matrimony are twin sacraments of love and should be considered together, for both are directly concerned with the spread of God's kingdom of love' (1958: 111).

The missionary oath

In the Chapel of St Vedast, one of the side chapels dedicated in 1888, the stained-glass windows depict two events in English Benedictine history. As described in Chapter 2, this is part of a wider assertion of the stability of monastic identity within English history. But here, a specific continuity is being asserted. The upper window depicts Pope Gregory the Great (himself a monk, and the author of the hagiographical *Life* of St Benedict) sending Augustine (later known as St Augustine of Canterbury) and a group of monks to Kent at the end of the sixth century; a key moment in the history of England's conversion to Christianity. The lower window shows Abbot Philip de Cavarel giving a charter to the monastic community of St Gregory the Great in the seventeenth century from which exiled monks could return to work for the reconversion of England. The parallel is clear: the Benedictine presence in England has always been missionary.

As briefly outlined in Chapter 1, the origins of the current English Benedictine Congregation lie in exile (see Lunn 1980). Following the reformation and dissolution of the monasteries, English and Welsh men continued to enter monasteries on the European continent, particularly those of the Spanish and Cassinese Congregations. These monks petitioned Rome to be allowed to return as missionaries to their own people. This permission was granted to monks of the Cassinese Congregation in 1601 and to monks of the Spanish Congregation in 1602. Growing numbers entered monasteries on the continent in order to join this missionary work, leading to the establishment of houses specifically for these English and Welsh monks in the Spanish Netherlands and in France – as commemorated in the stained-glass window described above, depicting Philip de Cavarel, Abbot of St Vedast, Arras, who endowed the community and built the community's first church and monastery at Douai. This 'revived' English Congregation grew in size, leading to attempts to unify it with the English elements of the Spanish and Cassinese Congregations. Lengthy negotiations eventually led to the papal recognition of a restored English Congregation in 1619. Missionary work in England played an extremely large role in the life of the Congregation, with life on the mission being the ultimate destination of the majority of those who entered the monastic life. The Papal Bull *Plantata* issued in 1633 by Pope Urban VIII ratified the Congregation's missionary mandate and confirming the monks' 'Missionary Oath'.

'We are the direct and sole descendants and inheritors of St Augustine and his companions … There are far more persons in England to be converted to (true) Christianity at the present day than there were when St Augustine landed on the shores of Kent … In 1891 the population of England and Wales was 29,000,000, and if we deduct the 1,500,000 Catholics, it will leave 27,500,000 who did not know their right hand from their left; or, what is worse, who mistook their right hand for their left, and their left hand for their right.'[6] This was the view of Alphonsus Morrall, a monk of the community who had spent considerable time on the mission and, more locally to Downside, initiated the construction of the village's Catholic church in 1857 as a point of missionary contact between the monastery and the surrounding population. His assertion of the fundamental missionary character of the English Benedictine Congregation, and the importance of this work, came at a time of heated debate among the monks (see also Irvine 2010b). As noted in Chapter 1, the history of this conflict was one of the very first things I was directed to when I arrived at Downside, precisely because it played a crucial role in defining English Benedictine identity and the interpretation of monastic stability. For this reason, it is worth examining the debate in some detail.

6 In a letter of 23 May 1899 to the monks of Downside, Morrall Vol. 6, 239–41, Downside Archives.

A visitation[7] of the Congregation on the instructions of Pope Leo XIII in 1881 became a flashpoint in a growing conflict between those who sought to maintain this missionary identity, and those who questioned the existence of an oath by which monks were sent to live on parishes away from the monastery and the structure by which the monasteries themselves were subordinate to an overall Congregational hierarchy whose focus was on this missionary labour. Those eager for change used the visitation as an opportunity to express their views, while those who supported the existing structure and focus felt the visit was a prelude to unwanted reform – especially given the perceived sympathy of the visitor, Prior Krug of Monte Cassino, to the more reform-minded. Having been informed of Krug's view that 'One abbey would constitute more to the conversion of England, than all the missionary residences put together',[8] Alphonsus Morrall's response to this is emphatic – in the margins of his notes on Krug's report, he writes 'Bosh!' Those who sought to protect the missionary tradition were clearly frustrated by the idea that monks 'are to be sent to their monasteries to pray there all day, and leave the salvation of souls to seculars [diocesan clergy]'.[9]

The most open expression of his conflict was in the form of a pamphlet war, with both sides of the debate seeking to influence an audience within and beyond the Congregation, not only in England but also in Rome. The first of these pamphlets, distributed in August 1881, was *The Missionary Work of the Benedictines*, by Benedict Snow, an official within the Congregation who served on the mission. Snow paints a picture of the disintegration of the Roman Empire. Among the desolation and ruin, he writes, 'one power remained undisturbed … and that power was the monk'. He sees Benedictine monks taking up the work of regeneration: 'sent forth as apostles and Missionaries', they 'commenced that wondrous resuscitation and

7 A visit for the purpose of inspection by someone acting as a representative of the Pope.
8 O'Gorman's notes on Krug's Diaries, Morrall Vol. 1, 139, Item 451, Downside Archives.
9 O'Gorman, Letter of 29 June 1881, Morrall Vol. 6, 83, Item 456, Downside Archives.

reconstruction that the world has not before or since witnessed'. It is this understanding of history which allows Snow to claim that the Order was 'brought into existence by Divine Providence for a great Missionary work'.[10] By this view, Benedictines are agents of social transformation. The monk is not set apart from the history of civilisation, having retreated to his monastery. Instead, he has a significant role in shaping that history.

Beyond this assertion of historic purpose, there was also a question of the Congregation's survival and continuing health. Through the missions the monk 'makes the Abbey and the Order known … he fosters and spreads love for the Monastic life, thereby, through the blessing of God, inducing vocations'.[11] And alongside the need for vocations, there is also a need for material and financial security. It is from this perspective that Austin Bury, in *Le Consequenze Funeste alla Congregazione Anglicana della Perdita della sue Missioni*,[12] published anonymously in December 1881 (in Italian, with an intended Vatican audience), warns of the dangers of disengaging from missionary activity. While pointing out the 'serious evils' of 'depriving Catholics of the services of so many zealous priests',[13] he also argues that giving up the missions would lead to a large increase in expenses, as many more monks would need to be materially supported within the monasteries, while at the same time 'diminishing their profits',[14] depriving the Congregation of the income that the missions provide. The transactional logic here is stark: a recognition of the reciprocal relationship between the monks and a wider world within which they must survive (Silber 1995). The threat to withdraw from the missions is 'something that will head

---

10 Snow, *The Missionary Work of the Benedictines*, privately published pamphlet, 9.
11 *The Missionary Work of the Benedictines*, privately printed pamphlet, 21.
12 I have used the translation by Gilbert Dolan, which is found in Butler Box M (Item 789), Downside Archives, for all quotations, and page numbers here refer to that translation.
13 *Le Consequenze Funeste*, 8.
14 *Le Consequenze Funeste*, 6.

down the trunk of our Congregation and dry up its very roots'.[15] Anselm O'Gorman, who would become President of the Congregation in 1883, shares these fears in a letter of 1881: 'If our missions are cut off, we are doomed as a Congregation – we shall die out – go to the wall.'[16]

But can such engagement be justified if it entails an abandonment of the monk's vows? For those seeking reform, the very existence of a missionary oath undermined monastic stability. The next pamphlet to enter the fray (printed and distributed in English and Italian) was by Francis Weld, a priest who earlier in life had entered the novitiate at Downside, but had left out of frustration with the quality of religious life possible in the Congregation. Having given a retreat at Downside in 1880, Weld believed his views were shared by many in the community: 'I call myself "Their voice".'[17] His pamphlet attempts to convey the complete and lifelong separation from the cloister experienced by members of the Congregation. Sent on the mission a few years after being clothed, the monk 'is ordered to quit his monastery, never more to return. They never do return.'[18] As Weld points out – 'a case is hardly to be found of one ever returning to his monastery'[19] after being translated to the mission.

A preoccupation with service to the world had led to compromise with the world, it was argued. Weld claims that monastic observance is almost completely abandoned in the houses of missionary monks: 'The floors, the stairs, every part luxuriously carpeted; the choicest furniture; the house is really like the private residence of a gentleman of fortune.'[20] It is alleged that nothing has been done to keep up the spirit of monasticism among the missioners, and the monks are placed in serious danger of being corrupted by the world in which they live. 'Ladies ... go upstairs, downstairs, anywhere.' The missioners

15 *Le Consequenze Funeste*, 9.
16 In Letter of 29 June 1881, in Morrall Vol. 6, 84, Item 456, Downside Archives.
17 Weld, *The English Benedictines*, privately published pamphlet, 12.
18 *The English Benedictines*, 11.
19 *The English Benedictines*, 5.
20 *The English Benedictines*, 25.

'are contented with their lot, and find pleasure in the fleshpots of Egypt'.[21] Little wonder, then, that Weld's pamphlet was labelled as 'libellous'[22] in a reply by Bede Prest, Deputy President of the Congregation, and a petition was sent to the President, signed by Alphonsus Morrall and others, which states, 'If this ... writer had visited our Missions in Liverpool and those among the Colliers of the North of England and of the South of Wales, he would never have compared the work of the Mission in England to "the fleshpots of Egypt".'[23] Elsewhere, in response to Weld's views, Morrall lists the martyrs of the Congregation who suffered death while serving on the English mission.[24] Indeed, monks continued to die as martyrs of charity working in the crowded cities of nineteenth-century England; Burke (1910) records the death of four Benedictines in Liverpool's 1840 and 1847 typhus outbreaks.

Weld printed another pamphlet in May 1882, this time with the text not by himself, but by an unnamed Benedictine monk – subsequently attributed[25] to Elphege Cody, who had been professed at Downside, but in 1879 left to seek a monastery whose life was more in keeping with the *Rule*. Cody, writing in direct response to Snow's defence of missionary life, follows Weld in decrying the dominance of the missions. 'In England "the mission" ... is the one absorbing interest. To supply its ravenous appetite monasteries are thinned down to their lowest possible number, studies and other employments must give way to its interests.'[26]

This was a common theme among those who believed the Congregation had lost its fundamentally Benedictine identity: in the

---

21 *The English Benedictines*, 6.
22 Prest, *Notes on the Pamphlet 'I Benedettini Inglesi'*, privately published pamphlet, 12.
23 Petition to the President in Morrall Vol. 1, 314, Downside Archives.
24 Morrall Vol. 5, 291, Downside Archives.
25 See Theodore James' Bibliography of the Controversy of 1880–1900 (which incorporates bibliographical notes by Cuthbert Butler), in the papers of Cuthbert Butler, Box C, Item 3560, Downside Archives.
26 *A Reply to 'The Missionary Work of the Benedictines'*, privately published pamphlet, 11–12.

words of Cuthbert Butler, a key advocate for change in the Congregation (and subsequently Abbot of Downside), 'The monasteries had come to be ... little more than seminaries to provide priests for the mission'.[27] What was at stake here was the extent to which the commitment to missionary work should be allowed to fundamentally alter the character of Benedictine life as a life spent in community, growing across the life-course within a family through the vow of stability.

Butler's contribution to the pamphlet war, commissioned by his prior, Edmund Ford, was *Notes on the Origin and Early Development of the Restored English Benedictine Congregation, 1660–1661*, the publication of which, Butler tells us, was felt to be a 'declaration of war'[28]. Butler does not deny that the Congregation had as its goal the preservation and propagation of the Catholic faith in England, but draws attention to the intention that the Congregation should exist in continuity with the Benedictine life which existed in England before the Reformation. For Butler, this was a point of great significance, leading him to argue that any 'differences which may exist ... are accidental; for no essential difference could be introduced without loss of identity'.[29] A central argument here is that no particular work should be seen as an essential characteristic of Benedictine life: it is life in community itself which is the essential characteristic. While the Congregation committed itself to missionary labour to meet the challenges of the times, Butler argued that this should not be seen as the abandonment of a monastic for a missionary identity. The monastic life was never a 'mere gate to the mission'.[30] Rather, the mission was understood as a temporary undertaking to be carried out without abandoning the continuation of monastic observance. Why would monks be asked to promise

---

27 Butler, 'The Downside Movement', notes from February 1905, 8, in Butler Box B, Item 1435, Downside Archives.
28 Butler, 'The Downside Movement', notes from February 1905, 51.
29 Butler, *Notes on the Origin and Early Development of the Restored English Benedictine Congregation, 1600–1661*, privately printed pamphlet, 7.
30 Butler, *Notes on the Origin and Early Development of the Restored English Benedictine Congregation, 1600–1661*, 49.

obedience, stability, and *conversatio morum* from the earliest days of the Congregation's restoration if the intention was that monks would always be deprived of the opportunity to live according to those vows, sent after a few years to live away from their monastery for the rest of their lives?

'After a life of nearly three centuries, after passing through a revolution ... after a return of the monasteries to England, it would surely be affectation to pretend there is nothing to amend, no adjustment to altered circumstances called for.'[31] This argument for change ultimately won out, in the sense that the Bulls *Religiosus Ordo* (in 1890) and *Diu Quidem* (in 1899) restructured the constitution and structure of the Congregation. The missionary oath was abolished, the monasteries were raised to the status of self-governing abbeys, no longer subject to the government of an overall Congregational hierarchy, and the Missions placed under the jurisdiction of the monasteries. Such reforms change the relationship between the monasteries and the work they carry out: the emphasis is on the autonomy of the community living together as a family as an end in itself, and not on the monastery as a vehicle for a particular form of work in the service of an overarching body.

Stanley Tambiah (1976: 362), in describing how the Thai Buddhist monk 'moves from wat [monastery] to wat in pursuit of his vocation' directly contrasts this with Benedictine stability and its attachment to place. He describes Thai monks' movement within a potential network of relations where 'active' ties of the past give way to newly established ties throughout a monastic career. 'Thus on the whole one can say that a monk's relations with his peers tend to be both short-lived and fragile, with his past patrons durable but sporadic, with his present sponsors frequent and continuing' (1976: 350). The contrast is important in defining the focus of the monastic life-course: on the one hand, as movement within an 'egocentric' (1976: 345) network of shifting ties activated and deactivated over a monastic career; on the other hand, as an enduring structure into which life cycles are enrolled. What the debate above reveals is the

---

31 Butler, *Notes on the Origin and Early Development of the Restored English Benedictine Congregation, 1600–1661*, 11–12.

tension generated by a mismatch between these models following the redirection of Benedictine life to a particular work – monks who have taken a vow of stability but then spend their life-course within a network of shifting relations owing to their missionary oath.

Following the allocation of parishes instructed by *Religiosus Ordo*, Downside had responsibility for 20 mission parishes, spread across the country. This remained an important element of the monks' work, though, over the subsequent century, the majority of these parishes were handed over to diocesan priests. At the time of my fieldwork in 2006, only Beccles and Bungay in Suffolk and Little Malvern in Worcestershire survived as residual remains of the parish commitments requiring monks to live away from the house of profession, and in 2022 these too were relinquished. Yet as a fundamental question of English Benedictine identity, even in the absence of the missionary oath, the tension examined above remains.

This tension was clear in the novice master's ambivalence when talking to me about work. On the one hand, he was of the mind that work with people was better for monks than having them do 'factory-style' work – making jam doesn't necessarily strengthen the spiritual life, whereas contact with people does. However, when it comes to running parishes, he has seen it takes a special kind of person to do this. Such a monk has to have the discipline to manage their own timetable and create their own structure of prayer; here, he noted that Augustine Baker's teaching on prayer (see Chapter 5) was good preparation for this. Most, however, need the support of the community close at hand. Given these challenges, a short timescale for such parish work seems best, so that the monk doesn't experience a sense of estrangement from their community. But this is not always the best thing for the parish, which has its own need for stability – 'although if it comes to the personal salvation of the monk against the needs of a parish, the parish needs to be told "go hang!"' In the end, the monastery is only doing this work to assist, 'although the need of assistance is great, and something people have been martyred for, compared to which people missing Vespers seems a small sacrifice!'

The monastic school

One day in the archives, I was shown a photograph of Abbot Cuthbert Butler with a pitchfork in his hand, working the lands around the monastery. The picture is somewhat iconic: an image of renewed monastic life, of monks returning to their monasteries to live out the *Rule*.

Though the symbolism is clear, in reality the consequence of the reforms described above was not primarily a recentring of work around *labor manuum*. In fact, in the decades that followed, the key development was the growth of the school run by the monastery. Cuthbert Butler himself saw education as perhaps the most appropriate domain of work for a monastery in the twentieth century: 'it may be thought that the work in modern times which is most conformable in character to Saint Benedict's agriculture is the cultivation of the minds and characters of the young, the eradication of faults, and the implanting of virtues and of knowledge' (Butler 1919: 376). The compatibility was also in its apparent ability to preserve stability by providing a form of pastoral work in the vicinity of the monastery and its rhythms of communal life.

By the time of my fieldwork, while the headmaster of the school was a monk, the vast majority of teaching at the school was undertaken by lay staff; only one other member of the monastic community had a full-time teaching role, though three more had chaplaincy roles. Yet the historic significance of the school as a form of work, its association with the monks in the public eye, and its conjoined presence in the complex of buildings around the monastery meant that it exerted an influence on monastic life even though its operations involved fewer monks. A further significance was that historically the school had been an important place of recruitment to the monastic community: a number of the monks had been educated at the school before entering the monastery, though in recent decades this route had all but ceased – a change the monks attributed to a shift in discernment, with postulants entering the monastery at a later age rather than immediately after school.

Some form of school had been part of the community's work

since the earliest days of its establishment in exile. Birt (1902: 10), in his history of the Downside school, cites a letter written in 1624 by Rudesind Barlow, President of the Congregation, referring to a monastic school at Douai with around 50 youths of 'good family', housed in their own dormitory and with their own refectory, who 'come to learn Latin, singing, and music', and then return to their own country. Again, there is a transactional character here: the scholars were a source of revenue for the monastery;[32] and for wealthy English Catholics there was a possibility of sending their children for an education that was illegal at home.

During the period from 1900 to 1914, the number of boys at the school had doubled from 100 to 200, with a significant building programme to accommodate the expansion. This process of growth continued (reflecting something of a shift in focus from missionary parishes to the school), reaching a peak of around 600 students in the 1960s. There were around 450 students in the school at the time of my fieldwork. Significantly, this growth was accompanied by changes to the kind of education it offered.

The term 'public school', used for the most elite English independent schools, is a contested accolade. The attainment of this status is linked to the imitation and incorporation of a set of behaviours associated with schools reported on by the Clarendon Commission, a Royal Commission set up in 1864 to investigate the status and running of elite schools including Eton, Harrow, and Rugby. Crucially, these schools were seen by the Commission as providing not only an intellectual education, but also an education in character for the 'governing class' (see Simon 1974). Some of the important contributing elements of this education are outlined by Walford (1986): the importance of boarding at the school; the institution of a 'house system', where students are separated into a number of distinct residential and social groups to which they develop a sense of belonging; the establishment of a cadet corps in the school (now

---

32 The economic motivation is apparent in a letter of Leander Jones, prior of the community, cited by Birt (1902: 11–12): 'Necessity compels us to have as boarders with us some English youths committed to our care, whom their parents confide to us solely for the purpose of being brought up in good manners and learning.'

known as the 'Combined Cadet Force', formerly known as the 'Officers' Training Corps'); and the importance of extracurricular activities, especially sports (with particular sports, such as cricket and rugby, considered most in keeping with the ethos of the public school).

The important point here is that in the early twentieth century, the school run by the monastery systematically took on this symbolic apparatus of the public school. David Knowles, who entered the school as a student in 1910 and subsequently entered the monastic community in 1914, outlines this transformation in his autobiography (a closed archival manuscript held at Downside Abbey) – as we shall see, he presents this information to contextualise his subsequent unease about the direction of the community. Describing his return to school after the summer of 1912, he notes, 'The term began a new period in Downside history. The old organization was to be swept away and the basic elements of a public school put in its place: housemasters, house prefects and school prefects. In addition there was to be a changeover from Soccer to Rugger.'[33] Cricket was well established in the school; in the words of Benedict Snow (1903: 172) – a monk we encountered above in the debate around the Congregation's missionary identity – 'The anomaly of an English School without cricket has, we hope, never yet been attempted. A thoroughly national sport, it enters the national life, and is an important formation of the national character.' Clubs for a number of other sports began to be set up around this time, including a golf club which played at a nearby course, societies for shooting, and the Downside Beagles for fox hunting.[34] An Officers' Training Corps was established in 1909.

What does this mean in terms of the kind of work the monks were engaged in? As with the situation around missionary parishes, here again we see the shift Weber (1968: 1167) described whereby the monastic impulse is 'reinterpreted into a means, not primarily of attaining individual salvation in one's own way, but of preparing

---

33 Knowles, Autobiography (Part 1) 67, closed archive at Downside.
34 See Mangan and McKenzie (2006) on the importance of field sports to the idea of the elite school.

the monk for work on behalf of the hierocratic authority'; in other words, monastic life becoming, in service of the wider Church, a means to an external end rather than an end in itself. But here this takes on a particular character. In a national context where public schools dominate the higher-ranking domains of politics, the banking sector, the military, Civil Service, Foreign Service, and judiciary, this is a form of schooling which is about access to the elite (see Maxwell and Aggleton 2015). What is therefore interesting is the attempt to construct a simulacrum of a particular model in order to provide a route of elite education for Catholics within English society, and a direct claim to a social status from which Catholics had been excluded. The significance of such a simulacrum has been highlighted in a different context by Srivastava (1998), writing about the Doon School, an Indian school that deliberately adopted the style and pattern of the English public school as an apparatus through which to promote a particular ideal of Indian nationhood among boys who would become part of the Indian political and economic elite. Seeing how the English public school becomes the model for the public school of the post-colony, we recognise its potency in sustaining a privileged 'world apart' (see also Courtois 2018). In terms of what that means for the monastery in relationship with society, especially when we note these developments occurring at the same time as the grand architectural assertion of a restored role for monasticism and Catholicism in England (see Chapter 2), the school becomes a route for the assertion of prestige and the place of Catholicism at the elite levels of national life. The 'mission' of the English Benedictine Congregation is served by working to restore Catholicism's place within the social order.

Again, there was an ambivalence around this element of work for the contemporary community. On the one hand, many of the monks who had taught clearly felt a strong sense of the importance of this work, the value of a pastoral and pedagogical role, and the distinctiveness of an education offered in the environment of a religious community and its rhythm of prayer. Monks involved in teaching also spoke warmly of the bond some pupils retained after their time at the school. The annual return of many alumni for the Easter triduum at the abbey was eagerly anticipated, and invitations to weddings from former pupils were among the notices pinned outside the calefactory – indeed, several monks have been celebrants at these weddings (as one remarked with a chuckle, 'I think some of them are just interested in the chance of a day out and a good dinner'). On the other hand, there were open questions about the compatibility of the school as a form of work.

Some shared fundamental concerns about the place occupied by this work: 'Of course people discerning their vocation learn of the particular apostolate of the Congregation, and of course the abbot has responsibility for finding suitable work. But the point remains, it does not automatically come with a vocation to the monastic life that you'll be a capable teacher, or suited to working with the young.' In addition, foreshadowing concerns raised by the Independent Inquiry into Child Sexual Abuse (see Chapter 8), some pointed to the safeguarding issues inherent in having the buildings of a monastic residence connected to those of a school.

Others reflected on the compatibility of the school with stability and *conversatio morum*. 'The school gives the illusion of stability, because the monks are working on site as it were. But it's just that, an illusion.' In fact, the novice master explained how commitments to the school exert a pull away from the rhythm of the monastic household. 'It's too easily done. You find yourself making excuses for missing Vigils, missing Midday Office. Not being able to take meals at the set times. Housemasters having to return to the school during the hours of silence.' We saw in Chapter 3 the importance of time discipline to monastic life, but the school has its own distinct institutional time discipline; as another monk pointedly put it, 'there's a whole different set of bells down there'.

In 2019 the school was legally separated from the abbey, a step that had become necessary following failures of child protection. But fundamental concerns about the compatibility of the school with monastic discipline have a longer history, and were central to a notable episode of conflict at Downside.

David Knowles, a monk who subsequently became estranged from the community, describes in his autobiography the atmosphere around the school in the 1920s and 30s, and the impact he perceived this had on monastic observance. 'The school ... was becoming more and more showy and expensive. [The headmaster] himself when away from Downside, stayed at country houses, shooting in Norfolk or on Scottish moors. At Downside a small group of four monks played golf regularly at Masbury twice a week ... Silence was frequently dispensed with in the monastery and numbers in choir for early morning offices fell low.'[35] Here, a core concern with the impact school work has on communal life and, in particular, with participation in the liturgy as the work of God is combined with unease with the worldliness of an elite school, through which monks are drawn into unsuitable habits of high society. Consequently, 'I began to feel that tension which was common at Downside then, and perhaps is still, between the school with all its human and mental interests, and life in the monastery felt as the only reality and true vocation.'[36]

Matters came to a head in 1933, with Downside expanding its commitments by establishing a new dependant priory in order to run a preparatory school.[37] At this point, believing that 'To accept the status quo would not be to fulfil, but to deny my vows,'[38] Knowles, together with several other monks of the community, composed and submitted to Abbot John Chapman a proposal for a new monastic foundation.[39] The proposal is revealing in the relationship it envisages with work: 'The aim would be to be as self-supporting as possible with dairy produce, eggs, vegetables and fruit ... producing for ourselves what we could by our own labour' (cited in Morey 1979: 146). The monastery would run neither school nor parishes; instead 'work should be of a kind compatible with a life of prayer, that is, allowing the worker to remain really recollected as much as possible' (1979: 147). So rather than redirecting the monks to external ends,

---

35 Knowles, Autobiography (Part 1) 195, closed archive at Downside.
36 Knowles, Autobiography (Part 1) 142, closed archive at Downside.
37 The foundation that would become Worth Abbey.
38 Knowles, Autobiography (Part 1) 202, closed archive at Downside..
39 As well as the account in Knowles's autobiography, this episode is described by Morey (1979) and Sillem (1991), both of whom were monks of the community at the time.

'All work should be regarded as St Benedict regarded it, merely as a means to the end, which is the perfection of the soul of the worker' – a direct critique of the working arrangements that persisted at Downside.

The proposal failed, and such a foundation was never to see the light of day. Two of the monks who supported Knowles in his proposal left Downside to undertake a second novitiate at Solesmes Abbey in France. Knowles himself was sent away by the abbot to reside at Ealing, then a priory of the monastery, and subsequently became estranged from Downside. His career as a historian led to him becoming Regius Professor of Modern History at the University of Cambridge, but he never returned to Benedictine community life.

Tambiah (1970) contrasts the Benedictine ideal of removal from the laity with Theravada Buddhist monasticism, where contact with the laity is institutionalised through the material dependence of monks on the laity, and laity's desire for the monks' spiritual services. Indeed, what we have seen in this chapter seems to invert the ideal of St Benedict's monastery as presented by Tambiah (1970: 88): 'Its inmates were to serve God and sanctify their souls apart from the life of the world. No work done within its walls was to be directed to an end outside them, even should it give material or spiritual relief to dependants or those in the neighbourhood' – but here it is noteworthy that this description follows immediately after a citation from David Knowles's compilation of writings *Saints and Scholars* (Knowles 1962). So Tambiah draws on Knowles for his account of the monastery as a self-contained and self-sufficient unit, and Knowles became estranged from Downside precisely because in its apparent concessions to pastoral work it failed to live up to his expectations of what a monastery should be.

Work and stability

Work in Benedictine life is a space of encounter with God in the everyday. The instruction in the *Rule* that the cellarer should treat the monastery's kitchen utensils as if they were sacred vessels of the altar[40] shows the place of even the most mundane tasks within the rhythm of prayer. The abbot insisted on a number of occasions that even administrative and bureaucratic work, often considered deadly dull, should be carried out reverently 'in the service of God'. He told me of a time when, while working in Rome as secretary to the Abbot Primate, he casually remarked to his superior that he was looking forward to doing some 'real priest work' deputising in a parish one weekend; his superior forcefully made the point that the administrative work they were doing was also 'real priest work', and that lives were affected by it. This rebuke, he said, had stayed with him all his life. Indeed, the abbot had occasion to pass on the rebuke: during a lecture at the monastery given by the Bishop of Clifton, attended by monks and laity, one of the audience members commented that priests in the diocese should be freed from paperwork so that they can concentrate on their religious duties. The abbot immediately took it upon himself to respond that for those priests, paperwork *was* a religious duty.

In this chapter we have seen how this general sense of work became largely directed to a particular external end: pastoral work in the service of society, as priests 'on the mission' to England and in schools. Here, the influence of the monks expands beyond the boundaries of the community. This expresses a sense of responsibility within English history. But there is also a transactional logic here, as the services brought to society by the monks are a source of revenue, a means for the community to support itself, and have in the past been considered a path to recruitment. The scope for disruption here has been noted in similar contexts: Campbell-Jones (1979), for example, in her ethnographic study of female religious congregations in England shows how the work the sisters undertake is essential for their own wellbeing and brings benefits to society, but is nevertheless a potential source of disruption to the very basis of religious life. In this context, she suggests, symbolic boundaries with the outside world – such as the place of silence – become particularly important to avoid dilution of the community's core values.

40 *Rule* of St Benedict, Chapter 31.

Concerns about the erosion of stability and of communal life have been a recurring theme in the monastery's history: external work responsibilities exerting a gravitational pull away from the *horarium* and the daily dynamics of life within the monastic family. Frustration about this could occasionally spill over, for example over tea at the point in time where the *Antiphonale Monasticum* was being introduced (see Chapter 4). 'What's the point in trying to have a proper liturgy, or trying to get us to learn how to sing these antiphons, when half of the community is away on parishes and the other half are down in the school?' Afterwards, taking our teacups to the dishwasher, another tried to explain a little the source of the problem. For him, it was about how easily, left unchecked, the independence that was a necessary element of some roles led to a drift away from the discipline of a life shared with others: 'So you have your parish, and so you need to live away from the monastery or even if it's nearby you need your own car to get to your parish. And then you need access to a bank account to manage your parish's finances. And then … you can see what I'm saying? And you're not at office, and you're having to sit at second table.[41] Well you have to ask, is that Benedictine life?' The monk who had initially vented their frustration chimed in again: 'Every day's a month day!' Month day is a traditional day of rest for the monks when, on the first Thursday of each month, aspects of monastic observance are relaxed; the monks can enjoy some recreation and have the freedom to take a trip away from the monastery – a long walk, for example. The implication here was that because of factors drawing the monks away from communal life, such freedom from monastic observance was not the exception but had become – in his view – all too commonplace. Work itself becomes a space of individualism.

We have seen the rhythms and structures through which the monks express what they call the 'charism of community living'. Work,

---

41 'Second table' refers to a meal taken after the rest of the monks have eaten and left the refectory; generally, this was when the reader and the monk who had been serving the food sat down to eat, but sometimes they are joined by others who had duties at the communal time of the meal. Silence is not observed at second table.

within a pattern of prayer and social interaction, is part of this rhythm, but also a point of contact and responsibility for a wider world. In this dynamic we see a recurrent tension: work is at the core of monastic stability but also has the capacity to erode that very stability.

CHAPTER 8

Abuse and the failure of responsibility

The institutional context of abuse

In July 2014 Theresa May, then UK Home Secretary, announced the establishment of an Independent Inquiry into Child Sexual Abuse, examining failings in duty of care by public and other institutions. Cases of abuse within the Catholic Church in England and Wales led to the extent of its failures to protect children becoming a particular focus of the Inquiry, and the nature and extent of abuse within the English Benedictine Congregation was examined over three weeks of proceedings between 27 November and 15 December 2017.

The English Benedictine Congregation became a focus of the inquiry as a result of a string of cases of abuse from the 1960s into the 2000s. High-profile cases led to Downside's inclusion as a case study: in 2004 a monk was jailed for possession of child pornography, and in 2012 a monk was jailed for sexually abusing two children at the school in the 1980s. Additionally, a monk had been cautioned in the 1960s for sexual abuse against a pupil, while another monk was cautioned in relation to sexual offences with a vulnerable adult taking place in the 1980s. Beyond these cases, allegations of inappropriate sexual behaviour had been made against a further four monks.

The ethnography presented in this book cannot be quarantined from this history of harm. Indeed, it is compromised by the proximity of my fieldwork to the 2004 conviction, and while that monk was no longer living with the community (and was subsequently laicised), it is now apparent that a known offender was living with the community at the time of my fieldwork and that some aspects of other cases would have been known at the time to those in authority. In this context my desire as a researcher not to appear prurient or sensationalist ends up seeming quite naive. As noted in Chapter 1, this has inevitably led me to question the value and purpose of the whole endeavour. Of course, such doubt is insignificant and irrelevant compared to the impact on the lives of those abused. It is also trivial compared to that experienced by monks for whom coming to terms with the abuse in their midst has led to disillusionment with their life in the community or even with their vocation. However, on a basic level, it recognises a silence around these themes in my ethnographic material.

Yet this is a context that cannot be ignored. This is primarily because the experience of those abused compels us to see abuse *within* the reality of the institution (see also Orsi 2017: 290–1). Following from this moral imperative, analytically this means that rather than bracket out such cases as instances of individual deviance, we require a social understanding of a social problem (Keenan 2011). Of course, ethnographers also have an ethical responsibility to the community they work with; this is built on the dialogue that emerges from relationships built up over time. It is important for the anthropologist to bring an honesty to that dialogue, and the impulse for this analysis emerges from conversations I have had with members of the community over recent years. Accordingly, I have offered some of the monks drafts of what I have written here for comment, with their feedback being part of the ongoing dialogue. In short, I see this chapter, and the application of an anthropological lens to the issues that became apparent, as part of that long-term ethical relationship.

As noted above, there are limitations to what I can provide for such an analysis from my field material directly; but at the same time, dynamics that could be observed during my fieldwork, and which I have described in the preceding chapters, are relevant to understanding the institutional context in which abuse occurred. This became apparent over the weeks of testimony relating to

Downside and the English Benedictine Congregation at the Independent Inquiry into Child Sexual Abuse in which survivors, agencies, and the monks themselves reflected on the factors involved. Accordingly, my approach in this chapter will be to focus on the evidence given at the Inquiry and how it connects with themes at the heart of this ethnography. As Orsi (2017: 286) challenges anthropologists and others to address what the abuse crisis 'reveals about Catholicism itself', my contention here is that the Inquiry provides insights into core elements of the English Benedictine community and of monasticism as a form of life.

The autonomous household

To begin with the household as a core unit of Benedictine life: the very identity of the monastery as an autonomous entity comes under scrutiny. It becomes clear that the English Benedictine organisational structure confounds expectations of how a 'religious order' should work. On the second day of evidence, the Abbot President of the Congregation explains that, unlike the centralised and top-down structure of a global organisation under a single worldwide head (as in the case of the Dominicans or Jesuits), which is then divided into regional provinces which operate individual houses of residence, for Benedictines the 'basic unit is the individual monastery, and rather than having an order divided into provinces, you have monasteries which group together into congregations'.[1] So there are limits to the extent of the Abbot President's jurisdiction over the monasteries themselves, which have autonomy in their affairs under the authority of their own abbot.

From a Benedictine perspective, the emergence of centralised orders is a historical trajectory that postdates the *Rule* of St Benedict by several centuries. As Knowles (1966) describes, constitutional arrangements that envision a hierarchical network directed towards central goals emerge from a very different historical moment to that of the *Rule*, with its idea of monks coming together as a localised

---

1   IICSA public hearing transcript, 28 November 2017, 92.

community to support one another in their pursuit of the spiritual life. Crucially, these later constitutional developments emerge in relation to an idea of the religious life increasingly directed to external ends in the service of the Church. As discussed in previous chapters, in fact in the centuries following their seventeenth-century restoration in exile, the English Benedictines adopted a congregational structure with greater constitutional centralisation. It was precisely in reaction to this that a return to the 'normal' Benedictine state of monastic houses having autonomy from the start of the twentieth century was such an important turning point in English Benedictine history, occupying a key place in the monks' identity. But in the wake of abuse, the value of autonomy is interrogated in light of different concerns: as a potential lack of oversight and accountability.

A perception that the Congregation is evading overarching responsibility when insisting on the independence of each monastery comes through clearly in an uncomfortable exchange between the former Abbot President and one of the lawyers representing survivors of abuse:[2]

> *Do you accept that the English Benedictine Congregation bears a moral responsibility to those people that have been abused by its monks?*
>
> I accept that the monasteries of the English Benedictine Congregation have a responsibility which is both moral and in many cases may be legal. The Congregation as a whole, as I have said, regrets, is sorry for and is ashamed of abuse which has been committed in any monastery.
>
> *Why don't you say that the EBC has a moral responsibility for the survivors of abuse? Why do you give an answer which says that, 'Well, we are very sorry, but don't accept moral responsibility'?*
>
> Because I think that the primary responsibility must be with the individual monastery ... I'm not certain that saying the EBC accepts moral responsibility – I'm not certain what that means.

2 IICSA public hearing transcript, 28 November 2017, 154–5.

> You, Abbot President ex of the EBC, are saying that you don't understand what the words 'moral responsibility' mean? Are you saying that?
>
> I'm saying that I'm not certain what the EBC accepting moral responsibility implies.

Constitutionally, the autonomy of monasteries is reflected in the limited jurisdiction the Abbot President has over each monastery's affairs. Primarily, the Abbot President carries out periodic visitations of each monastery (every four years), at which point they speak with the community, make observations about the functioning of the monastery, and can make any recommendations they have to the abbot; where necessary this can take the form of an Act of Visitation, which is a specific instruction requiring a change to be implemented. Only in 2013 were the constitutions changed to give the Abbot President oversight outside the time of visitation, creating scope to intervene in circumstances of failure and specifically in safeguarding cases (although even then he has no power to compel an abbot to resign) – this change was in response to problems around abuse, attempting to enhance structures of accountability beyond the monastery itself.[3]

A further aspect of the monastery's autonomy was its independence from diocesan governance. It was only in 2013, following pressure from the Catholic Safeguarding Advisory Service, and after the high-profile cases discussed above, that Downside came under diocesan oversight by aligning itself with the Clifton Diocese safeguarding office.[4] It seems that this lack of formal structures of external accountability was exacerbated by a sense among some within the community that it was best to deal with matters 'in house' rather than to go 'running to the authorities'[5] – autonomy breeding what the monastic school's first lay headmaster described as a

---

3   IICSA public hearing transcript, 12 December 2017, 60–2.
4   IICSA public hearing transcript, 7 December 2017, 107.
5   IICSA public hearing transcript, 6 December 2017, 94.

'culture of monastic superiority',[6] a belief that the community knew best and had little need for interlopers.

Of course, this autonomy is not simply a constitutional feature, but the expression of a core value. 'The concept of family is central to Benedictine monasticism and so each community exists as a separate family.'[7] We have seen how crucial this emphasis on family is, and that household dynamic is inevitably important for understanding the institutional response to abuse.

Stability, community and individualism

An emphasis on the household exhibits the tension at the heart of English Benedictine identity and, crucially, its relationship with stability. The centrality of living together as a family for the spiritual life of the monks – their charism of community living – is built around a lifelong relationship with the monastery as home. As we shall see, this presents particular difficulties in the context of the response to abuse, and to safeguarding in general. At the same time, it is striking that in seeking to identify factors that might have contributed to this history of harm, those who have held positions of authority in the monastery point to the limits of stability and cracks in the fabric of community living as key problems. Stability as a promise and as a core value comes under renewed scrutiny.

The responsibility to family members and the importance of maintaining those family bonds is key to Benedictine life: the monk grows in their relationship with God not in isolation, but living with his brothers. Crucially, this means that community is not merely the backdrop to monastic life. Rather, it plays a crucial role in the monks' salvation – a role that becomes all the more important if the monk is in moral difficulty, as it is through the social support of the community that they might overcome those difficulties. In the words of a former abbot of the community, 'we like to say the

---

6 IICSA public hearing transcript, 7 December 2017, 91.
7 IICSA witness statement INQ006922 001 003.

community is like a family, and I suppose in a family, you know, it is hopefully, anyway, the one place where you can return, even if you have been arrested or whatever, I don't know, but family support, as an institution, it is much more complex, especially these days.'[8] The imperative here is to provide a lifelong home. As per the first chapter of the *Rule*, flitting from place to place means that there are no checks on your own appetites – it is through living with others that self-will can be checked. But also, within the home there is a relationship of care and love that builds up through time within a family that cannot be discarded, precisely because that relationship of care and love is an expression of the love of God. In short, an intimacy of kinship lies at the heart of the form of life. Consequently, in the words of a subsequent abbot, 'I think that the monastery should be a place of trust … I think that normally speaking, the monastery is the home to which the monks return, but I don't think that is an absolute.'[9]

The context of this qualification that it may not be an absolute is important. Both abbots made decisions around the appropriate housing of a monk who was known to have abused two boys at the school; although initially sent away from Downside, placed in a number of other (primarily monastic) contexts while receiving psychological evaluation, he was subsequently allowed to return to the monastery. Although he did not return to work in the school, and restrictions were placed on his activities so that none of his responsibilities involved contact with children, the very problem of the spatial overlap between the monastic and school grounds[10] and buildings in and of itself involved risk.

What this demonstrates is the central conflict of interest discussed by each of the superiors called to give evidence: the abbot has responsibility for the welfare of his monks, and to encourage their perseverance in community life. However, when as a result of the monastery running a school, the abbot also has

---

8   IICSA public hearing transcript, 8 December 2017, 72.
9   IICSA public hearing transcript, 12 December 2017, 72.
10 As discussed by the Deputy Head of the school, IICSA public hearing transcript, 11 December 2017, 101.

Abuse and the failure of responsibility

responsibility for governance there – as was historically the case at Downside, with the abbot also chairman both of the trustees and of the school governing body – the abbot's focus on what is best for the monks and the community under his care can be in tension with what is in the interests of the welfare of children in the school. The suggestion that the focus was more on the welfare of the monks than on the victims was a key motif repeated throughout the proceedings. Legally, the Children's Act 1989, makes clear that the welfare of the child is the paramount consideration in decisions around safeguarding (known as the paramountcy principle). Here, the monk's stability is overridden by other considerations that might require them to leave home and live without the support of their monastic family, and consequently 'abbots are quite torn between two ideals, you might say. You want to comply with the law, but you also want to keep the family together. It's an almost impossible thing to actually get right the whole time.'[11]

So kinship is an important lens for understanding the response to abuse (see also Farkas and Miller 2007). On the one hand, we see the importance of the family unit in supporting the offender's rehabilitation and even in preventing reoffending (a specifically stated reason for keeping offenders living in a community context,[12] where their behaviour can be better monitored than if living alone). In the context of the monastic family, this takes the form, as we have seen, of an ongoing moral responsibility. These are ties that cannot be casually severed, and the nature of monastic stability implies an enduring commitment, demonstrated in material support for those who have to leave the household,[13] or in becoming part of the support group for one of the brothers coming out of prison.[14] They hope for the possibility of redemption: 'to see a sinner repent is a joyful thing and something to be celebrated'.[15]

11 IICSA public hearing transcript, 12 December 2017, 73–4.
12 IICSA public hearing transcript, 13 December 2017, 31.
13 IICSA public hearing transcript, 28 November 2017, 136.
14 IICSA public hearing transcript, 8 December 2017, 148.
15 IICSA public hearing transcript, 28 November 2017, 132.

Of course, we also see the strains placed on a family – the difficulty of living with people who have committed crimes, frustration that these kinship responsibilities might seem to be taking priority over the welfare of children.[16] Then there is the disillusionment that comes from realising the deep failings of people you had admired and respected, calling into question the things that had led you to become part of the family in the first place. This contributed to one former abbot leaving the monastic life altogether: 'I was angry about the fact that the life to which I had dedicated myself seemed to have been not what I originally sought.'[17]

Yet if the idealised stability of the household created bonds of loyalty[18] that contribute to a conflict of interest, it also figures as an object of self-reflection as those in authority reflect on the factors undermining stability by drawing monks away from community living. Recognising the *Rule*'s condemnation of the 'gyrovague' who in wandering from place to place has no check on his own whims and appetites,[19] a recurrent theme was that a 'culture of individualism' had been allowed to develop in the monastery and that this contributed to an environment where abuse could occur, with individual behaviours not sufficiently held to account. As observed by the Prior Administrator at the time of the Inquiry, 'The culture at Downside Abbey has, for some time, been relatively individualistic. By this I mean monks are given individual responsibilities as teachers, in parish work ... and so on; they seldom work together as a team which can encourage isolation and individualism and a degree of secrecy. In the past, where monks were becoming isolated by this individualism, they were not often challenged.'[20] Previous abbots shared this view, noting, for example, how a view that monks should be left to get on with their business without interference came to be seen as a virtue,[21] leading to members of

---

16 IICSA public hearing transcript, 6 December 2017, 120.
17 IICSA public hearing transcript, 11 December 2017, 76.
18 IICSA public hearing transcript, 12 December 2017, 43.
19 *Rule* of St Benedict, Chapter 1.
20 IICSA witness statement BNT006645, 1–2.
21 IICSA public hearing transcript, 8 December 2017, 101

the community operating independently to a high degree, only coming together at the times of collective prayer and meals – and even here (as seen in Chapters 3 and 7), work and other duties can lead to (or be used to justify) a drift away from this collective routine. Here, the very grounding of stability in shared time and space appears brittle – the risk is that the monk becomes the 'gyrovague' condemned in the first chapter of the *Rule*, wandering according to their own whims.

One consequence of this, as noted above, is that such individualism can lead to isolation. In spite of the family structure at the heart of Benedictine monasticism, we have seen how in English Benedictine history the reality for many monks was that they were required to pursue individual work away from the monastery. What emerges here is that even as the focus has shifted from the missionary parishes, structures of isolation – even when resident in community – can persist, for example, in the way monks were allocated responsibilities in the school. As Keenan (2011: 160–1) notes in her study of sexual abuse of children by Catholic priests in Ireland, the context of social isolation repeatedly figures in the accounts of abusers, while the associated 'emotional loneliness sets the stage for self-serving behaviors'. Successive abbots depict a picture of Downside having historically a formal dynamic, starved of opportunities for everyday conversation and interaction. Of course, Downside was not necessarily exceptional here, as historically this kind of formality could be traced across other institutions, and indeed family relationships. Nevertheless, the sense of monks 'keeping their contacts to strictly business'[22] makes clear the possibility of such loneliness.

A further consequence is the limited opportunity for the monks to express moral concern for one another, talking openly and critically when there are potential issues around behaviour. 'It is not really part of our tradition to go up and say to somebody, you know, "Why are you always late for office?"'[23] The fraternal correction of faults that Asad (1993: 161) treats as crucial to the building up of

22 IICSA public hearing transcript, 8 December 2017, 115
23 IICSA public hearing transcript, 8 December 2017, 115

the moral self within the monastery is restricted by social disengagement.

It is therefore notable that a key element of the monastery's response to institutional failure has been its attempt to address this culture of individualism. To some extent these responses build on slightly longer-term developments in the community. Trying to shift beyond a purely formal mode of interaction, from the 1990s onwards there were more relaxed opportunities to gather as a community and chat during the day.[24] The emergence of shared *lectio divina* (see Chapter 6) against a backdrop of deeply individual tradition of private prayer might also be seen in the context of these wider developments. In a somewhat more formal mode, from the late 2000s the abbot instituted a nightly community meeting after Vespers. The process of reflection in the wake of the abuse cases, including recommendations following Visitations, has led to an increased recognition of the need for 'fraternal correction and exhortation to virtue' with the goal of creating 'a community culture, rather than one of the individual'.[25]

Obedience and the limits of authority

The dynamics described above also shine a light on the nature of obedience within the monastery. For Scheper-Hughes and Devine (2003: 16), the role of hierarchy and 'almost totalitarian' authority is crucial to understanding abuse within the Church, both in creating forms of dependency among clergy (2003: 28) and in marshalling cover-ups. Yet there is also an important interplay between authority and isolation, as noted by Keenan (2011). A focus on individualism shows something of the complexity of this dynamic.

On the one hand, the abbot as *paterfamilias* (Nuzzo 1996) is a sole locus of authority within the monastery. As we have seen, in the rite of profession monks promise obedience to the abbot and are expected to accept responsibilities given in a spirit of humility.

---

24 IICSA public hearing transcript, 8 December 2017, 70–1.
25 IICSA witness statement BNT006645, 2.

Given the monastery's character as an autonomous household, this places the abbot in a position of some power. This comes across clearly in an exchange during the Inquiry: 'As abbot, did you answer to anyone?' 'Well, apart from the Almighty, not a lot. It was a rather curious arrangement ... it reflected a sort of medieval setup, so to speak, a feudal setup, dating from the days when some abbots were great sort of land magnates and things like that.'[26]

Yet in the interpersonal reality of the monastery, the limits of this authority become clear. As the Diocesan safeguarding officer observed, in the dynamic of day-to-day living, trying to get on with people within a household and managing 'strong personalities', it was not always easy to assert the need for obedience if someone was behaving in a wayward manner. 'It's different for us ... we go home in the evenings ... and they live and work and do everything together. So I think it's quite hard for an abbot, actually, to exert authority.'[27] Similarly, a safeguarding audit carried out by the Social Care Institute for Excellence identified cases where the monastic superior found it difficult to exert control over monks who apparently struggled with Benedictine obedience.[28]

In several cases, monks used opportunities for autonomy to navigate within the interstices of the abbot's oversight. When monastic obedience became strained, a loss of control seems apparent. This was explicitly acknowledged in relation to certain events: for example, a monk living away from the monastery on parish work who went against the abbot's intention that he should live with two other monks (in an attempt to keep his drinking in check) and instead appears to have manoeuvred a way of living on his own: 'I was not at all happy about this arrangement but I felt that it would be seen as disproportionate to order [him] to move ... and thus threaten him with dismissal from the religious life if he refused ... nevertheless, I felt that I had not exercised the level of control over him that I should

---

26 IICSA public hearing transcript, 8 December 2017, 87.
27 IICSA public hearing transcript, 6 December 2017, 72.
28 Safeguarding Audit of Downside Abbey and School, Social Care Institute for Excellence, February–March 2018, 25.

have done.'[29] The Inquiry also brought to light occasions in which monks with restrictions on their behaviour nonetheless flouted those restrictions.

A key element of this autonomy comes through the way the monastic identity enabled some monks, through their own charisma, to build up a reputation as wise and respected figures in their own right. One example of this comes through in concerns raised by a teacher that one of the monks serving as chaplain in the school had been 'cultivating a kind of guru-like status amongst the pupils using the chaplaincy as a vehicle'.[30] Precisely because of the popularity of this monk among pupils and parents, any decision to remove the monk from the school in response to these concerns was seen as a bit of a 'political tightrope'.[31] Notably, this was in spite of the misgivings of the headmaster at the time – a monk himself – who 'always had a sense of unease, however, about him, because the charismatic aspects of his character had something disturbing about them that I couldn't quite put my finger on'.[32] Rather than acting in their position of authority, the abbot left the decision in the hands of the headmaster, who prevaricated, and the monk remained in the school.

Weber (1968: 241–5), in his discussion of charismatic authority, makes clear the ways in which it can come into conflict with other modes of authority precisely because it has the potential to repudiate institutional structures through force of personality and an appeal to more immediate reactions of subjectivity and enthusiasm. In this sense it is 'naturally unstable' (1968: 1114). Interestingly, Winthrop (1985: 32) argues that Benedictine monasticism sits in contrast to this as a situation where 'traditional and charismatic authority are not opposed but complementary' because 'their point of balance is the monastic leader' as caring and respected father and interpreter of monastic tradition and continuity with the *Rule*. This, however, is potentially to underestimate the extent to which

---

29 IICSA witness statement, BNT006439, 22.
30 IICSA public hearing transcript, 7 December 2017, 37.
31 IICSA public hearing transcript, 7 December 2017, 39.
32 IICSA public hearing transcript, 12 December 2017, 15–16.

monasteries are spaces where multiple personalities interact and potentially become sources of authority in their own right. In the face of the following and respect cultivated by a revered monk, the abbot's own authority can seem rather fragile.

Conversatio morum and the character of celibacy

While Benedictine monks do not make an explicit vow of celibacy, this is taken to be implicitly included in the commitment to *conversatio morum* (Rees et al. 1978: 154), which embeds celibacy within the pursuit of life in community. But, to quote a statement by the superior at the time of the Inquiry, 'As history has taught us, however, vows do not make members of the English Benedictine Congregation ... less susceptible to temptation and failing to fulfil their vows.'[33]

Given this, the question of celibacy itself comes under scrutiny, firstly in relation to the suitability of the monks for a celibate life. Primarily this was framed in relation to individual psychological maturity: as one former abbot explained, since the late 1990s 'any candidate for the monastic life has been asked to undergo a psychological assessment ... So we are aware of the issue, and I think we are dealing with it.' However, with this came the recognition that 'From earlier years, I think people who are immature probably were accepted,'[34]

The concept of 'identity foreclosure' (Marcia 1966) – a premature commitment to an identity without having considered alternatives – was used to express a recognition that monks may have made their solemn profession without fully grasping the implication of the lifelong vows they were entering into in the context of their own development: 'young people coming into the community who think they know what their identity is but they haven't interrogated it'.[35]

33 IICSA witness statement BNT006645, 12.
34 IICSA public hearing transcript, 12 December 2017, 74.
35 IICSA public hearing transcript, 12 December 2017, 44.

Another observation was that alongside a lack of psychological assessment, until recently throughout the novitiate – and more generally – there was a reluctance to discuss sexual acts and accordingly a failure to actively consider the monk's sexual development and self-awareness. Recognising this, in more recent decades 'monastic formation has begun to include specific training in human formation and introduces candidates to a fuller and more objective awareness of their sexual identity and stages of development and to management of relationships in the context of celibacy.'[36] Notably, however, this increased attention to developmental suitability for monastic life did not necessarily involve direct consideration of the candidate's suitability to teach children, in spite of the fact that this had been such a key work for monks in the community.[37]

Yet, while here we see the question of individual suitability for a celibate life being considered, clearly the abuse crisis has led to a confrontation with the suitability of the institution of celibacy itself. For Scheper-Hughes and Devine (2003), mandatory celibacy is a source of ongoing harm, while Keenan (2011: 263) argues that 'The Church still promotes an institutional practice that is bound to fail. Cruelty and abuse are bound to arise from such impossible tasks.' Here, of course, we need to avoid the false conflation of failed celibacy with abusive behaviour. Nevertheless, the silence that it imposes around sexuality and the secrecy that emerges are obvious sources of danger.

The approaches above focus in turn on the psychological incompatibility of individuals with their vows, and on the strains generated by the vows themselves. What do we learn if we take the contradiction itself as our analytical focus (see also Berliner et al. 2016)? The reality we face here is of monks living formally committed lives and yet acting in ways that run sharply contrary to those commitments – sometimes in criminal and deeply harmful ways. Bastide (1955) in his study of Catholic participation in Afro-Brazilian rituals highlights how apparently contradictory behaviours can be sustained without inner conflict: by way of the *principe de coupure* (literally

---

36 IICSA witness statement BNT006645, 7.
37 IICSA public hearing transcript, 12 December 2017, 45; 74–6.

'principle of cutting', though more often translated as compartmentalisation principle), people inhabit multiple identities not in opposition but in separation. Such compartmentalisation offers a model for a particularly troubling aspect of the dynamic we see here: how monks may have felt that they were occupying sacred roles *sincerely* even as they engaged in behaviours that gravely contradict the life they have committed to. For Mayblin (2019), this points to a doubleness that she sees as fundamental to the life of the Church. While vocation fuses the individual with the Church, a priest relates to the faithful not only as an individual but representing a Church that expands beyond the capacity of any individual in time and space. As such, the priest is not purely acting as themselves but expressing something *beyond* themselves.

Anthropological discussion of the nature of this permanent ontological transformation enabling this mediation between the human and the divine has scrutinised its relationship with abuse (Orsi 2017; O'Neill 2020). What Mayblin (2019: 528) shows in her ethnographic engagement with Brazilian Catholic priesthood are the everyday ways in which this relation is managed through a 'cultivation of space between self and other'. We see this at the very heart of the priest's identity in the temporally circumscribed transformation by which he acts *in persona Christi* in the action of the Mass. Mayblin notes the way in which this transformation is stage-managed in dress and deportment, 'moments of parentheses' enacting a separation from the everyday self. More widely, she discusses how priests reflect on the need to keep a 'meticulous exterior' (2016: 526) to serve the greater good of the faithful, even if this means practices of secrecy. Crucially, this separation brought about by this profoundly transformative role-shifting not only creates spaces in which sexual deviation from the norms of the Church can operate – 'a stable instability at the heart of the Church' (2016: 519) – but can also generate the pressure that leads to a desire for such spaces of escape.

While all of this is clearly relevant to the monks' role as priests, as highlighted in Chapter 7 this is itself a dual identity. In the normal course of things at Downside (and in the English Benedictine Congregation more generally), the solemnly professed monk is later ordained as priest, and this follows its own process of education and preparation; in other words, a vocation to the priesthood is located *within* a monastic vocation and its identity *follows* the first identity, which is that of monk. This is relevant not only because the separation of roles within a unity of vocation takes on a somewhat distinct dimension, but also because it brings into relation the different temporalities of the ontological transformation of priesthood and the monastic solemn vows. Anthropological discussion of priesthood highlights the permanence of the new state of personhood brought about by a single point of transformation in the sacrament of Holy Orders (for example, Mayblin 2016: 521; O'Neill 2020: 750–1). Yet the commitment to *conversatio morum* in a monk's profession is a process of continual reform. With regard to celibacy, this implies not simply the separating out of vocation from sexuality but a living *with* desire – a process which Coakley (2015), in a book specifically recommended to me by one of the monks in the wake of the abuse scandal, describes as an ordering of desire (including erotic desire) towards its telos of God; 'a "practice" managed only over a life-time' (2015: 127). This, however, returns us to the problem of stability and the means by which this lifelong process can be recovered and sustained following the serious impact of failure without sidestepping the impacts of those failures. In other words, it needs to be recognised that a key aspect of the Inquiry was to draw attention to the way in which a focus on the crimes as a source of moral harm to the perpetrator was often at the expense of attention to the harm inflicted on the victim (see also Keenan 2011: 167) and the possibility for future harm in the form of re-offending.

Status and deference

A final dimension to be considered is the social status of the abbey and its monks and how this contributed to a culture of abuse. In the words of a Diocesan safeguarding officer, 'I think there's a deference to the monastery that isn't helpful, and, you know, when you throw faith and religion into the mix in this context, it is quite a toxic mix in relation to trying to deal with safeguarding issues.'[38] This point was reflected in the statement of a former abbot, referring to the 'deferential attitude' by which external agencies left the monastery and school to deal with its own affairs – a dynamic exacerbated by the monastery's 'rather conservative, paternalistic, "we know best" approach to dealing with matters which would now be externally reported'.[39] So here we see, first of all, the extent to which a reputation as respected holy men shielded the monks from scrutiny.

In Chapter 7, we saw how the community attempted to build up the prestige of the school, but in essence this reflected a wider economy of prestige in the monastery. In its grandeur, the very architecture of the abbey (see Chapter 2) conveys a renewed stature and visibility for Catholicism and monasticism in Britain. So the idea of the monastery as a 'reservoir of religion' (Butler 1919: 383) in the midst of society has entailed the pursuit of prominence.

Alongside Downside's attempt to protect its institutional reputation, an especially disturbing aspect of the response to allegations of abuse has been how the community sought to leverage this high social status to discourage scrutiny. The Diocesan Safeguarding officer described the abbot – in what could be construed as a thinly veiled threat – making reference to friends in in the House of Commons who intended to raise concerns in parliament about how Downside was being treated by safeguarding agencies.[40] In a similar way a Detective with Avon and Somerset Police recalled having his attention drawn to the monks' 'high-ranking connections'.[41] These connections are brought into view again in the Deputy Director of Children's Services from Somerset County Council's account of a phone call from the Secretary of State for Education making specific enquiries about the handling of a safeguarding matter relating to Downside.[42]

38 IICSA public hearing transcript, 8 December 2017, 14.
39 IICSA witness statement BNT006403, 7.
40 IICSA public hearing transcript, 6 December 2017, 132.
41 IICSA public hearing transcript, 8 December 2017, 31.
42 IICSA public hearing transcript, 13 December 2017, 170–1.

If the point here is how social status becomes potentially a corrupting influence on proceedings, it is also to recognise status as a source of moral danger to the monks. Where prestige attracts deference, and deference elevates the monk to a position of assumed piety, this can run contrary to the very nature of the monastic vocation.

In an argument I will return to again in the final chapter, Søren Kierkegaard (using a pseudonym drawn from monastic history, Johannes Climacus[43]) reflects on monasticism while discussing the relationship between inwardness and externality. He discerns a danger in the monastic movement in that 'anyone entering a monastery was in all seriousness accounted a saint. So, if I went down the street and met a poor wretch who is perhaps a far better man than I, he would bow to me and take me in pathos and earnest for a holy man' (Kierkegaard [1846] 2009: 349). The problem here is that the inwardness of the monk, his impulse in entering monastic life to seek a relationship with God as absolute telos, is turned inside out and becomes an externality to be venerated: a sign of holiness. The monk's pursuit of an end is mistaken for an achievement.

The relevance of Kierkegaard's argument in relation to the circumstances discussed here is that it draws our attention to a core conflict in the social life of the monastery: the emphasis on the humanity of the monk in humble pursuit of a Christian life, in tension with the presumption of the monk's virtuosity that comes from the monastery's status as an exemplary community (Weber 1968: 453). Stability, obedience, and *conversatio morum* are by implication a recognition of the monk's need, the means of support by which flawed humans seek their salvation. From this perspective, the starting point of monasticism is sinfulness. But as communities coming together to live a way of life for God, they also become signs of virtue. Here, precisely, is the danger Kierkegaard points to – the risk of the passionate pursuit of God becoming a source of spiritual pride as the character of the virtue is mistaken for something extraordinary, and those who pursue this life are deferred to and treated as saints. 'But entering the monastery must not be made

---

43 After the Syrian Christian monk Johannes Climacus c. 579–649.

out to be something meritorious. On the contrary, this step must be taken humbly before God and not without a certain shame' (Kierkegaard [1846] 2009: 348). As a source of deference, the monastery's externality – its status in relation to the world – can undermine the very core of monasticism.

In this chapter, the focus has been on understanding the failures around sexual abuse in relation to the institutional character of Benedictine monasticism, while also considering what those failures reveal about English Benedictine life itself and its place as a 'reservoir of religion'. As expressed by the English Benedictine Congregation's Theology Commission in the wake of the Second Vatican Council, 'Monasticism should be a witness to the Kingdom. Sadly, a monastic community … can become a counter-witness if it substitutes other values for the gospel, suffers from corporate pride, and fails to live up to its vocation' (Rees et al. 1978: 3–4).

CHAPTER 9

Leaving home

Uprooting

Compline again. The cycle of the day nearing its close. The darkened abbey church and the same three psalms, familiar companions leading us into the *summum silentium*. Repetition. 'The Lord grant us a quiet night and a perfect end.'

The monks make their way from the choir stalls to stand before the statue of the Blessed Virgin Mary. From my seat in the nave, I angle myself to face it too. A blackened limewood carving, thought to be the work of a fifteenth-century Flemish sculptor, it shows Mary with a faint smile as she holds her child close to her face, Jesus' hand touching the curled hair that flows down his mother's back. It has a domesticity to it, although perhaps that comes as much from its familiarity in the routine of daily life as from the apparent ease of the family relationship it shows.

We chant *Ave Regina Caelorum*, a final plea for Mary, Queen of Heaven, to intercede for us with her son. The sound of the chant echoes. I remember the monks who once stood here and are now buried in the cemetery. I remember the time the solemn chant was accidentally pitched too high after a festal supper, with the community bravely struggling through to the end in falsetto. I remember conversations beneath the statue; discussions about Mary and the sense in which her motherhood of Christ made her our mother; conversations asking after my own mother, who I had introduced to some of the monks as they made their way from the choir stalls to the cloister.

In 2019, the community put the statue up for sale. In the wake of the findings of the Independent Inquiry into Child Sexual Abuse, the monastic community and the school legally separated in September of that year, leaving the governance and day-to-day running of the school entirely independent of the monastery. This, nonetheless, left the Downside Abbey General Trust in the position, effectively, of landlord to the school and in this role they agreed to pay £4,000,000 for repairs of the historic school buildings. The sale of the statue was intended to raise a significant part of this money. While the sale was initially approved by the Southern Historic Churches Committee, this was subsequently overturned on appeal (initiated by an old boy of the school) as causing harm to the character and appearance of the church and running contrary to the laws protecting listed buildings.[1] The community were nonetheless allowed to proceed with the sale of two renaissance paintings.

Benedictine monasticism, as we have seen, embodies the *Rule* as a form of life (Agamben 2013), through rhythms of movement in space and time. What does it mean when the material forms that anchor these rhythms are set aside?

On 28 August 2020, the community made a public statement: 'The separation of Downside Abbey and Downside School in September 2019 has enabled the Monastic Community to concentrate on discerning their future. They have now unanimously decided to make a new start and to seek a new place to live in.' In March 2022, on the feast day of their patron St Gregory the Great, they celebrated the 'last Mass' in the abbey church, before moving as an interim measure to Southgate House in the grounds of Buckfast Abbey, Devon, another English Benedictine monastery. This move was considered a 'stepping stone', while they reflect on their longer-term future as a household.

The geographical aspect of monastic stability – stability of place – can be understood as the expression of a desire for rootedness:

---

1 The abbey church is a Grade I listed building, the highest grade of listing in the register maintained by Historic England, designating a 'building of exceptional interest'.

as articulated by the Congregation's Theology commission in the 1970s, 'This human need to be rooted in a particular locality is behind the monastic exercise of stability with reference both to material objects and to people ... A man usually comes to know himself, and in that knowledge to know God, when he dwells for long periods in a stable relationship to places and persons' (Rees et al. 1978: 141). So what happens when there is an uprooting? The place memory that builds up through habit, through the repeated inscription of body in place (Connerton 2009) is a social memory, the accumulation of interaction – in essence, the very location of the building-up of the social self as the everyday expression of the monk's relationship with God. In the context of the monastery, this also expands through generational time: the community living at any one moment is an expression of the interactions that have built up over centuries, the visible part of an institution that emphasises its endurance through time. Even if their portraits hadn't been looking down at us in the refectory, the sense in which everyday life readily engaged with the voices of past members of the community was testament to this.

For the Australian Cistercian monk Michael Casey (2005: 242), explaining how the lifelong commitment of stability localises the history of salvation within the microcosm of the community and its everyday interactions, 'one of the beautiful results of spending the bulk of one's life in a single place is that one retains and cherishes the memories of past years, surrounded as one is by so many reminders. We mellow alongside the trees we plant.' Yet such reminders are not always pleasant: 'we are always confronted by our past'. At Downside, the statement about the community's departure expressed its 'sorrow' for the 'failures in the care for children entrusted to them', and in the context of abuse at Downside, the memory of wrongdoing is also enmeshed in monastic stability.

When I made my final visit to the community before their departure from Downside, the monks were caught up in preparations for the move. A sense of loss was unavoidable – especially among fellow guests to the community who recalled how long they had been coming here on retreat and felt bereft that this would be their last stay – but in chatting with the monks, another prevalent mood was enthusiasm about future projects: a monk who performs conjuring tricks chatting about taking the time and opportunity to film these after the move; the monk with whom I worked in the carpentry workshop discussing the workshop facilities in the new location. Others were focused on the sheer logistics of the move, and how to pack the articulated lorries that would take the contents of the monks' cells and the other accumulated property of the household from Somerset to Devon. Thinking in the *longue durée*, I was repeatedly reminded that this would, in fact, be the third move in the community's history. The bowls from which the monks drank coffee at breakfast bore the coat of arms of the community, surrounded by the dates of arrival in its first three locations: Douay 1605, Acton Burnell 1795, Downside 1814. (The practice of drinking morning coffee from bowls, I had been told, was itself a material memory of its continental exile.) For the monk who had taught me carpentry, the lesson of this history – recalling that not only was the community's origin on the European continent a contingency, but also that their move to England was forced by the circumstances of the French Revolution – was that a monastic family should be 'open to providence'. The departure of the monks therefore gives cause for reflection on stability as a commitment to the future; while leaving behind a site so tied up with a particular relation between the monastery and society prompts reflection on what the relation will be in the future.

Proximity

A key theme of this ethnography has been an understanding of how stability embeds the life of the monk in the rhythms of the everyday. The idea of the monastery as a site where a Christian vocation is pursued through the *fundamental human calling of social life* is central to English Benedictine identity. This rejection of monastic exceptionalism could be seen, for example, in the monk making a rhetorical comparison between the 'superhero' saints who sought God through the most extraordinary feats, and the simplicity of a

Benedictine life where God is sought (and, he believed, found) within the ordinary.

Such self-representation has a significant presence in English Benedictine history. Cuthbert Butler, for example, set out a contrast between Benedictine moderation and the deliberate hardship of earlier modes of monasticism. He described the Desert Fathers in fourth-century Egypt each prolonging their fasts, pushing for greater and greater feats of endurance: 'Before St Benedict the practice of these bodily austerities had been looked on as a chief means for attaining the spiritual end of the monastic life. But he prescribed for his monks sufficient food, ample sleep, proper clothing' (Butler 1919: 40). Crucially, for Butler this was a contrast between spiritual individualism and the communitarian ideal of the Benedictine Rule. He wrote of the Desert Fathers that 'they loved to "make a record" in austerities, and to contend with one another in mortifications' (1919: 13); whereas Benedict broke with the past through 'the elimination of austerity and … the sinking of the individual in the community' (1919: 45). Again, the monks of the Congregation's Theology Commission in the 1970s wrote that 'the monk has traditionally sought to train and discipline himself by voluntary acts of self-denial. Historically this custom often led to exaggerations … An exaggerated emphasis on negative ascetical practices often makes people gloomy and irritable, whereas the result of true love is always a spirit of mercy, peace, and joy' (Rees et al. 1978: 151–2).

A key idea for the social science of monasticism has been Max Weber's notion of the 'virtuoso', someone recognised for their particular talent and skill (in this case, for prayer and living the religious life). This virtuosity, both by its exceptional nature and by the time, resources, and opportunity required to dedicate one's life to it, sets the specialist apart from the general population; and, in particular, as Weber (1963: 162–3) implies, it is usually developed through separation from the secular world. But in this English Benedictine emphasis on moderation and denial of exceptionalism, what manner of virtuoso is the monk? In many respects, their witness is one of proximity, stressing the continuity between the monastic and wider human life, rather than the sharp contrasts.

The English Benedictine is certainly no virtuoso of asceticism.

The emphasis on food sharing displaces any focus on extremes of fasting, which are seen as disruptive to the social life of the community. They stress their identity as a Christian household, granting this domestic commensality a sacred role and looking to the continuities with wider family life.

Even in those areas where one might expect the Benedictines to claim expertise, such as the work of prayer, there is little attempt to occupy a plateau unreachable by wider society. The Liturgy of the Hours is performed with a small number of simple tones, and the psalms are chanted in relatively easy-to-understand English. We saw in Chapter 4 the rejection of a 'museum mentality' – pushing against the idea that monasteries should become the repositories of liturgical forms that had been transformed or had fallen into disuse elsewhere. Instead, the community's own reform of the liturgy was linked to the wider transformation of Catholic ritual in the 1960s and '70s. Likewise, the English Benedictine's virtuosity does not lie in claims of mystical union inaccessible to others. Quite the opposite: the community has historically stressed the universality of the desire (and therefore the need) for personal prayer. Butler (1932: 212) saw contemplation as 'a legitimate practical possibility for good souls in general', and in Chapter 5 we saw the significance of a universal and 'democratising' idea of contemplation. *Lectio divina* (as seen in Chapter 6) is not only an area which monks are keen to share with a wider audience, but in which developments within the monastery have learned from wider lay innovations.

So instead of claiming realms of virtuosity that are radically discontinuous with the experience of wider society, such as ritual fastidiousness or mystical elitism, what is striking about the monks' self-representation is its emphasis on the search for God in the everyday (see also Irvine 2017). What they look to embody is a 'charism of community' – a potential that by seeking God in the pulse of social relationships, the monk might over a lifetime become a kind of virtuoso of ordinary life.

In and out of the world

But this rejection of exceptionalism cannot be the whole story. Firstly, we have seen in Chapter 7 the role that the Congregation's 'missionary identity' has played in shaping its history. The assertion of stability and community living at the heart of Benedictine life, then, emerges precisely from a historic recognition of the gravitational pull of external commitments away from this stability. But this highlights a shift in the monk's focus from a fundamental task of living with others to a specific and special role with responsibility for others. A tension is identified by Weber (1968: 1166–8) in his account of monasticism's two 'very different' meanings; the first is a concern with 'individual salvation through finding a personal, direct path to God'. He sees monks banding together and living in community as a continuing expression of this concern, given that the individual salvation of the community's members remains the focus of life. However, he suggests that the need for the hierocratic apparatus of the Church to deal with the exclusive monastic community within its ranks leads to an ongoing process of interpretation of the 'role' of monasticism, at first as a 'specific "vocation" within its own ranks'. Eventually (and this is what Weber describes as the second 'meaning' of monasticism), 'asceticism is completely reinterpreted into a means, not primarily of attaining individual salvation in one's own way, but of preparing the monk for work on behalf of the hierocratic authority – the foreign and home mission and the struggle against competing authorities' (Weber 1968: 1167). In such an incorporation, the end of monasticism shifts from an internal to an external focus.

Secondly, we have seen how this can lead to a shift in social status. The abbey church is an architecture of stability (Chapter 2), the heart of prayer in the life of the household but, in its assertion of the restored status of Catholicism and monasticism, it is also an expression of the pursuit of prominence (and prestige). In this relationship of witness to society, monasticism is not only lived, but made visible. Here, however, is what Kierkegaard ([1846] 2009: 340) in the *Concluding Unscientific Postscript* describes as 'the questionable character of the monastic movement'. Adopting a pseudonym that engages with monastic history – the name of Johannes Climacus, a notable Desert Father – Kierkegaard repeatedly offers 'all due respect for the medieval monastic movement' for its passionate pursuit of the innerness in which nothing is preferred to the telos of God. Yet this innerness 'received its striking expression, presumably in order to afford a properly vigorous demonstration of its existence, in a distinctive and special outwardness, through which, however much one twists and turns, it came to differ only relatively from all other outwardness'. As the internality becomes an externality, the show of monasticism's virtue leads to conceit, especially as other people start treating the monk as special – a holy man. This brings critical focus to the monastery's economy of prestige, and to the problem of deference to the monks (which as we have seen in Chapter 8, can have damaging consequences). Misrecognising the character of the monk's virtue as something extraordinary, the monk is puffed up and the very goal of the transcendence of the self is undermined.

For Kierkegaard ([1846] 2009: 386) the due respect for the monastic movement is in its pursuit of 'self-annihilation' as 'the essential form of the God-relationship', which must not be expressed in the external. But this itself draws us to a key tension within the ethnography. On the one hand, a core aspect of English Benedictine identity is the potential for transcendence through 'the sinking of the individual in the community' (Butler 1919: 45). On the other hand, the monks recognise how a culture of individualism can emerge within the household (Chapter 8). Indeed, in the central importance given to contemplative prayer (Chapter 5), the freedom afforded by the withdrawal of the self from the social remains a vital space of encounter with God: the question of how to integrate this crucial freedom into a renewed community and liturgical life remains a live point. The theologian Christopher Insole (2001: 479) taking as his target 'some sloppier modern constructions of the apophatic God' (Insole 2001: 479), warns against a tendency to see experience as closed in on the individual and so personal as to be incommunicable – the 'phony-privatisation of the inner world of each hermetically sealed individual' (2001: 481). The God for whom this individual looks becomes, like the searcher, 'unfathomable', a projection of the 'intensely private romantic self' (2001: 482). Nothing can be revealed, and so each individual is separated by their claim to a knowledge that cannot be shared. And as nothing can be said of the experience of God – it can only be understood in the private world – God can neither be spoken in the public domain, nor affect it: His inexpressibility renders Him socially and politically impotent.

Insole makes it clear that his intention is not to attack the apophatic tradition, but rather to warn about the risk of self-indulgence in the closure of the self to the means of communication with others. Nevertheless, I think his warning raises an important point for our understanding of the social life of the monastery: how the space of solitude, recognised as the crucial freedom in which to be 'alone with the alone', nonetheless, as an exaggerated individualism, becomes something exclusive of the experience of others in a way that tugs against the Benedictine life's social impulse. This is the crucial dilemma of engagement and disengagement that lies at the heart of monasticism; the 'double movement' (Kierkegaard ([1846] 2009: 344) of severance and return, how to be a 'stranger in the world of the finite' while nonetheless 'taking the God-relationship along in everything every day' ([1846] 2009: 398).

Stability and departure

I recall one day, during my fieldwork, the chant seemed threadbare and for some reason there were very few monks at the liturgy of the hours. I had been working in the library and, after he had listed some of the pressing engagements that had drawn so many away from the enclosure, the librarian turned to me and smiled: 'in the future, I suppose, monasteries will be built on aeroplanes'. It was a world where everyone always had somewhere else to be; in the end, were monks any different? And with that, the bell rang and he headed away to the midday office.

But, of course, stability mattered dearly to him. For half a century, his days were shaped by the rhythm of the liturgy of the hours, by his responsibilities for the community, who in turn were shaped by his diligence, his prayer, and his laughter at teatime and in the calefactory: a life cycle bound to a family who cared for him to his last days. His bodily remains now lie alongside those of his brothers in the abbey grounds, still part of the place, still within the community of prayer.

There is something significant about this stability in the contemporary world because of the contrast it invites. The intimate sense of place contrasts with the anonymity of the non-place (Augé 1995); the enduring social bonds contrast with a world of networking and fleeting social interactions. This is the 'witness value of stability' (Rees et al. 1978: 142), a visible expression of how we might better understand ourselves if only we would (or could) reject the life symbolised by the gyrovague,[2] a life turned around and around, and instead seek a community in which to root ourselves.

Stability shines out in all these ways but, in doing so, it risks being romanticised as a kind of comfortable domesticity. In fact, there is a deep intensity to close social interaction. One of the times I was hearing how monks would sometimes push notes under one another's door during the *summum silentium* so as not to let the sun set on their anger, it was pointed out just how much harder it was for people to live with one another as numbers dwindled. The larger the community, the more scope you had to choose who to spend time with, and the more opportunity there was to avoid certain monks. 'As the community gets smaller, the call to holiness in how we interact with one another gets even harder. In a close community it's hardest of all, but really it's in these everyday acts of love that the gospel is communicated authentically.'

All of this, of course, reiterates the value of staying put as a grounding for the monks' growth through 'the development of Christian social sanctity' (Gasquet 1896: xiv). But this brings us back to the question: in the context of such a commitment to stability, what does it mean to leave home?

This is a matter of special significance in the English Benedictine Congregation, because historic circumstances led to a particular

---

2 *Rule* of St Benedict, Chapter 1.

emphasis on the fundamental character of *local* stability, expressed perhaps most forcefully by Cuthbert Butler (1924: 133–4). This was, as we have seen, a reaction to a previous state of affairs in which monks took a missionary oath that, in a sense, superseded the vow of stability: it led to them being transferred from monastery to parish (Chapter 7) and not ordinarily having an opportunity to spend their lives within a monastic community. The building-up of Downside Abbey (Chapter 2) and the other great English Benedictine homes was a reassertion of stability after the abolition of the missionary oath, a material expression of the lifelong commitment to a particular household that had been recovered. Leaving such a home behind might seem to call all this into question.

While the value and importance of local stability remains integral, as some monks of the community have nevertheless pointed out (see, for example, Yeo 1982: 352), the danger of its fetishisation is that it comes to be seen as an end in itself, rather than a means to an end. At the heart of stability is the goal of perseverance – described to me as 'standing firm in Christ'. Crucially, this is not just about the comfort of the familiar, but about keeping going in the face of the unknown – ultimately in the face of death.

This is important, as a misapprehension of the 'localised' nature of stability might leave it seeming rather trivial. The architecture of stability is not just about home comforts, but the intensity of a life lived with others and, within that relationship, coming to know God. The rhythm of stability is not simply a shared routine, but an expression of time's relation to eternity. In this sense, stability has a paradoxically *unsettling* quality. The local is opened up through its relationship with the transcendent.

Here we return to the monk lying on the funeral pall, prayed for by his brothers. Dead to the world, the monk confronts the infinitude of time and space. Resurrected to the world, he returns to a particular time and a particular space: the challenge of living out that relationship with the absolute through the relationships of everyday life. In this sense, stability is fundamentally about making a home, but this is a way of being at home that necessarily begins with a departure.

REFERENCES

Agamben, Giorgio. 2013. *The Highest Poverty: Monastic Rules and Form-of-Life*, trans. Adam Kotsko. Stanford: Stanford University Press.

Applebaum, Herbert. 1992. *The Concept of Work: Ancient, Medieval, and Modern*. Albany: State University of New York Press.

Arnstein, Walter L. 1982. *Protestant versus Catholic in Mid-Victorian England: Mr. Newdegate and the Nuns*. Columbia, MO: University of Missouri Press.

Asad, Talal. 1993. *Genealogies of Religion: Discipline and Reasons of Power in Christianity and Islam*. Baltimore: John Hopkins University Press.

Augé, Marc. 1995. *Non-Places: Introduction to an Anthropology of Supermodernity*, trans. John Howe. London: Verso.

Baker, Augustine. 1657. *Sancta Sophia, or, Directions for the prayer of contemplation*, ed. Serenus Cressy. Douai: John Patte and Thomas Fievet.

Barry, Patrick. 2005. *A Cloister in the World*. St Louis: The Abbey of St Mary and St Louis.

Bastide, Roger. 1955. 'Le Principe de coupure et le comportement afro-brésilien'. In *Anais do XXXI Congresso internacional de Americanistas*, ed. Herbert Baldus, 493–503. São Paulo: Editora Anhembi.

Bazzanella, Carla. 2011. 'Redundancy, repetition, and intensity in discourse'. *Language Sciences* 33 (2): 243–54.

Bergeron, Katherine. 1998. *Decadent Enchantments: The Revival of Gregorian Chant at Solesmes*. Berkeley: University of California Press.

Berliner, David, Michael Lambek, Richard Shweder, Richard Irvine, and Albert Piette. 2016. 'Anthropology and the study of contradictions'. *HAU: Journal of Ethnographic Theory* 6 (1): 1–27.

Bielo, James S. 2009. *Words upon the Word: An Ethnography of Evangelical Group Bible Study*. New York: New York University Press.

Birt, Henry Norbert. 1902. *Downside: The History of St Gregory's School from Its Commencement at Douay to the Present Time*. London: Kegan Paul, Trench, Trubner.

Bloch, Maurice. 1968. 'Tombs and Conservatism Among the Merina of Madagascar'. *Man*, N. S. 3(1): 94–104.

Bloch, Maurice. 1974. 'Symbols, Song, Dance and Features of Articulation: Is religion an extreme form of traditional authority?' *European Journal of Sociology* 15 (1): 55–81.

Bloch, Maurice. 1986. *From Blessing to Violence: History and Ideology in the Circumcision Ritual of the Merina of Madagascar*. Cambridge: Cambridge University Press.

Bloch, Maurice. 2004. 'Ritual and Deference'. In *Ritual and Memory: Toward a Comparative Anthropology of Religion*, ed. Harvey Whitehouse and James Laidlaw, 65–78. Walnut Creek, CA: Altamira Press.

Bossy, John. 1970. 'The Counter-Reformation and the People of Catholic Europe'. *Past and Present* 47 (1): 51–70.

Bourdieu, Pierre. 1963. 'The Attitude of the Algerian Peasant Toward Time.' In *Mediterranean Countrymen: Essays in the Social Anthropology of the Mediterranean*, ed. Julian Pitt-Rivers, 55–72. Paris: Mouton.

Bowman, Marion. 2004. 'Procession and Possession in Glastonbury: Continuity, Change and the Manipulation of Tradition'. *Folklore* 115 (3): 273–85.

Boyarin, Jonathan. 1989. 'Voices Around the Text: The Ethnography of Reading at Mesivta Tifereth Jerusalem.' *Cultural Anthropology* 4 (4): 399–421.

Braudel, Fernand. 1972. *The Mediterranean and the Mediterranean World in the Age of Philip II: Volume I*, trans. Siân Reynolds. New York: Harper and Row.

Burke, Thomas. 1910. *Catholic History of Liverpool*. Liverpool: C. Tinling and Co.

Butler, B. C. 1959. 'English Spiritual Writers: John Chapman'. *Clergy Review* 44: 641–62.

Butler, B. C. 1961. *Prayer: An Adventure in Living*. London: Darton, Longman and Todd.

Butler, B. C. 1967. *The Theology of Vatican II*. London: Darton, Longman and Todd.

Butler, Edward Cuthbert. 1919. *Benedictine Monachism: Studies in Benedictine Life and Rule*. London: Longmans, Green and Co.

Butler, Edward Cuthbert. 1926. *Western Mysticism: The Teaching of SS. Augustine, Gregory and Bernard on Contemplation and the Contemplative Life*, second edition. London: Constable.

Butler, Edward Cuthbert. 1932. *Ways of Christian Life: Old Spirituality for Modern Men*. London: Sheed and Ward.

Campbell-Jones, Suzanne. 1979. *In Habit: An Anthropological Study of Working Nuns*. London: Faber and Faber.

Cannell, Fenella. 2005. 'The Christianity of Anthropology'. *Journal of the Royal Anthropological Institute* 11 (2): 335–56.

Cannell, Fenella. 2006. 'The Anthropology of Christianity'. In *The Anthropology of Christianity*, ed. Fenella Cannell, 1–50. Durham, NC: Duke University Press.

Casey, Michael. 2005. *An Unexciting Life: Reflections on Benedictine Spirituality*. Petersham, MA: St Bede's Publications.

Chapman, John. 1935. The Spiritual Letters of Dom John Chapman O. S. B., ed. Roger Hudleston. London: Sheed and Ward.

Clark, J. P. H. 2004. 'Augustine Baker, O. S. B.: Towards a Re-Assessment'. *Studies in Spirituality* 14: 209–24.

Coakley, Sarah. 2002. *Powers and Submissions: Spirituality, Philosophy and Gender*. Oxford: Blackwell.

Coakley, Sarah. 2015. *The New Asceticism: Sexuality, Gender and the Quest for God*. London: Continuum.

Coleman, Simon. 2000. 'Meanings of Movement, Place and Home at Walsingham'. *Culture and Religion* 1 (2): 153–69.

Coleman, Simon. 2019. 'From Excess to Encompassment: Repetition, Recantation, and the Trashing of Time in Swedish Christianities'. *History and Anthropology* 30 (2): 170–89.

Connerton, Paul. 2009. 'How Modernity Forgets'. Cambridge: Cambridge University Press.

Cook, Joanna. 2010. 'Ascetic Practice and Participant Observation, or, the Gift of Doubt in Field Experience.' In *Emotions in the Field: The Psychology and Anthropology of Fieldwork Experience*, ed. James Davies and Dimitrina Spencer, 239–65. Stanford: Stanford University Press.

Cook, Joanna. 2010. *Meditation in Modern Buddhism: Renunciation and Change in Thai Monastic Life*. Cambridge: Cambridge University Press.

Corwin, Anna I. 2021. *Embracing Age: How Catholic Nuns Became Models of Aging Well*. New Brunswick, NJ: Rutgers University Press.

Courtois, Aline. 2018. *Elite Schooling and Social Inequality: Privilege and Power in Ireland's Top Private Schools*. London: Palgrave Macmillan.

Crapanzano, Vincent. 2000. *Serving the Word: Literalism in America from the Pulpit to the Bench*. New York: New Press.

Deflem, Mathieu. 1991. 'Ritual, Anti-Structure, and Religion: a Discussion of Victor Turner's Processual Symbolic Analysis'. *Journal for the Scientific Study of Religion* 30 (1): 1–25.

Dohrn-van Rossum, Gerhard. 1996. *History of the Hour: Clocks and Modern Temporal Orders*, trans. Thomas Dunlap. Chicago: University of Chicago Press.

Duffy, Eamon. 1992. *The Stripping of the Altars: Traditional Religion in England, 1400–1580*. New Haven: Yale University Press.

Egan, Harvey D. 1978. 'Christian Apophatic and Kataphatic Mysticisms'. *Theological Studies* 39 (3): 399–426.

Eickelman, Dale F. 1978. 'The Art of Memory: Islamic Education and Its Social Reproduction'. *Comparative Studies in Society and History* 20 (4): 485–516.

Eickelman, Dale F. 1992. 'Mass Higher Education and the Religious Imagination in Contemporary Arab Societies'. *American Ethnologist* 19 (4): 643–55.

El Guindi, Fadwa. 2008. *By Noon Prayer: The Rhythm of Islam*. Oxford: Berg.

Engelke, Matthew. 2007. *A Problem of Presence: Beyond Scripture in an African Church*. Berkeley: University of California Press.

Evans, Nicholas. 2023. 'Exemplars'. In *The Cambridge Handbook for* the *Anthropology of Ethics*, ed. James Laidlaw, 433–59. Cambridge: Cambridge University Press.

Farkas, Mary Ann, and Gale Miller. 2007. 'Reentry and Reintegration: Challenges Faced by the Families of Convicted Sex Offenders'. *Federal Sentencing Reporter* 20 (2): 88–92.

Faubion, James. 2013. 'The Subject That is Not One: on the Ethics of Mysticism'. *Anthropological Theory* 13 (4): 287–307.

Fortin, John R. 2003. 'The Reaffirmation of Monastic Hospitality'. *Downside Review* 121 (423): 105–18.

Foster, David. 2005. *Reading with God: Lectio Divina*. London: Continuum.

Foster, David. 2015. *Contemplative Prayer: A New Framework*. London: Bloomsbury.

Foster, David. 2021. 'Lectio Divina: Reading in the Rule of St Benedict'. *CounterText* 7 (1): 30–45.

Freeman, Laurence. 2001. 'Baker and the Contemplative Ideal'. In *That Mysterious Man: Essays on Augustine Baker OSB 1575–1641*, ed. Michael Woodward, 191–201. Abergavenny, Monmouthshire: Three Peaks Press.

Gasquet, Francis Aidan. 1895. *The Last Abbot of Glastonbury and His Companions: An Historical Sketch*. London: S. Marshall, Hamilton, Kent and Co.

Gasquet, Francis Aidan. 1896. 'Sketch of Monastic Constitutional History'. Introduction to *The Monks of the West from St. Benedict to St. Bernard* by Charles Forbes, comte de Montalembert. London: J. C. Nimmo.

Goldman, Marion, and Steven Pfaff. 2014. 'Reconsidering Virtuosity: Religious Innovation and Spiritual Privilege'. *Sociological Theory* 32 (2): 128–46.

Goodier, Alban. 1935. 'Abbot Chapman on Prayer.' *The Month* 165: 493–503.

Granfield, Patrick. 1967. 'An interview with Abbot Christopher Butler.' *Review for Religious* 26 (1): 46–59.

Guarino, Maria S. 2018. *Listen with the Ear of the Heart: Music and Monastery Life at Weston Priory*. Rochester, NY: University of Rochester Press.

Hall, Michael. 2000. 'What Do Victorian Churches Mean? Symbolism and Sacramentalism in Anglican Church Architecture, 1850–1870.' *Journal of the Society of Architectural Historians* 59 (1): 78–95

Han, Byung-Chul. 2020. *The Disappearance of Rituals: A Topology of the Present*, trans. Daniel Steur. Cambridge: Polity.

Harvey, Peter. 1969. Introduction to *The Experience of Prayer* by Sebastian Moore and Kevin Maguire, 3–8. London: Darton, Longman and Todd.

Hedley, John Cuthbert. 1894. *A Retreat: Thirty-Three Discourses With Meditations for the Use of Clergy, Religious, and others*. London: Burns and Oates.

Herzfeld, Michael. 2004. *The Body Impolitic: Artisans and Artifice in the Global Hierarchy of Value*. Chicago: University of Chicago Press.

Hill, Rosemary. 2007. *God's Architect: Pugin and the Building of Romantic Britain*. London: Allan Lane.

Hirschkind, Charles. 2001. 'The Ethics of Listening: Cassette-Sermon Audition in Contemporary Egypt'. *American Ethnologist* 28 (3): 623–49.

Hobsbawm, Eric. 1983. 'Inventing Traditions'. In *The Invention of Tradition*, ed. Eric Hobsbawm and Terence Ranger, 1–14. Cambridge: Cambridge University Press.

Horn, Walter. 1973. 'On the Origins of the Medieval Cloister'. *Gesta* 12 (1/2): 13–52.

Hudleston, Roger. 1935. 'Abbot Chapman on Prayer: A Reply to an Article in "The Month" for June 1935'. *Downside Review* 53 (3): 286–306.

Humphrey, Caroline. 1997. 'Exemplars and Rules: Aspects of the Discourse of Moralities in Mongolia'. In *The Ethnography of Moralities*, ed. Signe Howell, 25–47. London: Routledge.

Ingram, Philip. 1991. 'Protestant Patriarchy and the Catholic Priesthood in Nineteenth-Century England'. *Journal of Social History* 24 (4): 783–97.

Insole, Christopher. 2001. 'Anthropomorphism and the Apophatic God'. *Modern Theology* 17 (4): 475–83.

Irvine, Richard D. G. 2010a. 'The Experience of Fieldwork in an English Benedictine Monastery; Or, Not Playing at Being a Monk.' *Fieldwork in Religion* 5 (2): 146–60.

Irvine, Richard D. G. 2010b. 'The Mission and the Cloister: Identity, Tradition, and Transformation in the English Benedictine Congregation'. *Saeculum* 61 (2): 111–28.

Irvine, Richard D. G. 2010c. 'How to Read: Lectio Divina in an English Benedictine Monastery'. *Culture and Religion* 11 (4): 395–411.

Irvine, Richard D. G. 2011a. 'The Architecture of Stability: Monasteries and the Importance of Place in a World of Non-Places.' *Etnofoor* 23 (1): 29–49.

Irvine, Richard D. G. 2011b. 'Eating in Silence in an English Benedictine Monastery'. In *Food and Faith in Christian Culture*, ed. Ken Albala and Trudy Eden, 221–37. New York: Columbia University Press.

Irvine, Richard D. G. 2017. 'The Everyday Life of Monks: English Benedictine Identity and the Performance of Proximity'. In *Monasticism in Modern Times*, eds Isabelle Jonveaux and Stefania Palmisano, 191–208. London: Routledge.

Irvine, Richard D. G. 2018. 'Our Lady of Ipswich: Devotion, Dissonance, and the Agitation of Memory at a Forgotten Pilgrimage Site'. *Journal of the Royal Anthropological Institute* 24 (2): 366–84.

Irvine, Richard D. G. 2020. 'The Social Life of the Inexpressible: English Benedictine Mysticism, the Ineffable, and the Sublime'. In *Capturing the Ineffable: An Anthropology of Wisdom*, eds Philip Y. Kao and Joseph S. Alter, 45–63. Toronto: University of Toronto Press.

Irvine, Richard D. G. 2021a. 'Experts in Self-Isolation? Monastic Outreach During Lockdown'. *Religions* 12: 814.

Irvine, Richard D. G. 2021b. 'Points of Resistance to Lectio Divina: An Anthropological Perspective'. *CounterText* 7 (1): 46–52.

James, Augustine. 1961. *The Story of Downside Abbey Church*. Stratton-on-the-Fosse, Somerset: Downside Abbey Press.

Jamison, Christopher. 2006. *Finding Sanctuary: Monastic Steps for Everyday Life*. London: Weidenfeld and Nicolson.

Johnson, Christopher D. L. 2010. *The Globalization of Hesychasm and the Jesus Prayer: Contesting Contemplation*. London: Continuum.

Jonveaux, Isabelle. 2018. *Moines, corps et âme: une sociologie de l'ascèse monastique contemporaine*. Paris: Cerf.

Keane, Webb. 2006. 'Anxious Transcendence'. In *The Anthropology of Christianity*, ed. Fenella Cannell, 308–23. Durham, NC: Duke University Press.

Keane, Webb. 2007. *Christian Moderns: Freedom and Fetish in the Mission Encounter*. Berkeley: University of California Press.

Keenan, Marie. 2011. *Child Sexual Abuse and the Catholic Church: Gender, Power, and Organizational Culture*. New York: Oxford University Press.

Kelly, James E. 2021. 'Political Mysticism: Augustine Baker, the Spiritual Formation of Missionaries and the Catholic Reformation in England'. *Journal of Ecclesiastical History* 72 (2): 300–22.

Kelty, Christopher M. 2019. *The Participant: A Century of Participation in Four Stories*. Chicago: University of Chicago Press.

Kierkegaard, Søren [1846] 2009. *Concluding Unscientific Postscript to the Philosophical Crumbs*, trans. Alistair Hannay. Cambridge: Cambridge University Press.

Klauser, Theodor. 1969. *A Short History of the Western Liturgy: An Account and Some Reflections*, trans. John Halliburton. Oxford: Oxford University Press.

Knowles, David. 1940. *The Monastic Order in England: A History of Its Development From the Times of St. Dunstan to the Fourth Lateran Council, 943–1216*. Cambridge: Cambridge University Press.

Knowles, David. 1962. *Saints and Scholars: Twenty-Five Medieval Portraits*. Cambridge: Cambridge University Press.

Knowles, David. 1966. *From Pachomius to Ignatius: A Study in the Constitutional History of the Religious Orders*. Oxford: Clarendon Press.

La Fontaine, Jean. 1977. 'The Power of Rights'. *Man* N. S. 12 (3/4): 421–37.

Lambert, Ambrose. 1997. *Mendip: A Journey Around the Ornate Parish Church Towers of the Somerset Mendip Hills*. Radstock, Somerset: Fosseway Press.

Larsen, Timothy. 2014. *The Slain God: Anthropologists and the Christian Faith*. Oxford: Oxford University Press.

Lester, Rebecca J. 2005. *Jesus in Our Wombs: Embodying Modernity in a Mexican Convent*. Berkeley: University of California Press.

Livingston, Eric. 1995. *An Anthropology of Reading*. Bloomington, IN: Indiana University Press.

Luhrmann, T. M. 2004. 'Metakinesis: How God Becomes Intimate in

Contemporary U.S. Christianity'. *American Anthropologist* 106 (3): 518–28.

Luhrmann, T. M. 2007. 'How Do You Learn to Know That it is God Who Speaks?' In *Learning Religion: Anthropological Approaches*, eds David Berliner and Ramon Sarró, 83–102. Oxford: Berghahn.

Luhrmann, T. M. 2012. *When God Talks Back: Understanding the American Evangelical Relationship With God*. New York: Knopf.

Luhrmann, T. M. and Rachel Morgain. 2012. 'Prayer as Inner Sense Cultivation: An Attentional Learning Theory of Spiritual Experience'. *Ethos* 40 (4): 359–89.

Lunn, David. 1975. 'Augustine Baker (1575–1641) and the English Mystical Tradition'. *Journal of Ecclesiastical History* 26 (3): 267–77.

Lunn, David. 1980. *The English Benedictines, 1540–1688: From Reformation to Revolution*. London: Burns and Oates.

Lynch, Andrew P. 2017. 'The Benedictine Tradition Since Vatican II: Catholic Monasticism in the Modern World'. In *Monasticism in Modern Times*, eds Isabelle Jonveaux and Stefania Palmisano, 13–28. Abingdon, Oxon: Routledge.

Main, John. 1980. *Word into Silence*. London: Darton, Longman and Todd.

Mair, Jonathan. 2015. 'The Discourse of Ignorance and the Ethics of Detachment Among Mongolian Tibetan Buddhists in Inner Mongolia, China'. In *Detachment: Essays on the Limits of Relational Thinking*, eds Matei Candea, Joanna Cook, Catherine Trundle and Thomas Yarrow, 236–55. Manchester: Manchester University Press.

Mangan, J. A. and Callum McKenzie. 2006. 'The Other Side of the Coin: Victorian Masculinity, Field Sports, and English Elite Education'. In *A Sport-Loving Society: Victorian and Edwardian Middle-Class England at Play*, ed. J. A. Mangan, 45–64. London: Routledge.

Marchand, Trevor H. J. 2010. 'Embodied Cognition and Communication: Studies with British Fine Woodworkers''. *Journal of the Royal Anthropological Institute* 16 (S1): S100–S120.

Marchand, Trevor H. J. 2022. *The Pursuit of Pleasurable Work: Craftwork in Twenty-First Century England*. Oxford: Berghahn.

Marcia, James E. 1966. 'Development and Validation of Ego-Identity Status'. *Journal of Personality and Social Psychology* 3 (5): 551–8.

Martini, Carlo Maria. 1994. *The Joy of the Gospel: Meditations for Young People*, trans. James McGrath. Collegeville, MN: Liturgical Press.

Mauss, Marcel. [1925] 1954. *The Gift: Forms and Functions of Exchange in Archaic Societies*, trans. Ian Cunnison. London: Cohen and West.

Maxwell, Claire, and Peter Aggleton. 2015. 'The Historical Construction of an Elite Education in England'. In *Elite Education: International Perspectives*, eds Claire Maxwell and Peter Aggleton, 15–28. Abingdon, Oxon: Routledge.

Mayblin, Maya. 2017. 'The Lapsed and the Laity: Discipline and Lenience in the Study of Religion'. *Journal of the Royal Anthropological Institute* 23 (3): 503–22.

Mayblin, Maya. 2019. 'A Brilliant Jewel: Sex, Celibacy, and the Roman Catholic Church'. *Religion* 49 (4): 517–38.

McGinn, Bernard. 2021. *The Crisis of Mysticism: Quietism in Seventeenth-Century Spain, Italy, and France*. New York: Crossroad.

McKenty, Neil. 1986. *In the Stillness Dancing: the Journey of John Main*. London: Darton, Longman and Todd.

Moore, Sebastian, and Kevin Maguire. 1969. *The Experience of Prayer*. London: Darton, Longman and Todd.

Morey, Adrian. 1979. *David Knowles: A Memoir*. London: Darton, Longman and Todd.

Mumford, Lewis. 1934. *Technics and Civilization*. New York: Harcourt Brace Jovanovich.

Murcott, Anne. 1997. 'Family Meals – A Thing of the past?', in *Food, Health and Identity*, ed. Pat Caplan, 32–49. Abingdon, Oxfordshire: Routledge.

Murray, Gregory. 1977. *Music and the Mass: A Personal History*. Leigh-on-Sea, Essex: Kevin Mayhew.

Naumescu, Vlad. 2012. 'Learning the "Science of Feelings": Religious Training in Eastern Christian Monasticism'. *Ethnos* 77 (2): 227–51.

Neveling, Patrick, and Susanne Klein. 2010. 'Tradition Within and Beyond the Framework of Invention'. In *Tradition Within and*

Beyond the Framework of Invention: Case Studies from the Mascarenes and Japan, eds Susanne Klein and Patrick Neveling, 1–51. Halle: ZIRS, Martin-Luther-Universität Halle-Wittenberg.

Nuzzo, James L. J. 1996. 'The Rule of Saint Benedict: the Debates Over the Interpretation of an Ancient Legal and Spiritual Document'. *Harvard Journal of Law and Public Policy* 20 (3): 867–86.

O'Donnell, Roderick. 1981. 'Pugin Designs for Downside Abbey'. *The Burlington Magazine* 123 (937): 230–3.

O'Neill, Kevin Lewis. 2020. 'The Unmaking of a Pedophilic Priest: Transnational Clerical Sexual Abuse in Guatemala'. *Comparative Studies in Society and History* 62 (4): 745–69.

Orsi, Robert A. 2017. 'What is Catholic about the Clergy Sex Abuse Crisis?' In *The Anthropology of Catholicism: A Reader*, eds Kristin Norget, Valentina Napolitano and Maya Mayblin, 282–92. Oakland, CA: University of California Press.

Ortner, Sherry B. 1978. *Sherpas Through Their Rituals*. Cambridge: Cambridge University Press.

Parkins, Wendy. 2004. 'Out of Time: Fast Subjects and Slow Living'. *Time and Society* 13 (2–3): 363–82.

Paz, Denis G. 1992. *Popular Anti-Catholicism in Mid-Victorian England*. Stanford: Stanford University Press.

Pevsner, Nikolaus. 1958. *The Buildings of England: North Somerset and Bristol*. Harmondsworth: Penguin.

Philips, Peter. 2024. *Christopher Butler: Monk, Theologian, Bishop*. Upper Woolhampton, Berks.: Weldon Press.

Pietrykowski, Bruce. 2004. 'You Are What You Eat: The Social Economy of the Slow Food Movement'. *Review of Social Economy* 62 (4): 307–21.

Pina-Cabral, João de. 2018. 'Modes of Participation'. *Anthropological Theory* 18 (4): 435–55.

Pink, Sarah. 2009. 'Urban Social Movements and Small Places: Slow Cities as Sites of Activism'. *City* 13 (4): 451–65.

Platt, Tristan. 2012. 'Between Routine and Rupture: The Archive as Field Event'. In *Sage Handbook of Social Anthropology*, eds Richard Fardon and Olivia Harris, 21–37. London: Sage.

Post, Paul. 2001. 'The Creation of Tradition: Rereading and Reading Beyond Hobsbawm'. In *Religious Identity and the Invention of*

Tradition, eds A. W. J. Houtepen and Jan Willem van Henten, 41–59. Assen: Royal Van Gorcum.

Powers, Alan. 1999. *Francis Pollen: Architect, 1926–1987*. Oxford: Robert Dugdale.

Prince, Ruth, and David Riches. 2000. *The New Age in Glastonbury: The Construction of Religious Movements*. Oxford: Berghahn.

Pryce, Paula. 2018. *The Monk's Cell: Ritual and Knowledge in American Contemplative Christianity*. New York: Oxford University Press.

Pugin, Augustus Welby. 1841a. *Contrasts: or, A Parallel Between the Noble Edifices of the Fourteenth and Fifteenth Centuries, and Similar Buildings of the Present Day; Showing the Present Decay of Taste*, second revised and expanded edition. London: Charles Dolman.

Pugin, Augustus Welby. 1841b *The True Principles of Christian or Pointed Architecture*. London: J. Weale.

Qirko, Hector. 2004. 'Altruistic Celibacy, Kin-Cue Manipulation, and the Development of Religious Institutions'. *Zygon* 39 (3): 681–706.

Ralls, Walter. 1974. 'The Papal Aggression of 1850: A Study in Victorian Anti-Catholicism'. *Church History* 43 (2): 242–6.

Ranger, Terence. 1993. 'The Invention of Tradition Revisited: The Case of Colonial Africa'. In *Legitimacy and the State in Twentieth-Century Africa*, eds Terence Ranger and Olufemi Vaughan, 62–111. London: Palgrave Macmillan.

Rees, Daniel and others. 1978. *Consider Your Call: A Theology of Monastic Life Today*. London: SPCK.

Reid, Alcuin. 2004. *The Organic Development of the Liturgy: The Principles of Liturgical Reform and Their Relation to the Twentieth-century Liturgical Movement Prior to the Second Vatican Council*. Farnborough, Hampshire: St Michael's Abbey Press.

Robbins, Joel. 2001. 'God is Nothing But Talk: Modernity, Language and Prayer in a Papua New Guinea Society'. *American Anthropologist* 103 (4): 901–12.

Robbins, Joel. 2007. 'Continuity Thinking and the Problem of Christian Culture: Belief, Time, and the Anthropology of Christianity'. *Current Anthropology* 48 (1): 5–38.

Robbins, Joel. 2018. 'Where in the World Are Values? Exemplarity, Morality, and Social Process'. In *Recovering the Human Subject:*

Freedom, Creativity and Decision, eds James Laidlaw, Barbara Bodenhorn and Martin Holbraad, 174–92. Cambridge: Cambridge University Press.

Sarris, Marios. 2004. 'Pitfalls of Intellection: Pedagogical Concerns on Mount Athos'. *Journal of Modern Greek Studies* 22 (2): 113–35.

Scheper-Hughes, Nancy and John Devine. 2003. 'Priestly Celibacy and Child Sexual Abuse'. *Sexualities* 6 (1): 15–40

Scott, Geoffrey. 1992. *Gothic Rage Undone: English Monks in the Age of Enlightenment*. Bath: Downside Abbey Press.

Seasoltz, R. Kevin. 1974. 'Monastic Hospitality'. *American Benedictine Review* 25 (4): 427–51.

Silber, Ilana Friedrich. 1995. *Virtuosity, Charisma, and Social Order: A Comparative Sociological Study of Monasticism in Theravada Buddhism and Medieval Catholicism*. Cambridge: Cambridge University Press.

Sillem, Aelred. 1991. 'Father David and the Monastic and Spiritual Life'. In *David Knowles Remembered*, eds Christopher Brooke, Roger Lovatt, David Luscombe and Aelred Sillem, 27–46. Cambridge: Cambridge University Press.

Simon, Brian. 1974. *The Two Nations and the Educational Structure 1780–1870*. London: Lawrence & Wishart.

Snow, Terence Benedict. 1903. *Sketches of Old Downside*. London: Sands and Co.

Sorg, Rembert. 1951. *Towards a Benedictine Theology of Manual Labor*. Lisle, IL: Benedictine Orient.

Spearritt, Placid. 1974. 'The Survival of Medieval Spirituality Among the Exiled English Black Monks'. *American Benedictine Review* 25 (3): 287–316.

Srivastava, Sanjay. 1998. *Constructing Post-Colonial India: National Character and the Doon School*. London: Routledge.

Stamp, Gavin. 2011. 'Downside Abbey and Sir Giles Gilbert Scott', 177–99. In *Downside Abbey, An Architectural History*, ed. Aidan Bellenger. London: Merrell.

Stockford, Cyprian. 1964. 'Monastic Renewal and the Work of God'. *Downside Review* 82 (269): 312–26.

Studzinski, Raymond J. 2009. *Reading to Live: The Evolving Practice of Lectio Divina*. Collegeville, MN: Liturgical Press.

Tambiah, S. J. 1968. 'The Magical Power of Words'. *Man* (N. S.) 3 (2): 175–208.

Tambiah, S. J. 1970. *Buddhism and the Spirit Cults in North-east Thailand*. Cambridge: Cambridge University Press.

Tambiah, S. J. 1976. *World Conqueror and World Renouncer: A Study of Buddhism and Polity in Thailand Against a Historical Background*. Cambridge: Cambridge University Press.

Tambiah, S. J. 1981. 'A Performative Approach to Ritual'. *Proceedings of the British Academy* 65: 113–69.

Temple, Liam Peter. 2017. 'The Mysticism of Augustine Baker, OSB: A Reconsideration'. *Reformation and Renaissance Review* 19 (3): 213–30.

Temple, Liam Peter. 2019. *Mysticism in Early Modern England*. Woodbridge, Suffolk: Boydell and Brewer.

Thompson, E. P. 1967. 'Time, Work-Discipline, and Industrial Capitalism'. *Past and Present* 38: 56–97.

Tolle, Eckhart. 1997. *The Power of Now: A Guide to Spiritual Enlightenment*. Vancouver: Namaste Publishing.

Tomlinson, Matt, and Matthew Engelke. 2006. 'Meaning, Anthropology, Christianity'. In *The Limits of Meaning: Case Studies in the Anthropology of Christianity*, eds Matthew Engelke and Matt Tomlinson, 1–37. Oxford: Berghahn.

Trethowan, Illtyd. 1942. *What is the Liturgy?* Exeter: Catholic Records Press.

Trethowan, Illtyd. 1952. *Christ in the Liturgy*. London: Sheed and Ward.

Trethowan, Illtyd. 1971. *The Absolute and the Atonement*. London: Allen and Unwin.

Troeltsch, Ernst. 1931. *The Social Teaching of the Christian Churches*, trans. Olive Wyon. London: Allen and Unwin.

Turner, Victor. 1969. *The Ritual Process: Structure and Anti-Structure*. Chicago: Aldine.

Turner, Victor. 1972a. 'Passages, Margins, and Poverty: Religious Symbols of Communitas' (Part I). *Worship* 46 (7): 390–412.

Turner, Victor. 1972b. 'Passages, Margins, and Poverty: Religious Symbols of Communitas' (Part II). *Worship* 46 (8): 482–94.

Turner, Victor. 1975. *Revelation and Divination in Ndembu Ritual*. Ithaca, NY: Cornell University Press.

Turner, Victor. 1976. 'Ritual, Tribal and Catholic'. *Worship* 50 (6): 504–26.
van Gennep, Arnold. 1909. *Les rites de passage*. Paris: Émile Nourry.
Vergunst, Jo, and Anna Vermehren. 2012. 'The Art of Slow Sociality: Movement, Aesthetics and Shared Understanding'. *Cambridge Anthropology* 30 (1): 127–42.
Verkaaik, Oskar. 2012. 'Designing the "Anti-Mosque": Identity, Religion and Affect in Contemporary European Mosque Design'. *Social Anthropology* 20 (2): 161–76.
Verkaaik, Oskar. 2020. 'The Anticipated Mosque: The Political Affect of a Planned Building'. *City and Society* 32 (1): 118–36.
Vermeiren, Korneel. 1999. *Praying with Benedict: Prayer in the Rule of St Benedict*, trans. Richard Yeo. London: Darton, Longman and Todd.
Wajcman, Judy. 2014. *Pressed for Time: The Acceleration of Life in Digital Capitalism*. Chicago: University of Chicago Press.
Walford, Geoffrey. 1986. *Life in Public Schools*. London: Methuen.
Watkin, Aelred. 1958. *The Enemies of Love*. London: Burns and Oates.
Weber, Max. 1963. *The Sociology of Religion*. Translated by Ephraim Fischoff. Boston: Beacon Press.
Weber, Max. 1968. *Economy and Society: An Outline of Interpretive Sociology*, eds Guenther Roth and Claus Wittich, trans. Ephraim Fischoff, Hans Gerth, Alexander M. Henderson, Ferdinand Kolegar, Charles Wright Mills, Talcott Parsons, Max Rheinstein, Guenther Roth, Edward Shils and Claus Wittich. New York: Bedminster.
Webster, Joseph. 2013. 'The Immanence of Transcendence: God and the Devil on the Aberdeenshire Coast'. *Ethnos* 78 (3): 380–402.
Wells, Arthur. 2002. 'Bishop Christopher Butler at Vatican II: His Role in Dei Verbum'. *Downside Review* 120 (419): 129–54.
Wichroski, Mary Anne. 1997. 'Breaking Silence: Some Fieldwork Strategies in Cloistered and Non-Cloistered Communities'. In *Reflexivity and Voice*, ed. Rosanna Hertz, 265–82. Thousand Oaks, CA: Sage.
Winthrop, Robert H. 1985. 'Leadership and Tradition in the Regulation of Catholic Monasticism'. *Anthropological Quarterly* 58 (1): 30–8.

Wittel, Andreas. 2001. 'Toward a Network Sociality'. *Theory, Culture and Society* 18 (6): 51–76.

Wright, Peter Poyntz. 1981. *The Parish Church Towers of Somerset: Their Construction, Craftsmanship and Chronology*. Amersham, Buckinghamshire: Avebury.

Yaneva, Albena. 2012. *Mapping Controversies in Architecture*. Farnham, Surrey: Ashgate.

Yates, Luke, and Alan Warde. 2017. 'Eating Together and Eating Alone: Meal Arrangements in British Households'. *British Journal of Sociology* 68 (1): 97–118.

Yelle, Robert A. 2003. *Explaining Mantras: Ritual, Rhetoric, and the Dream of a Natural Language in Hindu Tantra*. London: Routledge.

Yeo, Richard. 1975. 'The Renewal of the Monastic Office'. *Downside Review* 93 (311): 144–8.

Yeo, Richard. 1982. *The Structure and Content of Monastic Profession: A Juridical Study, With Particular Regard to the Practice of the English Benedictine Congregation Since the French Revolution*. Rome: Pontificio Ateneo S. Anselmo.

Yeo, Richard, and Leo Maidlow Davis. 1982. 'Abbot Cuthbert Butler, 1858–1934'. In *Commentaria in S. Regulam*, ed. Jean Gribomont, 91–108. Rome: Pontificio Ateneo S. Anselmo.

Zerubavel, Eviatar. 1980. 'The Benedictine Ethic and the Modern Spirit of Scheduling: on Schedules and Social Organization'. *Sociological Enquiry* 50 (2): 157–69.

Zerubavel, Eviatar. 1981. *Hidden Rhythms: Schedules and Calendars in Social Life*. Chicago: University of Chicago Press.

INDEX

abbot, role of the 8, 10–11, 99–100, 179, 207–8
   as *paterfamilias* 9, 70, 211–12
   role within the *horarium* 65–6, 68, 71–2, 117
Abbot President of the English Benedictine Congregation, role of the 101, 163, 203–5
acedia 59–61, 69
Acton Burnell 23, 224
Agamben, Giorgio 6, 8, 73, 222
Antiphonale Monasticum 104-106, 199
apophatic prayer 130–1, 134–5, 138, 140, 228–9
Augustine of Canterbury 39, 182
autonomy of monasteries 6, 24, 47, 105, 189, 203–6
archaism 89, 97-9, 111
Asad, Talal 26, 135, 175–6, 210
Baker, Augustine 123–7, 137–8, 141–2, 147–8, 190
bells 59, 61–2, 64, 82, 117, 195
Bloch, Maurice 41–2, 87, 91, 103, 109, 112–13
brutalism 50–1
Buckfast Abbey 26, 222
Bury, Austin 14–15
Butler, Christopher, Seventh Abbot of Downside 95, 101, 121, 137–8
Butler, Cuthbert, Second Abbot of Downside 23, 24–5, 188–9, 225–6, 228, 231
calefactory 49, 71, 230
Cambrai 124, 141-142
celibacy 13, 38–9, 14–7, 186–7, 214–7
cemetery 48, 51, 221
cenobitic life 7, 63
Chapman, John, Fourth Abbot of Downside 122, 127-129, 133-138, 143-146, 196-197
chapter house 11, 49, 70
chapter meeting 49, 70, 99
choir stalls 25, 40, 52, 65–72
clocks 61–2, 64, 72–8, 174
cloister 17, 31–2, 49–52
clothing ceremony 8
Coakley, Sarah 137, 145–156, 216
commensality 52–56, 69, 93

Index 249

Compline 71–2, 100, 103, 151, 221
constitutional controversy (1880–1900) 18–19, 23–24, 45–47, 183–190
contemplative prayer 117–30, 133–6, 140–51, 157–8, 226
    democratisation of 137–40, 153, 167
    suspicion of 140–4
contributory autonomy 87, 92–3, 111, 114
conversatio morum 10, 13, 181, 195, 214–7
counterfactual architecture 42, 44–5, 58
COVID lockdown 7, 48, 59–61
deference 217–20
departure from Downside Abbey 26–7, 222–4
Dei Verbum 163
Diu Quidem 24, 47, 189
dissolution of the monasteries 4, 37–8, 40, 182
divided consciousness 129, 133–7, 145
Divine Office 6, 62, 65–73, 78–81, 94–9, 102–103, 113, 173, 221
    priority of the Divine Office 100, 148, 194, 190, 195
    reduction of the number of hours 86, 98, 100
Douai 22, 23, 45, 192, 224
Downside Abbey church
    architecture 16, 31–51, 77, 87, 227
    organ 93–4

Downside School 27, 181, 191–6, 201, 203–10, 212–18
    Separation from Downside Abbey 27, 195, 222
Dunn, Archibald 34–5, 62
Ealing Abbey 139, 197
Easter 12, 68, 174, 194
enclosure 16–17, 65, 180, 229
exemplars 24, 28, 219–20
exile in continental Europe 22, 45, 124, 182–3, 224
family 13, 22–4, 47, 55–8, 98, 188–9, 206–11
food 24–6, 52–6, 61, 167–8, 177
Ford, Edmund, First Abbot of Downside 34–5, 47, 188
French Revolution 23, 95, 189, 224
Garner, Thomas 35, 47
Gasquet, Aidan 34, 37–8, 40, 47, 141, 230
Glastonbury Abbey 36–8, 46
Gothic revival 34–6, 42–5
Guarino, Maria 10, 86, 113
Guéranger, Prosper 94–5, 101
Guigo II 155–6, 162
Gregorian Chant 94–5, 104–6
gyrovagues 63, 209–10, 230
Hansom, Edward 34–5, 62
hebdomadary 52–3, 65
Holy Orders 178–82
horarium 52, 59, 62–3, 65–73, 118, 195
hospitality 15–16, 31, 44, 51
idiorhythmic tendencies 63–4, 77, 82

Ignatius of Loyola 121, 131–2, 143, 165
Independent Inquiry into Child Sexual Abuse 27, 195, 201, 203–15, 217–8, 222
individualism 81–2, 101, 119, 133, 147–9, 151, 199, 209–11, 225, 228–29
infirmary 48–49, 51, 112–13
intentionality 88–91, 95–97, 102–3, 112–15, 122
invention of tradition 41–3, 57, 95, 109
immanence 4, 9, 78, 197–8, 224–5, 231
John of the Cross 133–4, 146
kataphatic prayer 130–2, 134, 143, 165
Keane, Webb 87, 96, 144–5
Kierkegaard, Søren 219–20, 227–9
kitchen 5, 177, 197, 199
Knowles, David 6, 193, 195–7, 203–4
Latin as liturgical language 86, 89–90, 98–9, 105–6
Latin Mass Society 106–7, 110
Lauds 52, 66–68, 70, 103, 117
lectio divina 6-7, 151–69
  group *lectio* 165–7
Lester, Rebecca 133–5
library 19, 51, 76, 229
limestone 16, 32, 39–40
liminality 10–12, 108–9, 111–12, 149, 151
listening 7, 53–5, 66, 123, 157–8, 161, 168–9

liturgical reform 50, 85–7, 94, 99–100, 106–9
liturgy of the hours *see* Divine Office
Liverpool 147, 187
Main, John 139–40
manual labour 6, 18–19, 173–7, 190–1, 196
Manquehue movement 166–7
martyrdom 22, 38, 179, 187, 190
Mass 40, 68–9, 88–93, 106–7, 113, 135, 178–80, 216
Maundy Thursday 54, 180
Mayblin, Maya 25–6, 216–17
mealtimes 17, 52–5, 68–71, 93, 224
medievalism 34–5, 37, 42, 95, 97
Midday Office 52, 69, 229
minority religion 33, 38–9, 183, 194
Missionary identity 46, 77, 148, 182–9, 198, 227
Missionary Oath 22, 24, 45–6, 183, 186, 231
  abolition 24, 189
moderation 18, 24–6, 61, 65, 224–26
month day 199
Mount St Bernard Abbey 38–9
Morrall, Alphonsus 36, 46, 183–4, 187
Mumford, Lewis 73–5
Murray, Gregory 85, 88–92, 94–5, 105–6
music 90–5, 98, 104–6, 180
national identity 38–9, 193

non-place 57–58, 230
novitiate 7–8, 48
obedience, vow of 9, 13, 99, 179, 211–14
parish work 18, 45–6, 64, 147, 173, 177, 209, 212
    reduction of parish commitments 27, 190
    tensions between parish work and *cenobitic* life 46, 118, 184–90, 196, 199
participation 87–93, 110–11, 114–15
Perfectae Caritatis 161, 163
perseverance 8, 28, 30, 150–1, 231
Plantata 22, 183
Pollen, Francis 50–1
prayer without ceasing 5, 73, 104, 118
private prayer 7, 52, 55, 117–23, 129–30
Pryce, Paula 16, 21, 75, 140, 149–50
psalms 60, 65–71, 80, 101–2, 113, 221
public schools, characteristics of 192–94
Pugin, Augustus 43–5
Quietism 142–5
reading 5–6, 123–4, 141, 154–64, 168–9
    reading in the refectory 53–5, 69–71
refectory 15, 17–18, 52–5, 68–71, 169, 177, 199, 222
Reformation 4, 35, 40, 43–5, 109, 182

Religiosus Ordo 24, 189–90
repetition 102–3, 156–8, 169, 221
renunciation of property 9, 13, 75, 199
rite of passage 3, 10–13, 178, 181
ritual reversion 100–6
Rule of St Benedict 3, 5–7, 24–6, 47, 50, 72–7, 175, 203, 225
    Prologue 6, 26, 161
    Chapter 1 63, 207, 209, 230
    Chapter 3 9
    Chapter 19 115
    Chapter 31 5, 197–8
    Chapter 43 65, 104, 148
    Chapter 48 155–6, 173, 177
    Chapter 53 15
    Chapter 72 7
    Chapter 73 26
Sacrosanctum Concilium 86
Scott, Giles Gilbert 35, 40–1, 62
second table 199
Second Vatican Council 50, 85–6, 92, 106, 109, 162–3
sexual abuse 27–8, 146, 195, 201–18
Shepherd, Laurence 36–7, 45–6
silence 15, 17, 52–5, 66, 120, 196, 198
simple profession 8–9
slowness 153, 155–6, 167–8
Snow, Benedict 184–5, 193
social media 7, 48, 59–61
solemn profession 3, 10–13, 20, 181, 231
Solesmes Abbey 94–5, 101, 104, 197

Somerset Tower 40–1
stability 9, 15, 30, 47–50, 115,
    150–51, 206–11, 229–31
  disruptions to stability 82,
    86, 195, 199, 210, 227
  stability and becoming a
    family 47–8, 55–6, 206–7,
    230
  stability of place 9, 26,
    188–9, 222–3, 231
  stability within time 64–5,
    76–8
  witness value of stability
    56–8, 168, 230
Stanbrook Abbey 36
statio 70, 80–1
summum silentium 56, 65, 68,
    72, 118
sundials 76
Suscipe 11
Tambiah, Stanley 21, 96, 99,
    102–3, 189, 197
teatime 4–5, 25, 67, 70, 141,
    160, 177, 199, 230
*Thesaurus Liturgiae Horarum
    Monasticae* 102
time discipline 61–5, 72–7, 81–2,
    117–18
Tolle, Eckhart 136–7
Turner, Victor 10–11, 87, 108–9,
    111–13, 115, 151, 178

transcendence 4, 98–9, 103,
    108–15, 145, 231
Trent, Council of 106, 109
Trethowan, Illtyd 87–9, 98–9,
    108
Troeltsch, Ernst 21, 118–19, 133,
    138, 148
universality of prayer 137–40,
    226
van Gennep, Arnold 10–11, 178
Vatican II *see* Second Vatican
    Council
vernacular language in the
    liturgy 86, 88–9, 97–9, 113
Vespers 52, 67, 70–1, 80, 105
Vigils 65–6, 103, 118
virtuoso 21, 24, 137, 225–6
vocation 5, 25, 31, 47–8, 57, 216,
    220, 224
  relationship between
    monastic vocation and
    vocation to the priesthood
    178, 180–2, 190, 199, 216–17
Walsingham 35
Watkin, Aelred 181–2
Weber, Max 20–1, 24, 193–4,
    213, 219, 225, 227
Weld, Francis 44–5, 186–7
Westminster Cathedral 21–3, 90
workshop 18–19, 25, 78, 173–7
Worth Abbey 10, 50, 196

www.ingramcontent.com/pod-product-compliance
Lightning Source LLC
Chambersburg PA
CBHW031145020426
42333CB00013B/519